Compiled by ROY McCORMACK and AUSTIN BARRETT
Published by SCOTTISH MEDIA NEWSPAPERS LTD.,
195 Albion Street, Glasgow, G1 1QP.

www.weeredbook.co.uk

BIG GAME DATES

EUROPEAN INTERNATIONAL CHAMPIONSHIP

Saturday, September 4 . . . . . . Bosnia-Herzigovina v SCOTLAND
Wednesday, September 8 . . . . Estonia v SCOTLAND
Wednesday,October 6. . . . . SCOTLAND v Bosnia-Herzigovina
Saturday, October 9 . . . . SCOTLAND v Lithuania

LEAGUE CUP

Saturday, July 31 . . . . FIRST ROUND
REMAINDER OF COMPETITION DATES STILL TO BE DECIDED BY SCOTTISH LEAGUE

TENNENTS SCOTTISH CUP

Saturday, December 11, 1999 . . . . FIRST ROUND
Saturday, January 8, 2000. . . . . SECOND ROUND
Saturday, January 29. . . . . THIRD ROUND
Saturday, February 19 . . . . FOURTH ROUND
Saturday, March 11 . . . . QUARTER-FINALS
Saturday, April 8 . . . . SEMI-FINALS
Saturday, May 27 . . . . FINAL

EUROPEAN CHAMPIONS LEAGUE

(Tuesdays/Wednesdays)

July 14 and 21, 1999 . . . . FIRST QUALIFYING PHASE
July 28 and August 4 . . . . SECOND QUALIFYING PHASE
August 10/11 and 24/25 . . . . THIRD QUALIFYING PHASE

FIRST GROUP PHASE (32 clubs, six matches each)
September 14/15, 21/22, 28/29, October 19/20, 26/27, November 2/3

SECOND GROUP PHASE (16 clubs, six matches each)
November 23/24, December 7/8
February 29, 2000/March 1, 7/8, 14/15, 21/22

April 4/5 and 18/19 . . . . QUARTER-FINALS
May 2/3 and 9/10 . . . . SEMI-FINALS
May 24 . . . . FINAL

UEFA CUP

(Thursdays apart from the final)

August 12 and 26. . . . . QUALIFYING PHASE
September 16 and 30 . . . . FIRST ROUND
October 21 and November 4. . . . . SECOND ROUND
November 25 and December 9 . . . . THIRD ROUND
March 2 and 9, 2000 . . . . FOURTH ROUND
March 16 and 23 . . . . QUARTER-FINALS
April 6 and 20 . . . . SEMI-FINALS
May 17 . . . . FINAL

EUROPEAN SUPER CUP FINAL

August 27. . . . . Manchester United v Lazio (Monaco)

LEAGUE CUP DRAW

FIRST ROUND: Brechin v Dumbarton, Stenhousemuir v Inverness, Montrose v Hamilton Accies, Stranraer v Raith Rovers, Ross County v Forar, East Fife v Stirling Albion, Cowdenbeath v Livingston, Albion Rovers v Clyde, Partick Thistle v Alloa, Queen of the South v Arbroath, Queen's Park v Berwick, Clydebank v East Stirling.

SECOND ROUND: Dundee v Brechin or Dumbarton, Stenhousemuir or Inverness v St Mirren, Ayr United v Montrose or Hamilton Accies, Stranraer or Raith v Motherwell, Dundee United v Ross County or Forfar, East Fife or Stirling v Airdrie, Aberdeen v Cowdenbeath or Livingston, Albion Rovers or Clyde v Hibs, Morton v Partick Thistle or Alloa, Queen of the South or Arbroath v Hearts, Dunfermline v Queen's Park or Berwick, Clydebank or East Stirling v Falkirk.

FINAL LEAGUE TABLES 1998-99

PREMIER DIVISION

	P	W	D	L	F	A	Pts
Rangers	36	23	8	5	78	31	77
Celtic	36	21	8	7	84	35	71
St Johnstone	36	15	12	9	39	38	57
Kilmarnock	36	14	14	8	47	29	56
Dundee	36	13	7	16	36	56	46
Hearts	36	11	9	16	44	50	42
Motherwell	36	10	11	15	35	54	41
Aberdeen	36	10	7	19	43	71	37
Dundee Utd	36	8	10	18	37	48	34
Dunfermline	36	4	16	16	28	59	28

DIVISION TWO

	P	W	D	L	F	A	Pts
Livingston	36	22	11	3	66	35	77
Inverness Cal.	36	21	9	6	80	48	72
Clyde	36	15	8	13	46	42	53
Queen of Sth.	36	13	9	14	50	45	48
Alloa	36	13	7	16	65	56	46
Stirling	36	12	8	16	50	63	44
Arbroath	36	12	8	16	37	52	44
Partick	36	12	7	17	36	45	43
East Fife	36	12	6	18	42	64	42
Forfar	36	8	7	21	48	70	31

DIVISION ONE

	P	W	D	L	F	A	Pts
Hibernian	36	28	5	3	84	33	89
Falkirk	36	20	6	10	60	38	66
Ayr	36	19	5	12	66	42	62
Airdrie	36	18	5	13	42	43	59
St Mirren	36	14	10	12	42	43	52
Morton	36	14	7	15	45	41	49
Clydebank	36	11	13	12	36	38	46
Raith	36	8	11	17	37	57	35
Hamilton	36	6	10	20	30	62	28
Stranraer	36	5	2	29	29	74	17

DIVISION THREE

	P	W	D	L	F	A	Pts
Ross County	36	24	5	7	87	42	77
Stenh'semuir	36	19	7	10	62	42	64
Brechin	36	17	8	11	47	43	59
Dumbarton	36	16	9	11	53	40	57
Berwick	36	12	14	10	53	49	50
Queen's Park	36	11	11	14	41	46	44
Albion	36	12	8	16	43	63	44
East Stirling	36	9	13	14	50	48	40
Cowdenbeath	36	8	7	21	34	65	31
Montrose	36	8	6	22	42	74	30

REEBOK CENTRAL LEAGUE 1998-99

PREMIER DIVISION

	P	W	D	L	F	A	Pt
Shotts	22	15	6	1	52	19	51
Maryhill	22	14	3	5	45	32	45
Arthurlie	22	12	3	7	43	32	39
Benburb	22	9	9	4	35	23	36
Neilston	22	10	3	9	38	32	33
Lanark	22	8	6	8	28	29	30
Petershill	22	7	7	8	31	30	28
Pollok	22	6	6	10	41	43	24
Lesmahagow	22	6	4	12	28	36	22
Baillieston	22	7	1	14	25	43	22
Cambuslang	22	4	7	11	29	48	19
Glencairn	22	6	1	15	29	57	19

FIRST DIVISION

	P	W	D	L	F	A	Pt
Blantyre V	26	18	5	3	54	20	59
Johnstone	26	17	5	4	51	27	56
Shettleston	26	15	5	6	43	32	50
Larkhall	26	13	8	5	48	30	47
Greenock	26	14	4	8	53	32	46
Renfrew	26	11	5	10	38	36	38
V of Leven	26	9	8	9	53	52	35
V of Clyde	26	10	5	11	46	48	35
Rob Roy	26	10	5	11	52	48	34
Carluke	26	6	10	10	36	45	28
Kilsyth	26	6	6	14	36	50	24
Cumbern'ld	26	5	5	16	30	61	20
St Roch's	26	5	6	17	37	64	19
Forth	26	4	4	18	27	58	16

SECOND DIVISION

	P	W	D	L	F	A	Pt
Dunipace	24	17	6	1	63	23	57
E Kilbride	24	14	5	5	45	27	47
St Anthony's	24	13	6	5	41	27	45
P Glasgow	24	13	5	6	64	40	44
Perthshire	24	12	3	9	59	41	39
Ashfield	24	10	4	10	42	47	34
Bellshill	24	8	7	9	39	36	31
Stonehouse	24	9	3	12	38	49	30
Royal Albert	24	7	8	9	32	32	29
Yoker Ath	24	9	5	10	37	50	32
Thorniewood	24	6	5	13	26	40	23
Coltness	24	3	5	16	31	57	14
Wishaw	24	2	4	18	19	67	10

WESTERN SCOTTISH LEAGUE 1998-99

FIRST DIVISION

	P	W	D	L	F	A	Pt
Kilwinning	20	18	1	1	80	17	55
Auchinleck	20	17	2	1	60	15	50
Cumnock	20	13	0	7	59	29	39
Kilbirnie	20	10	3	7	38	25	33
Glenafton	20	9	2	9	43	30	29
Beith	20	8	3	9	32	32	27
Dalry Th	20	8	2	10	35	35	26
Troon	20	7	3	10	43	50	24
Largs Th	20	6	3	11	29	39	21
Ardrossan	20	4	1	15	19	61	13
Annbank U	20	0	0	20	16	120	0

SECOND DIVISION

	P	W	D	L	F	A	Pt
Irvine M	22	20	1	1	95	13	61
Irvine V	22	14	3	5	60	37	45
Lugar	22	13	5	4	60	27	44
Muirkirk	22	12	7	3	50	26	43
Ardeer Th	22	12	4	6	59	44	40
Craigmark	22	9	3	10	43	49	30
Kello Rov	22	9	2	11	55	61	29
Saltcoats	22	8	5	9	34	43	29
Hurlford	22	6	2	14	28	54	20
Maybole	22	3	6	13	44	59	15
Darvel	22	3	4	15	32	71	13
Whitletts	22	2	0	20	24	100	6

BANK OF SCOTLAND PREMIER LEAGUE 1999-2000

● DENOTES LIVE SKY TV GAME

Saturday, July 31, 1999
Dundee Utd v Dundee
Hibs v Motherwell
Rangers v Kilmarnock
St Johnstone v Hearts
Sunday, August 1
Aberdeen v Celtic●
Saturday, August 7
Celtic v St Johnstone
Hearts v Rangers
Kilmarnock v Aberdeen
Motherwell v Dundee Utd
Sunday, August 8
Dundee v Hibs●
Saturday, August 14
Aberdeen v Dundee
Dundee Utd v Celtic
Hibs v Hearts
St Johnstone v Kilmarnock
Sunday, August 15
Rangers v Motherwell●
Saturday, August 21
Dundee v Celtic
Kilmarnock v Motherwell
Rangers v Dundee Utd
St Johnstone v Hibs
Sunday, August 22
Hearts v Aberdeen●
Saturday, August 28
Aberdeen v St Johnstone
Celtic v Hearts
Dundee Utd v Kilmarnock
Hibs v Rangers
Motherwell v Dundee
Saturday, September 11
Dundee Utd v Hibs
Hearts v Dundee
Rangers v Aberdeen
St Johnstone v Motherwell
Sunday, September 12
Kilmarnock v Celtic●
Saturday, September 18
Aberdeen v Dundee Utd
Celtic v Rangers
Dundee v St Johnstone
Hibs v Kilmarnock
Monday, September 20
Motherwell v Hearts●
Saturday, September 25
Dundee Utd v Hearts
Hibs v Celtic
Kilmarnock v Dundee
Motherwell v Aberdeen
Rangers v St Johnstone
Saturday, October 2
Aberdeen v Hibs
Celtic v Motherwell
Dundee v Rangers
Hearts v Kilmarnock
St Johnstone v Dundee Utd
Saturday, October 16
Celtic v Aberdeen
Hearts v St Johnstone
Kilmarnock v Rangers
Motherwell v Hibs
Sunday, October 17
Dundee v Dundee Utd●
Saturday, October 23
Aberdeen v Kilmarnock
Dundee Utd v Motherwell
Hibs v Dundee
Rangers v Hearts
Sunday, October 24
St Johnstone v Celtic●
Saturday, October 30
Aberdeen v Rangers
Celtic v Kilmarnock
Dundee v Hearts
Motherwell v St Johnstone
Sunday, October 31
Hibs v Dundee Utd●
Saturday, November 6
Dundee Utd v Aberdeen
Hearts v Motherwell
Kilmarnock v Hibs
Rangers v Celtic
St Johnstone v Dundee

Sunday, November 7
Rangers v Celtic●
Saturday, November 13
Aberdeen v Hearts
Celtic v Dundee
Dundee Utd v Rangers
Hibs v St Johnstone
Motherwell v Kilmarnock-
Saturday, November 20
Dundee v Motherwell
Hearts v Celtic
Kilmarnock v Dundee Utd
Rangers v Hibs
St Johnstone v Aberdeen
Saturday, November 27
Dundee Utd v St Johnstone
Hibs v Aberdeen
Kilmarnock v Hearts
Motherwell v Celtic
Rangers v Dundee
Saturday, December 4
Aberdeen v Motherwell
Celtic v Hibs
Dundee v Kilmarnock
Hearts v Dundee Utd
St Johnstone v Rangers
Saturday, December 11
Aberdeen v Celtic
Dundee Utd v Dundee
Hibs v Motherwell
Rangers v Kilmarnock
St Johnstone v Hearts
Saturday, December 18
Celtic v Dundee Utd
Dundee v Aberdeen
Hearts v Hibs
Kilmarnock v St Johnstone
Motherwell v Rangers
Monday, December 27
Aberdeen v Dundee Utd
Celtic v Rangers●
Dundee v St Johnstone
Hibs v Kilmarnock
Motherwell v Hearts
Saturday, January 22, 2000
Dundee Utd v Hibs
Hearts v Dundee
Kilmarnock v Celtic
Rangers v Aberdeen
St Johnstone v Motherwell
Saturday, February 5
Aberdeen v St Johnstone
Celtic v Hearts
Dundee Utd v Kilmarnock
Hibs v Rangers
Motherwell v Dundee
Saturday, February 12
Dundee v Celtic
Hearts v Aberdeen
Kilmarnock v Motherwell
Rangers v Dundee Utd
St Johnstone v Hibs
Saturday, February 26
Aberdeen v Hibs
Celtic v Motherwell
Dundee v Rangers
Hearts v Kilmarnock
St Johnstone v Dundee Utd
Saturday, March 4
Dundee Utd v Hearts
Hibs v Celtic
Kilmarnock v Dundee
Motherwell v Aberdeen
Rangers v St Johnstone
Saturday, March 11
Celtic v St Johnstone
Dundee v Hibs
Hearts v Rangers
Kilmarnock v Aberdeen
Motherwell v Dundee Utd
Saturday, March 18
Aberdeen v Dundee
Dundee Utd v Celtic
Hibs v Hearts
Rangers v Motherwell
St Johnstone v Kilmarnock
Saturday, March 25
Dundee Utd v Aberdeen
Hearts v Motherwell
Kilmarnock v Hibs
St Johnstone v Dundee
Sunday, March 26
Rangers v Celtic●

Saturday, April 1
Aberdeen v Rangers
Celtic v Kilmarnock
Dundee v Hearts
Hibs v Dundee Utd
Motherwell v St Johnstone
Saturday, April 8
Dundee v Motherwell
Hearts v Celtic
Kilmarnock v Dundee Utd
Rangers v Hibs
St Johnstone v Aberdeen
Saturday, April 15
Aberdeen v Hearts
Celtic v Dundee
Dundee Utd v Rangers
Hibs v St Johnstone
Motherwell v Kilmarnock
Saturday, April 22
Aberdeen v Motherwell
Celtic v Hibs
Dundee v Kilmarnock
Hearts v Dundee Utd
St Johnstone v Rangers

Saturday, April 29
Dundee Utd v St Johnstone
Hibs v Aberdeen
Kilmarnock v Hearts
Motherwell v Celtic
Rangers v Dundee
Saturday, May 6
Celtic v Aberdeen
Dundee v Dundee Utd
Hearts v St Johnstone
Kilmarnock v Rangers
Motherwell v Hibs
Saturday, May 13
Aberdeen v Kilmarnock
Dundee Utd v Motherwell
Hibs v Dundee
Rangers v Hearts
St Johnstone v Celtic
Saturday, May 20
Celtic v Dundee Utd
Dundee v Aberdeen
Hearts v Hibs
Kilmarnock v St Johnstone
Motherwell v Rangers

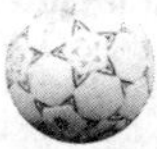

SCOTTISH LEAGUE DIVISION ONE 1999-2000

Saturday, August 7, 1999
Clydebank v Airdrie
Dunfermline v Inverness Cal
Falkirk v Morton
Livingston v Raith Rov
St Mirren v Ayr Utd
Saturday, August 14
Airdrie v Dunfermline
Ayr v Livingston
Morton v Clydebank
Inverness Cal v Falkirk
Raith Rov v St Mirren

Saturday, August 21
Clydebank v Raith Rov
Dunfermline v Morton
Falkirk v Ayr
Livingston v Airdrie
St Mirren v Inverness Cal
Saturday, August 28
Airdrie v Raith Rov
Ayr v Inverness Cal
Clydebank v St Mirren
Dunfermline v Falkirk
Morton v Livingston

Saturday, September 4
Falkirk v Clydebank
Inverness Cal v Morton
Livingston v Dunfermline
Raith Rov v Ayr
St Mirren v Airdrie

Saturday, September 11
Ayr v Airdrie
Dunfermline v St Mirren
Falkirk v Livingston
Inverness Cal v Clydebank
Morton v Raith Rov

Saturday, September 18
Airdrie v Falkirk
Clydebank v Ayr
Livingston v Inverness Cal
Raith Rov v Dunfermline
St Mirren v Morton

Saturday, September 25
Dunfermline v Ayr
Falkirk v St Mirren
Inverness Cal v Raith Rov
Livingston v Clydebank
Morton v Airdrie

Saturday, October 2
Airdrie v Inverness Cal
Ayr v Morton
Clydebank v Dunfermline
Raith Rov v Falkirk
St Mirren v Livingston

Saturday, October 16
Clydebank v Morton
Dunfermline v Airdrie
Falkirk v Inverness Cal
Livingston v Ayr
St Mirren v Raith Rov

Saturday, October 23
Airdrie v Clydebank
Ayr v St Mirren
Inverness Cal v Dunfermline
Morton v Falkirk
Raith Rov v Livingston

Saturday, October 30
Airdrie v Ayr
Clydebank v Inverness Cal
Livingston v Falkirk
Raith Rov v Morton
St Mirren v Dunfermline

Saturday, November 6
Ayr v Clydebank
Dunfermline v Raith Rov
Falkirk v Airdrie
Inverness Cal v Livingston
Morton v St Mirren

Saturday, November 13
Airdrie v St Mirren
Ayr v Raith Rov
Clydebank v Falkirk
Dunfermline v Livingston
Morton v Inverness Cal

Saturday, November 20
Falkirk v Dunfermline
Inverness Cal v Ayr
Livingston v Morton
Raith Rov v Airdrie
St Mirren v Clydebank

Saturday, November 27
Dunfermline v Clydebank
Falkirk v Raith Rov
Inverness Cal v Airdrie
Livingston v St Mirren
Morton v Ayr

Saturday, December 4
Airdrie v Morton
Ayr v Dunfermline
Clydebank v Livingston
Raith Rov v Inverness Cal
St Mirren v Falkirk

Saturday, December 11
Airdrie v Livingston
Ayr v Falkirk
Inverness Cal v St Mirren
Raith Rov v Clydebank
Morton v Dunfermline

Saturday, December 18
Clydebank v Airdrie
Dunfermline v Inverness Cal
Falkirk v Morton
Livingston v Raith Rov
St Mirren v Ayr

Monday, December 27
Ayr v Airdrie
Dunfermline v St Mirren
Falkirk v Livingston
Inverness Cal v Clydebank
Morton v Raith Rov

Monday, January 3, 2000
Airdrie v Falkirk
Clydebank v Ayr
Livingston v Inverness Cal
Raith Rov v Dunfermline
St Mirren v Morton

Saturday, January 8
Falkirk v Clydebank
Inverness Cal v Morton
Livingston v Dunfermline
Raith Rov v Ayr
St Mirren v Airdrie

Saturday, January 15
Airdrie v Raith Rov
Ayr v Inverness Cal
Clydebank v St Mirren
Dunfermline v Falkirk
Morton v Livingston

Saturday, January 22
Dunfermline v Ayr
Falkirk v St Mirren
Inverness Cal v Raith Rov
Livingston v Clydebank
Morton v Airdrie

Saturday, February 5
Airdrie v Inverness Cal
Ayr v Morton
Clydebank v Dunfermline
Raith Rov v Falkirk
St Mirren v Livingston

Saturday, February 12
Clydebank v Raith Rov
Dunfermline v Morton
Falkirk v Ayr
Livingston v Airdrie
St Mirren v Inverness Cal

Saturday, February 26
Airdrie v Dunfermline
Ayr v Livingston
Inverness Cal v Falkirk
Morton v Clydebank
Raith Rov v St Mirren

Saturday, March 4
Airdrie v Ayr
Clydebank v Inverness Cal
Livingston v Falkirk
Raith Rov v Morton
St Mirren v Dunfermline

Saturday, March 18
Ayr v Clydebank
Dunfermline v Raith Rov
Falkirk v Airdrie
Inverness Cal v Livingston
Morton v St Mirren

Saturday, March 25
Falkirk v Dunfermline
Inverness Cal v Ayr
Livingston v Morton
Raith Rov v Airdrie
St Mirren v Clydebank

Saturday, April 1
Airdrie v St Mirren
Ayr v Raith Rov
Clydebank v Falkirk
Dunfermline v Livingston
Morton v Inverness

Saturday, April 8
Airdrie v Morton
Ayr v Dunfermline
Clydebank v Livingston
Raith Rov v Inverness Cal
St Mirren v Falkirk

Saturday, April 15
Dunfermline v Clydebank
Falkirk v Raith Rov
Inverness Cal V Airdrie
Livingston v St Mirren
Morton v Ayr

Saturday, April 22
Airdrie v Clydebank
Ayr v St Mirren
Inverness Cal v Dunfermline
Morton v Falkirk
Raith Rov v Livingston

Saturday, April 29
Clydebank v Morton
Dunfermline v Airdrie
Falkirk v Inverness Cal
Livingston v Ayr
St Mirren v Raith Rov

Saturday, May 6
Airdrie v Livingston
Ayr v Falkirk
Inverness v St Mirren
Morton v Dunfermline
Raith Rov v Clydebank

DIVISION TWO 1999-2000

Saturday, August 7, 1999
Clyde v Alloa
Partick Th v Stenhousemuir
QOS v Arbroath
Ross Co v Hamilton
Stirling v Stranraer

Saturday, August 14
Alloa v Partick
Arbroath v Clyde
Hamilton v QOS
Stenhousemuir v Stirling
Stranraer v Ross Co

Saturday, August 21
Clyde v Stranraer
Partick v Arbroath
QOS v Alloa
Ross Co v Stenhousemuir
Stirling v Hamilton

Saturday, August 28
Alloa v Hamilton
Clyde v Stirling
Partick v QOS
Ross Co v Arbroath
Stenhousemuir v Stranraer

Saturday, September 4
Arbroath v Alloa
QOS v Clyde
Stirling v Ross Co
Stranraer v Partick

Sunday, September 5
Hamilton v Stenhousemuir

Saturday, September 11
Alloa v Ross Co
Arbroath v Stirling
Clyde v Partick
Hamilton v Stranraer
QOS v Stenhousemuir

Saturday, September 18
Partick v Hamilton
Ross Co v Clyde
Stenhousemuir v Arbroath
Stirling v Alloa
Stranraer v QOS

Saturday, September 25
Alloa v Stenhousemuir
Arbroath v Stranraer
Clyde v Hamilton
Partick v Ross Co
QOS v Stirling

Saturday, October 2
Hamilton v Arbroath
Ross Co v QOS
Stenhousemuir v Clyde
Stirling v Partick
Stranraer v Alloa

Saturday, October 16
Clyde v Arbroath
Partick v Alloa
QOS v Hamilton
Ross Co v Stranraer
Stirling v Stenhousemuir

Saturday, October 23
Alloa v Clyde
Arbroath v QOS
Hamilton v Ross Co
Stenhousemuir v Partick
Stranraer v Stirling

Saturday, October 30
Partick v Clyde
Ross Co v Alloa
Stenhousemuir v QOS
Stirling v Arbroath
Stranraer v Hamilton

Saturday, November 6
Alloa v Stirling
Arbroath v Stenhousemuir
Clyde v Ross Co
Hamilton v Partick
QOS v Stranraer

Saturday, November 13
Alloa v Arbroath
Clyde v QOS
Partick v Stranraer
Ross Co v Stirling
Stenhousemuir v Hamilton

Saturday, November 20
Arbroath v Ross Co
Hamilton v Alloa
QOS v Partick
Stirling v Clyde
Stranraer v Stenhousemuir

Saturday, November 27
Alloa v Stranraer
Arbroath v Hamilton
Clyde v Stenhousemuir
Partick v Stirling
QOS v Ross Co

Saturday, December 4
Hamilton v Clyde
Ross Co v Partick
Stenhousemuir v Alloa
Stirling v QOS
Stranraer v Arbroath

Saturday, December 18
Clyde v Alloa
Partick v Stenhousemuir
QOS v Arbroath
Ross Co v Hamilton
Stirling v Stranraer

Monday, December 27
Alloa v QOS
Arbroath v Partick
Hamilton v Stirling
Stenhousemuir v Ross Co
Stranraer v Clyde

Monday, January 3, 2000
Partick v Hamilton
Ross Co v Clyde
Stenhousemuir v Arbroath
Stirling v Alloa
Stranraer v QOS

Saturday, January 15
Alloa v Ross Co
Arbroath v Stirling
Clyde v Partick
Hamilton v Stranraer
QOS v Stenhousemuir

Saturday, January 22
Alloa v Stenhousemuir
Arbroath v Stranraer
Clyde v Hamilton
Partick v Ross Co
QOS v Stirling

Saturday, February 5
Hamilton v Arbroath
Ross Co v QOS
Stenhousemuir v Clyde
Stirling v Partick
Stranraer v Alloa

Saturday, February 12
Alloa v Hamilton
Clyde v Stirling
Partick v QOS
Ross Co v Arbroath
Stenhousemuir v Stranraer

Saturday, February 19
Arbroath v Alloa
Hamilton v Stenhousemuir
QOS v Clyde
Stirling v Ross Co
Stranraer v Partick

Saturday, February 26
Alloa v Partick
Arbroath v Clyde
Hamilton v QOS
Stenhousemuir v Stirling
Stranraer v Ross Co

Saturday, March 4
Clyde v Stranraer
Partick v Arbroath
QOS v Alloa
Ross Co v Stenhousemuir
Stirling v Hamilton

Saturday, March 11
Partick v Clyde
Ross Co v Alloa
Stenhousemuir v QOS
Stirling v Arbroath
Stranraer v Hamilton

Saturday, March 18
Alloa v Stirling
Arbroath v Stenhousemuir
Clyde v Ross Co
Hamilton v Partick
QOS v Stranraer

Saturday, March 25
Arbroath v Ross Co
Hamilton v Alloa
QOS v Partick
Stirling v Clyde
Stranraer v Stenhousemuir

Saturday, April 1
Alloa v Arbroath
Clyde v QOS
Partick v Stranraer
Ross Co v Stirling
Stenhousemuir v Hamilton

Saturday, April 8
Hamilton v Clyde
Ross Co v Partick
Stenhousemuir v Alloa
Stirling v QOS
Stranraer v Arbroath

Saturday, April 15
Alloa v Stranraer
Arbroath v Hamilton
Clyde v Stenhousemuir
Partick v Stirling
QOS v Ross Co

Saturday, April 22
Alloa v Clyde
Arbroath v QOS
Hamilton v Ross Co
Stenhousemuir v Partick
Stranraer v Stirling

Saturday, April 29
Clyde v Arbroath
Partick v Alloa
QOS v Hamilton
Ross Co v Stranraer
Stirling v Stenhousemuir

Saturday, May 6
Alloa v QOS
Arbroath v Partick
Hamilton v Stirling
Stenhousemuir v Ross Co
Stranraer v Clyde

DIVISION THREE 1999-2000

Saturday, August 7, 1999
Albion Rov v Dumbarton
East Fife v Berwick
Forfar v Brechin
Montrose v Cowdenbeath
Queen's Pk v East Stirling

Saturday, August 14
Berwick v Albion Rov
Brechin v Queen's Pk
Cowdenbeath v Forfar
Dumbarton v Montrose
East Stirling v East Fife

Saturday, August 21
Albion Rov v Brechin
East Fife v Dumbarton
Forfar v East Stirling
Montrose v Berwick
Queen's Pk v Cowdenbeath

Saturday, August 28
Berwick v Queen's Pk
Brechin v Dumbarton
East Fife v Montrose
East Stirling v Cowdenbeath
Forfar v Albion Rov

Saturday, September 4
Albion Rov v East Fife
Cowdenbeath v Brechin
Dumbarton v Berwick
Montrose v East Stirling
Queen's Pk v Forfar

Saturday, September 11
Albion Rov v Montrose
Berwick v Cowdenbeath
Brechin v East Stirling
Dumbarton v Queen's Pk
East Fife v Forfar

Saturday, September 18
Cowdenbeath v East Fife
East Stirling v Dumbarton
Forfar v Berwick
Montrose v Brechin
Queen's Pk v Albion Rov

Saturday, September 25
Albion Rov v East Stirling
Berwick v Brechin
Dumbarton v Cowdenbeath
East Fife v Queen's Pk
Montrose v Forfar

Saturday, October 2
Brechin v East Fife
Cowdenbeath v Albion Rov
East Stirling v Berwick
Forfar v Dumbarton
Queen's Pk v Montrose

Saturday, October 16
Albion Rov v Berwick
East Fife v East Stirling
Forfar v Cowdenbeath
Montrose v Dumbarton
Queen's Pk v Brechin

Saturday, October 23
Berwick v East Fife
Brechin v Forfar
Cowdenbeath v Montrose
Dumbarton v Albion Rov
East Stirling v Queen's Pk

Saturday, October 30
Cowdenbeath v Berwick
East Stirling v Brechin
Forfar v East Fife
Montrose v Albion Rov
Queen's Pk v Dumbarton

Saturday, November 6
Albion Rov v Queen's Pk
Berwick v Forfar
Brechin v Montrose
Dumbarton v East Stirling
East Fife v Cowdenbeath

Saturday, November 13
Berwick v Dumbarton
Brechin v Cowdenbeath
East Fife v Albion Rov
East Stirling v Montrose
Forfar v Queen's Pk

Saturday, November 20
Albion Rov v Forfar
Cowdenbeath v East Stirling
Dumbarton v Brechin
Montrose v East Fife
Queen's Pk v Berwick

Saturday, November 27
Albion Rov v Cowdenbeath
Berwick v East Stirling
Dumbarton v Forfar
East Fife v Brechin
Montrose v Queen's Pk

Saturday, December 4
Brechin v Berwick
Cowdenbeath v Dumbarton
East Stirling v Albion Rov
Forfar v Montrose
Queen's Pk v East Fife

Saturday, December 18
Albion Rov v Dumbarton
East Fife v Berwick
Forfar v Brechin
Montrose v Cowdenbeath
Queen's Pk v East Stirling

Monday, December 27
Berwick v Montrose
Brechin v Albion Rov
Cowdenbeath v Queen's Pk
Dumbarton v East Fife
East Stirling v Forfar

Monday, January 3, 2000
Cowdenbeath v East Fife
East Stirling v Dumbarton
Forfar v Berwick
Montrose v Brechin
Queen's Pk v Albion Rov

Saturday, January 15
Albion Rov v Montrose
Berwick v Cowdenbeath
Brechin v East Stirling
Dumbarton v Queen's Pk
East Fife v Forfar

Saturday, January 22
Albion Rov v East Stirling
Berwick v Brechin
Dumbarton v Cowdenbeath
East Fife v Queen's Pk
Montrose v Forfar

Saturday, February 5
Brechin v East Fife
Cowdenbeath v Albion Rov
East Stirling v Berwick
Forfar v Dumbarton
Queen's Pk v Montrose

Saturday, February 12
Berwick v Queen's Pk
Brechin v Dumbarton
East Fife v Montrose
East Stirling v Cowdenbeath
Forfar v Albion Rov

Saturday, February 19
Albion Rov v East Fife
Cowdenbeath v Brechin
Dumbarton v Berwick
Montrose v East Stirling
Queen's Pk v Forfar

Saturday, February 26
Berwick v Albion Rov
Brechin v Queen's Pk
Cowdenbeath v Forfar
Dumbarton v Montrose
East Stirling v East Fife

Saturday, March 4
Albion Rov v Brechin
East Fife v Dumbarton
Forfar v East Stirling
Montrose v Berwick
Queen's Pk v Cowdenbeath

Saturday, March 11
Cowdenbeath v Berwick
East Stirling v Brechin
Forfar v East Fife
Montrose v Albion Rov
Queen's Pk v Dumbarton
Saturday, March 18
Albion Rov v Queen's Pk
Berwick v Forfar
Brechin v Montrose
Dumbarton v East Stirling
East Fife v Cowdenbeath
Saturday, March 25
Albion Rov v Forfar
Cowdenbeath v East Stirling
Dumbarton v Brechin
Montrose v East Fife
Queen's Pk v Berwick
Saturday, April 1
Berwick v Dumbarton
Brechin v Cowdenbeath
East Fife v Albion Rov
East Stirling v Montrose
Forfar v Queen's Pk
Saturday, April 8
Brechin v Berwick
Cowdenbeath v Dumbarton
East Stirling v Albion Rov
Forfar v Montrose
Queen's Pk v East Fife
Saturday, April 15
Albion Rov v Cowdenbeath
Berwick v East Stirling
Dumbarton v Forfar
East Fife v Brechin
Montrose v Queen's Pk
Saturday, April 22
Berwick v East Fife
Brechin v Forfar
Cowdenbeath v Montrose
Dumbarton v Albion Rov
East Stirling v Queen's Pk
Saturday, April 29
Albion Rov v Berwick
East Fife v East Stirling
Forfar v Cowdenbeath
Montrose v Dumbarton
Queen's Pk v Brechin
Saturday, May 6
Berwick v Montrose
Brechin v Albion Rov
Cowdenbeath v Queen's Pk
Dumbarton v East Fife
East Stirling v Forfar

SCOT·FM
when did **you** last listen to the best sport coverage in Scotland?
100·3 WEST • 101·1 EAST

GRADE ONE REFEREES

KEVIN BISSET
TOM BROWN
BRIAN CASSIDY
● KENNY CLARK
MARTIN CLARK
GEORGE CLYDE
● HUGH DALLAS
● STUART DOUGAL
IAN ELMSLIE
JOHN FLEMING
● ALAN FREELAND
IAN FRICKLETON
IAN FYFE
ALAN GEMMILL
COLIN HARDIE
JIM HERALD
STEVE KANEY
CRAIG MACKAY
ERIC MARTINDALE
JIM McCLUSKEY
● MICHAEL McCURRY
DOUGLAS McDONALD
BRIAN McGARRY
CAMMY MELVILLE
GARRY MITCHELL
ROBERT ORR
MIKE RITCHIE
● JOHN ROWBOTHAM
GEORGE SIMPSON
DOUGIE SMITH
DAVID SOMERS
KEVIN TONER
JOHN UNDERHILL
● WILLIE YOUNG

● *DENOTES FIFA STATUS*

HUGH DALLAS

WILLIE YOUNG

FA CARLING PREMIER LEAGUE

● DENOTES LIVE SKY TV GAME

Saturday, August 7
Arsenal v Leicester
Chelsea v Sunderland
Coventry v Southampton
Leeds v Derby
Middlesboro v Bradford
Newcastle v Aston Villa
Sheff Wed v Liverpool
Watford v Wimbledon
West Ham v Tottenham
Sunday, August 8
Everton v Man Utd●
Monday, August 9
Tottenham v Newcastle●
Tuesday, August 10
Bradford v Chelsea
Derby v Arsenal●
Sunderland v Watford
Wimbledon v Middlesboro
Wednesday, August 11
Aston Villa v Everton
Leicester v Coventry
Liverpool v West Ham
Man Utd v Sheff Wed
Southampton v Leeds
Saturday, August 14
Bradford v Sheff Wed
Derby v Middlesboro
Leicester v Chelsea
Liverpool v Watford
Man Utd v Leeds
Sunderland v Arsenal
Tottenham v Everton
Wimbledon v Coventry
Sunday, August 15
Southampton v Newcastle●
Monday, August 16
Aston Villa v West Ham●
Saturday, August 21
Chelsea v Aston Villa
Coventry v Derby
Everton v Southampton
Leeds v Sunderland
Middlesboro v Liverpool
Newcastle v Wimbledon
Sheff Wed v Tottenham
Watford v Bradford
West Ham v Leicester
Sunday, August 22
Arsenal v Man Utd●
Monday, August 23
Leeds v Liverpool●
Tuesday, August 24
Arsenal v Bradford
Middlesboro v Leicester
Watford v Aston Villa
Wednesday, August 25
Chelsea v Tottenham
Coventry v Man Utd
Everton v Wimbledon
Newcastle v Sunderland
Sheff Wed v Derby
West Ham v Southampton
Saturday, August 28
Aston Villa v Middlesboro
Bradford v West Ham
Derby v Everton
Liverpool v Arsenal
Man Utd v Newcastle
Southampton v Sheff Wed
Tottenham v Leeds
Wimbledon v Chelsea
Sunday, August 29
Sunderland v Coventry●
Monday, August 30
Leicester v Watford●
Saturday, September 11
Arsenal v Aston Villa
Chelsea v Newcastle
Coventry v Leeds
Liverpool v Man U● (11.30)
Middlesboro v Southampton
Sheff Wed v Everton
Sunderland v Leicester
West Ham v Watford
Wimbledon v Derby
Sunday, September 12
Bradford v Tottenham●

Saturday, September 18
Aston Villa v Bradford
Derby v Sunderland
Everton v West Ham
Leicester v Liverpool
Man Utd v Wimbledon
Newcastle v Sheff Wed
Southampton v Arsenal
Tottenham v Coventry
Watford v Chelsea
Sunday, September 19
Leeds v Middlesboro●
Saturday, September 25
Arsenal v Watford
Coventry v West Ham
Derby v Bradford
Leeds v Newcastle
Leicester v Aston Villa
Man Utd v Southampton
Middlesboro v Chelsea
Sunderland v Sheff Wed
Sunday, September 26
Wimbledon v Tottenham●
Monday, September 27
Liverpool v Everton●
Saturday, October 2
Aston Villa v Liverpool
Bradford v Sunderland
Everton v Coventry
Newcastle v Middlesboro
Sheff Wed v Wimbledon
Tottenham v Leicester
Watford v Leeds
West Ham v Arsenal
Sunday, October 3
Chelsea v Man Utd●
Monday, October 4
Southampton v Derby●
Saturday, October 16
Arsenal v Everton
Coventry v Newcastle
Derby v Tottenham
Leeds v Sheff Wed
Leicester v Southampton
Liverpool v Chelsea
Man Utd v Watford
Wimbledon v Bradford
Sunday, October 17
Middlesboro v West Ham●
Monday, October 18
Sunderland v Aston Villa●
Saturday, October 23
Aston Villa v Wimbledon
Bradford v Leicester
Chelsea v Arsenal
Everton v Leeds
Sheff Wed v Coventry
Southampton v Liverpool
Tottenham v Man Utd
West Ham v Sunderland
Sunday, October 24
Watford v Middlesboro●
Monday, October 25
Newcastle v Derby●
Saturday, October 30
Arsenal v Newcastle
Derby v Chelsea
Leeds v West Ham
Leicester v Sheff Wed
Man Utd v Aston Villa
Middlesboro v Everton
Sunderland v Tottenham
Wimbledon v Southampton
Sunday, October 31
Coventry v Watford●
Monday, November 1
Liverpool v Bradford●
Saturday, November 6
Aston Villa v Southampton
Bradford v Coventry
Chelsea v West Ham
Liverpool v Derby
Man Utd v Leicester
Middlesboro v Sunderland
Sheff Wed v Watford
Tottenham v Arsenal
Sunday, November 7
Wimbledon v Leeds●
Monday, November 8
Newcastle v Everton●

Saturday, November 20
Arsenal v Middlesboro
Derby v Man Utd
Everton v Chelsea
Leeds v Bradford
Leicester v Wimbledon
Southampton v Tottenham
Sunderland v Liverpool
Watford v Newcastle
Sunday, November 21
West Ham v Sheff Wed●
Monday, November 22
Coventry v Aston Villa●
Saturday, November 27
Arsenal v Derby
Coventry v Leicester
Everton v Aston Villa
Leeds v Southampton
Middlesboro v Wimbledon
Newcastle v Tottenham
Sheff Wed v Man Utd
Watford v Sunderland
West Ham v Liverpool
Sunday, November 28
Chelsea v Bradford●
Saturday, December 4
Aston Villa v Newcastle
Bradford v Middlesboro
Derby v Leeds
Leicester v Arsenal● (11.30)
Man Utd v Everton
Southampton v Coventry
Sunderland v Chelsea
Wimbledon v Watford
Sunday, December 5
Tottenham v West Ham●
Monday, December 6
Liverpool v Sheff Wed●
Saturday, December 18
Arsenal v Wimbledon
Aston Villa v Sheff Wed
Bradford v Newcastle
Leicester v Derby
Liverpool v Coventry
Middlesboro v Tottenham
Sunderland v Southampton
Watford v Everton
West Ham v Man Utd
Sunday, December 19
Chelsea v Leeds●
Sunday, December 26
Coventry v Arsenal● (5pm)
Derby v Aston Villa
Everton v Sunderland
Leeds v Leicester
Man Utd v Bradford
Newcastle v Liverpool
Sheff Wed v Middlesboro
Southampton v Chelsea
Tottenham v Watford
Wimbledon v West Ham
Tuesday, December 28
Arsenal v Leeds
Aston Villa v Tottenham
Bradford v Everton
Leicester v Newcastle
Liverpool v Wimbledon
Middlesboro v Coventry
Sunderland v Man Utd●
Watford v Southampton
West Ham v Derby
Wednesday, December 29
Chelsea v Sheff Wed●
Monday, January 3, 2000
Coventry v Chelsea
Derby v Watford
Everton v Leicester
Leeds v Aston Villa
Man Utd v Middlesboro
Newcastle v West Ham
Sheff Wed v Arsenal
Southampton v Bradford
Tottenham v Liverpool
Wimbledon v Sunderland
Saturday, January 15
Arsenal v Sunderland
Chelsea v Leicester
Coventry v Wimbledon
Everton v Tottenham
Leeds v Man Utd
Middlesboro v Derby
Newcastle v Southampton
Sheff Wed v Bradford
Watford v Liverpool
West Ham v Aston Villa

Saturday, January 22
Aston Villa v Chelsea
Bradford v Watford
Derby v Coventry
Leicester v West Ham
Liverpool v Middlesboro
Man Utd v Arsenal
Southampton v Everton
Sunderland v Leeds
Tottenham v Sheff Wed
Wimbledon v Newcastle

Saturday, February 5
Aston Villa v Watford
Bradford v Arsenal
Derby v Sheff Wed
Leicester v Middlesboro
Liverpool v Leeds
Man Utd v Coventry
Southampton v West Ham
Sunderland v Newcastle
Tottenham v Chelsea
Wimbledon v Everton

Saturday, February 12
Arsenal v Liverpool
Chelsea v Wimbledon
Coventry v Sunderland
Everton v Derby
Leeds v Tottenham
Middlesboro v Aston Villa
Newcastle v Man Utd
Sheff Wed v Southampton
Watford v Leicester
West Ham v Bradford

Saturday, February 26
Arsenal v Southampton
Bradford v Aston Villa
Chelsea v Watford
Coventry v Tottenham
Liverpool v Leicester
Middlesboro v Leeds
Sheff Wed v Newcastle
Sunderland v Derby
West Ham v Everton
Wimbledon v Man Utd

Saturday, March 4
Aston Villa v Arsenal
Derby v Wimbledon
Everton v Sheff Wed
Leeds v Coventry
Leicester v Sunderland
Man Utd v Liverpool
Newcastle v Chelsea
Southampton v Middlesboro
Tottenham v Bradford
Watford v West Ham

Saturday, March 11
Aston Villa v Coventry
Bradford v Leeds
Chelsea v Everton
Liverpool v Sunderland
Man Utd v Derby
Middlesboro v Arsenal
Newcastle v Watford
Sheff Wed v West Ham
Tottenham v Southampton
Wimbledon v Leicester

Saturday, March 18
Arsenal v Tottenham
Coventry v Bradford
Derby v Liverpool
Everton v Newcastle
Leeds v Wimbledon
Leicester v Man Utd
Southampton v Aston Villa
Sunderland v Middlesboro
Watford v Sheff Wed
West Ham v Chelsea

Saturday, March 25
Arsenal v Coventry
Aston Villa v Derby
Bradford v Man Utd
Chelsea v Southampton
Leicester v Leeds
Liverpool v Newcastle
Middlesboro v Sheff Wed
Sunderland v Everton
Watford v Tottenham
West Ham v Wimbledon

Saturday, April 1
Coventry v Liverpool
Derby v Leicester
Everton v Watford
Leeds v Chelsea
Man Utd v West Ham
Newcastle v Bradford
Sheff Wed v Aston Villa
Southampton v Sunderland
Tottenham v Middlesboro
Wimbledon v Arsenal

Saturday, April 8
Arsenal v Sheff Wed
Aston Villa v Leeds
Bradford v Southampton
Chelsea v Coventry
Leicester v Everton
Liverpool v Tottenham
Middlesboro v Man Utd
Sunderland v Wimbledon
Watford v Derby
West Ham v Newcastle

Saturday, April 15
Coventry v Middlesboro
Derby v West Ham
Everton v Bradford
Leeds v Arsenal
Man Utd v Sunderland
Newcastle v Leicester
Sheff Wed v Chelsea
Southampton v Watford
Tottenham v Aston Villa
Wimbledon v Liverpool

Saturday, April 22
Aston Villa v Leicester
Bradford v Derby
Chelsea v Middlesboro
Everton v Liverpool
Newcastle v Leeds
Sheff Wed v Sunderland
Southampton v Man Utd
Tottenham v Wimbledon
Watford v Arsenal
West Ham v Coventry

Monday, April 24
Arsenal v West Ham
Coventry v Everton
Derby v Southampton
Leeds v Watford
Leicester v Tottenham
Liverpool v Aston Villa
Man Utd v Chelsea
Middlesboro v Newcastle
Sunderland v Bradford
Wimbledon v Sheff Wed

Saturday, April 29
Aston Villa v Sunderland
Bradford v Wimbledon
Chelsea v Liverpool
Everton v Arsenal
Newcastle v Coventry
Sheff Wed v Leeds
Southampton v Leicester
Tottenham v Derby
Watford v Man Utd
West Ham v Middlesboro

Saturday, May 6
Arsenal v Chelsea
Coventry v Sheff Wed
Derby v Newcastle
Leeds v Everton
Leicester v Bradford
Liverpool v Southampton
Man Utd v Tottenham
Middlesboro v Watford
Sunderland v West Ham
Wimbledon v Aston Villa

Sunday, May 14
Aston Villa v Man Utd
Bradford v Liverpool
Chelsea v Derby
Everton v Middlesboro
Newcastle v Arsenal
Sheff Wed v Leicester
Southampton v Wimbledon
Tottenham v Sunderland
Watford v Coventry
West Ham v Leeds

TENNENTS
SCOTTISH CUP

1998-99 REVIEW OF THE SEASON

July & August

JULY

22: The European adventure begins . . . Celtic disappoint as they draw 0-0 with Irish part-timers St Patrick's Athletic at Parkhead. Rangers find themselves 3-0 down to another Irish part-time team but fight back to win 5-3. Killie draw 1-1 in Bosnia with Zeljeznicar.

25: Celtic beat Tottenham Hotspur 2-1 in a friendly at Parkhead.

29: Celtic go through to the second European Cup qualifying round after a 2-0 second leg win over St Partick's in Dublin. Rangers progress in the UEFA Cup, courtesy of a 2-0 win over Shelbourne at Ibrox. Kilmarnock beat Zeljeznicar 1-0 at Rugby Park to also go through.

AUGUST

1: Celtic kick off the defence of their title with a 5-0 home win over Dunfermline.

2: Hearts open their campaign as they left the last one with a 2-1 win over Rangers at Tynecastle.

4: Ally McCoist signs for Kilmarnock on a free transfer and Colin Hendry completes his move to Rangers for £3.75m. Celtic draw 1-1 with Bolton.

8: Celtic lose 1-0 to Liverpool in another pre-season friendly at Celtic park.

10: Celtic are in embroiled in a bonus row on the eve of their crunch Champions League Qualifier with Croatia Zagreb.

11: Rangers beat PAOK Salonika 2-0 at Ibrox in the UEFA Cup. Kilmarnock go down 2-0 in the Czech Republic to SK Sigma.

12: Celtic beat Euro cracks Croatia Zagreb 1-0 at Parkhead.

15: Colin Hendry makes his Rangers debut and is impressive as Gers beat Motherwell 2-1 at Ibrox.

16: Aberdeen go to the top of the table after a remarkable 3-2 win over Celtic at Pittodrie. Dons are three up and Celts are awarded three penalties, missing two in a crazy match.

18: Rangers thump Alloa 4-0 to move into the quarter-finals of the League Cup. Ally McCoist scores an injury-time goal as Kilmarnock dump Livingston 3-1 but the shock of the round comes as Ayr beat Motherwell 2-0 at Rugby Park after travel boss John Boyle takes over the Fir Park side.

19: A Marvyn Wilson strike makes sure Airdrie dump holders Celtic out of the League Cup at the Shyberry Excelsior Stadium.

22: Teen hi-tkid Mark Burchill arrives on the scene for Celtic as he comes off the bench to score a last-minute winner against Dundee United in a 2-1 win. Meanwhile, Rangers move into top gear as they beat Kilmarnock 3-1 at Rugby Park, but Jorg Albertz and skipper Lorenzo Amoruso almost come to blows after a disagreement over a free kick. Hearts go top after a 2-0 win over Aberdeen.

25: Rangers draw 0-0 with PAOK Salonika in Greece to progress to the first round of the UEFA Cup. Killie lose 2-0 to SK Sigma at Rugby Park to go out 4-0 on aggregate.

26: Celtic are humiliated 3-0 by Croatia Zagreb and miss out on the Champions League.

1998-99 REVIEW OF THE SEASON

September

2: Rangers' midfielder Jonas Thern is on the verge of quitting football with damaged knee tendons.
4: Pat Nevin leaves Kilmarnock to join Motherwell as player and chief-executive. Paul Sturrock quits St Johnstone to take over as Dundee United boss after the resignation of Tommy McLean.
5: Scotland dismally draw 0-0 with Lithuania in a Euro Championship qualifier in Vilnius. Celtic's Henrik Larsson is part of the Swedish team which beats England 2-1 in Stockholm.
7: Sandy Clark leaves Hamilton to become new St Johnstone manager. Bertie Vogts sacked as boss of Germany after drastic start to Euro 2000 campaign. Seb Rozental arrives back at Ibrox to resume his career after recovering from injury in Chile.
8: Rangers progress to the semi-finals of the League Cup with a comfortable 2-0 win over Ayr at Somerset Park. Airdrie shock Kilmarnock after extra time with a 1-0 win at Rugby Park and St Johnstone thump Hibs 4-0 at McDiarmid Park.
9: Hearts scrape through on penalties after a 1-1 draw with Ross County in the League Cup at Tynecastle to set up a semi-final with St Johnstone, Rangers drawn against Airdrie.
10: Morten Wieghorst ruled out for season after operation on damaged knee ligaments. Ibrox chairman David Murray insists Rangers are set to clinch the signature of Brazilian hit-man Christian
11: Bobby Williamson signs a five-year-deal with Kilmarnock. Stuart McCall knocks back manager's job at Hamilton Accies. Rangers bid to sign Christian collapses as boss Dick Advocaat blames the player's THREE agents.
12: Celtic stumble to a 1-1 draw with Kilmarnock at Parkhead while Rangers also draw 0-0 at Dundee United, but stay top of the table.
14: Celtic survive stormy AGM, with Jock Brown taking abuse from the shareholders.
15: Celtic and Rangers pull off creditable results in Europe. Celtic post a 2-1 win over Vitoria Guimaraes while Rangers draw 1-1 with Beitar Jerusalem in Israel.
17: Hearts go down 1-0 to Real Mallorca in the Cup-Winners Cup first leg at Tynecastle.
20: Rangers and Celtic draw the first Old Firm game of the season 0-0 at Ibrox.
22: Celtic unveil new Norwegian signing Vidar Riseth from Austrian side Lask Linz
23: Celtic slump to a 1-0 home defeat to St Johnstone. Meanwhile, Rangers battle back to secure a 1-1 draw at Aberdeen.
26: Celtic slump to fifth in the table after 1-1 home draw with Hearts. Rangers stretch their lead at the top with a 2-0 win at Dunfermline, and Kilmarnock move into second after a 1-0 win over Aberdeen.
28: Rangers accept bid of £800,000 for Craig Moore from Crystal Palace.
29: Celtic win through to the second round of the UEFA Cup. The Bhoys beat Vitoria Guimaraes 2-1 at Parkhead.
30: Motherwell sign Derek Adams from Ross County

1998-99 REVIEW OF THE SEASON

October

1: Rangers go through to the second round of the UEFA Cup after a 4-2 win over Beitar Jerusalem at Ibrox. Hearts exit the Cup-Winners Cup in controversial circumstances. They go out 2-1 on aggregate to Real Mallorca after a 1-1 draw in Palma, but launch a protest after they find a 10cm difference in the height of the goalposts. Chairman Chris Robinson also suggests that the UEFA delegate at the match has indulged in a little too much of the local hospitality.

2: Celtic draw Swiss side FC Zurich and Rangers pull Germans Bayer Leverkusen out of the hat for the second round of the UEFA Cup.

4: Rangers complete a good week by surging five points clear at the top of the table after a 1-0 win over Dundee at Ibrox.

10: Scotland fight back to beat Estonia 3-2 at Tynecastle in the Euro 2000 qualifying clash. England draw 0-0 with Bulgaria at Wembley.

12: Jim Leighton quits international football after his poor performance against Estonia.

14: Billy Davies named new Motherwell manager. The 34-year-old replaces Harri Kampmann who quit after just eight months.

Scotland are again disappointing as they record a 2-1 win over the Faroes at Pittodrie.

16: Ex-Motherwell boss Harri Kampmann takes swipe at Pat Nevin. He says: "I had no confidence at the club after he arrived." Hearts lose their appeal to be reinstated to the Cup-Winners Cup after the goalpost debacle.

17: In the Premier League, Rangers stay on top with a 3-0 win over Hearts at Ibrox. Kilmarnock maintain their second spot with a 2-0 win at Dundee United, but Celtic stumble again after a 2-2 draw at Dunfermline.

20: Celtic draw 1-1 with FC Zurich at Parkhead in the UEFA Cup. Tom Boyd is sent off for handling a goal-bound shot on the line. The Swiss miss the penalty, but equalise in the second half.

22: Rangers record a sensational 2-1 UEFA Cup victory over Bayer Leverkusen in Germany.

25: Rangers go through to the League Cup final after a 5-0 thrashing of Airdrie at Parkhead.

27: Celtic sign Slovak midfielder Lubomir Moravcik for £300,000 from German side MVV Duisburg. Motherwell also move into the transfer market by signing Manchester City midfielder Ged Brannan and picking up John Spencer on loan from Everton. St Johnstone stun Hearts to set up a League Cup final clash with Rangers. The Perth men demolish Jim Jefferies' side 3-0.

28: Motherwell new boy John Spencer sinks Rangers with the only goal of the game in a league clash at Fir Park.

29: Brian Laudrup leaves Chelsea after just five months. The ex-Ibrox star signs for FC Copenhagen.

31: Celtic slump seven points behind Rangers when they lose 2-0 to Kilmarnock, while the Ibrox side stay a point ahead of the Rugby Parkers after a 2-1 win over Dundee United at home.

1998-99 REVIEW OF THE SEASON

November

2: Rangers are stunned by the news that Sebastian Rozental needs a fourth operation on his damaged knee.
3: Celtic hit rock-bottom as they crash out of the UEFA Cup to mediocre Swiss side FC Zurich. The Parkhead men go down 4-2 and Fergus McCann and Jock Brown need a police escort to reach their cars at Glasgow Airport.
4: Derek McInnes leaves Ibrox to join English First Division side Stockport County on loan.
5: Rangers complete a glorious UEFA Cup victory over Bayer Leverkusen after a 1-1 second leg draw at Ibrox to go through 3-2 on aggregate.
6: Rangers hit the Euro jackpot as they draw Italian giants Parma in the UEFA Cup third round and, on a busy day at Ibrox, French World Cup striker Stephane Guivarc'h signs on.
7: Jock Brown sensationally leaves Celtic and the team beat Dundee 6-1. Kilmarnock go down 2-1 at Hearts.
8: Stephane Guivarc'h comes off the bench to score twice in Rangers' incredible 7-0 thrashing of St Johnstone at Perth.
10: Parkhead legend Kenny Dalglish reveals he is head of a consortium, along with rock star Jim Kerr, bidding to buy Celtic.
11: Sebastian Rozental returns home to Chile for a fourth knee op. Jonathan Gould signs an improved contract at Parkhead which ties him to the club until 2003.
13: Dick Advocaat announces he expects to sign German international keeper Andreas Kopke. Dunfermline bid for former Ibrox hero Mark Hateley.
14: Celtic booed off the park after losing to St Johnstone as Rangers move a massive 10 points clear of the Parkhead men. Kilmarnock slip six points off the pace after a 1-1 draw at Dundee.
18: Celtic sign Swede Johan Mjallby from AIK Stockholm for £1.5m. Rangers pull the plug on Andreas Kopke after the German takes too long to agree a deal.
20: Darren Jackson joins Coventry on loan from Celtic.
21: Celtic trounce Rangers 5-1 at Parkhead in Old Firm clash at Parkhead. Lubo Moravcik (2), Henrik Larsson (2), and Mark Burchill score for Celts while van Bronckhorst hits the net for Rangers. Scott Wilson sees red in the first half as Celtic close the gap on their ancient rivals to seven points. Kilmarnock miss their chance to edge closer to Rangers when they draw 0-0 with Motherwell.
25: Rangers draw 1-1 with Parma in the first leg of their Euro clash. Celtic hit work permit problems in their bid to sign Mark Viduka from Croatia Zagreb.
28: Kilmarnock turn up the heat at the top with a 3-0 win at Dunfermline while Celtic beat Motherwell 2-0 at Parkhead, recording successive league wins for the first time all season.
29: Rangers win the League Cup with a 2-1 win over St Johnstone at Parkhead. Stephane Guivarc'h and Jorg Albertz are on the mark for Gers. Nick Dasovic scores for Saints

1998-99 REVIEW OF THE SEASON

December

2: Celtic finally complete the signing of Australian striker Mark Viduka from Croatia Zagreb for £3m.
3: Brian Kidd named new manager of Blackburn Rovers
5: Mark Viduka walks out on Celtic just two days after signing. The Aussie hit-man cites stress as the reason for his departure. Rangers slip-up in the title chase with a 1-1 draw with Dunfermline at Ibrox and Kilmarnock draw level at the top with a 4-0 demolition of Aberdeen.
6: Celtic, still reeling from Viduka's disapearance, crash dismally 2-1 to Hearts at Tynecastle.
8: Rangers lose 3-1 to Parma in the seond leg of their Euro clash in Italy. Gers look on for a tremendous victory after Jorg Albertz gives them a 28th-minute lead, but the roof caves in after Sergio Porrini gets sent off on the stroke of half-time. Fergus McCann flies out to Croatia in a bid to solve the Mark Viduka situation. Alex Miller sacked as manager of Aberdeen. Alex McLeish installed as favourite to take over, but the club appoint Paul Hegarty as temporary boss until the end of the season.
10: Rangers sign Neil McCann from Hearts for £2m. Mark Viduka surfaces in Australia. It's revealed that money may be the real motive for him going AWOL.
11: Partick Thistle directors are raging after the club is reported to be on the verge of a merger with Clydebank. Dick Advocaat tells Jorg Albertz he can leave the club if he feels threatened by the signing of Neil McCann.
12: Rangers win the top-of-the-table clash with Kilmarnock at Ibrox and stretch their lead to three points. Celtic manage to snatch a draw with a late goal from Henrik Larsson at Dundee United, but slip to seven behind Rangers, who have a game in hand.
14: St Mirren sack Tony Fitzpatrick and Mark Hateley emerges as front runner for the job.
18: Brian McLair leaves Motherwell and joins Blackburn as assistant manager.
19: Fergus McCann knocks back Kenny Dalglish's bid for Celtic. The Parkhead club record a 5-0 win over Dunfermline at home, while Rangers stay in front with a 3-2 win at Tynecastle, Killie stay close after a 2-0 win over Dundee United.
21: Kenny Dalglish says he will try again to bid for Celtic after Fergus McCann knocked back his consortium's original offer.
23: Stefan Klos signs for Rangers in a £700,000 deal.
24: Tom Hendrie is named new St Mirren manager after leaving Alloa.
26: Rangers beat St Johnstone 1-0 at Ibrox thanks to a goal from Sergio Porrini, but Kilmarnock keep up the pressure with a 1-0 win at Hearts as the Tynecastle men hit free fall into the relegation zone.
27: Celtic beat Dundee 3-0 at Dens Park.
29: Dick Advocaat reported to be stalling on a new deal at Ibrox after talks with chairman David Murray.
30: Rangers take a giant step towards the title with a last-gasp 2-1 victory over Dundee United at Tannadice. Rod Wallace nets the winner with seconds remaining to increase the Ibrox club's lead at the top to six points over Kilmarnock

1998-99 REVIEW OF THE SEASON

January

1: Kilmarnock kick-off the New Year in winning style with a 2-1 victory over Motherwell.
2: Rangers and Celtic fight out a 2-2 draw at Ibrox in an Old Firm thriller. Amato and Wallace net for Rangers while Stubbs and Larsson score for Celtic.
6: The Mark Viduka row rumbles on as it emerges the runaway striker will try settle his cash differences with the club before returning to Parkhead.
7: Motherwell open talks to sign John Spencer on a permanent basis from Everton as his Fir Park loan deal comes to a close. Dermot Desmond seems set to make a fresh bid for power at Celtic as Fergus McCann gears up to the leave the club in March.
11: Rangers set to bid for Dundee midfielder Dariusz Adamczuk and David Murray vows to step up the hunt for a shirt sponsor for the club after the departure of chief executive Bob Brannan. Gers are without a sponsor for the new campaign and that is reckoned to be the reason behind Brannan's departure.
12: Rangers jet out to Florida as Scottish football's first winter break gets under way. Dutch legend Johan Cruyff is named European footballer of the century.
13: Mark Viduka tries to board Celtic's plane as they head off for Spain on a winter break. The Aussie is ordered off by Fergus McCann. He wants Viduka to stay behind until a deal can be worked out when the club return.
14: Andy Goram joins Motherwell until the end of the season. Celtic pay the price for playing games on their break to Spain. Six players take serious injuries in a bruising clash with FC Balona which saw one of the Spanish players sent off.
17: Rangers fight a 2-2 draw with Brazilian side Atletico Miniero in Florida and Celtic keeper Stewart Kerr reveals he has knocked back a move to Leeds United. The Parkhead club accepted the Elland Road club's offer of £800,000, but Kerr refused to go.
22: Henrik Larsson named BBC Scotland Sports Personality of the Year for 1998.
23: In the third round of the Scottish Cup, Aberdeen crash out to Second Division Livingston, Ayr United knock out Kilmarnock, and Motherwell send holders Hearts spinning out of the competition. Celtic and Rangers go through after victories over Airdrie and Stenhousemuir.
25: Mark Viduka finally rejoins Celtic after his Australian exile and immediately gets into a fight with his new team-mates. His new Parkhead pals pelt him with snowballs as he arrives at training!
26: Mark Burchill signs a new four-and-a-half-year deal with Celtic. John Spencer finally seals a permanent move from Everton to Motherwell.
27: Rangers go seven points clear of Kilmarnock and 13 points clear of Celtic with a 4-0 win over Dundee at Dens Park.
30: Rangers stretch their lead at the top again with 4-2 win at Aberdeen and Kilmarnock slip further behind after a 0-0 draw with Dundee.
31: Celtic demolish St Johnstone 5-0 at Parkhead.

1998-99 REVIEW OF THE SEASON

February

1: Rangers striker Gabriel Amato on the verge of leaving Ibrox for a switch to Leicester City.
2: Zinidine Zidane named FIFA World Player of the Year.
4: Derek McInnes returns to Ibrox ready to fight for his first-team place after a three-month loan spell at Stockport County.
5: David Hannah signs for Dundee United from Celtic. Vinnie Jones has talks with Hearts over a possible move to Tynecastle. Darren Jackson knocks back a move to China because he can't stomach the food!
Dick Advocaat tells unsettles striker Gabriel Amato to grin and bear it at Ibrox.
6: Celtic keep up their fine form with a 3-0 win over Hearts, while Kilmarnock's hopes of title glory take another severe battering as they lose at Pittodrie.
7: Rangers keep ahead of the chasing pack with an impressive 3-0 thumping of Dunfermline at East End Park.
Andy Goram's future in doubt after it is reported he has links with Northern Ireland terrorists.
9: Kilmarnock midfielder Gary Holt, picked to play for Northern Ireland, discovers he can't play after all because his alleged parentage link doesn't exist.
10: Motherwell announce they will stand by shamed keeper Andy Goram.
12: Blackburn Rovers complete the signing of St Mirren starlets Burton O'Brien and David McNamee.
13: After the shocks of the last round, the big boys take over in the fourth round of the Scottish Cup. Celtic thrash Dunfermline 4-0 while Livingston, conquerors of Aberdeen, go down 3-1 to St Johnstone
14: Rangers trounce Hamilton 6-0 at Firhill with Neil McCann netting his first goal for the club since his move from Hearts.
17: Celtic end Kilmarnock's title challenge with a 1-0 win over the Ayrshire men at Celtic Park, Vidar Riseth heads the winner. Leaders Rangers remain a massive 10 points clear.
19: Motherwell announce they will not field Andy Goram against Celtic in case it sparks crowd trouble. The keeper asked the Fir Park club to axe him from the game.
20: Rangers thrash Dundee 6-1 at Dens Park to stay out in front in the title race. Hearts are firmly entrenched in the danger zone after losing 2-0 to St Johnstone.
21: Celtic destroy Motherwell 7-1 at Fir Park, Henrik Larsson scores four.
24: Hamilton Council announce they will honour the town's favourite son Davie Cooper. A bronze statue will be erected in honour of the Rangers legend.
26: Rangers striker Gordon Durie's season is over after an operation on an Achilles tendon injury.
27: Celtic come back from a goal down with 15 minutes to go to beat Dundee United as Mark Viduka comes off the bench to make his debut for the Parkhead club.
28: Rangers stay out in front in the title chase with a magnificent 5-0 demolition of Kilmarnock at Rugby Park.

1998-99 REVIEW OF THE SEASON

March

1: SFA supremo Jim Farry is suspended from his post of Chief Executive of the SFA. Celtic had complained to the governing body that Farry held up the registration of Jorg Cadete and ensured he would miss vital games in the championship run-in of the 1995/96 season, eventually won by Rangers by four points.
The Association cave in over Celtic's complaints and agree a compensation deal with Fergus McCann.
2: Rangers draw 4-4 with Middlesbrough in Alan McLaren's testimonial match at Ibrox.
6: Owen Coyle leaves Motherwell to join Dunfermline for £175,000. Rangers move into the semi-finals of the Scottish Cup with a 2-1 win over Falkirk at Ibrox. They are joined in the last four by St Johnstone who beat Motherwell 2-0 at Fir Park.
8: Celtic beat Morton 3-0 at Cappielow to move into the semis of the Scottish Cup with Mark Viduka hitting his first goal for the club.
9: Jim Farry is sacked by the SFA for delaying the transfer of Jorg Cadete.
10: John Lambie is the new boss at Partick Thistle as Tommy Bryce returns to the playing staff at Firhill.
12: Rangers' Lorenzo Amoruso and Giovanni van Bronckhorst declare that Scottish football is too easy in a newspaper article.
13: Dick Advocaat blasts the pair for their outburst and pins the offending article on the dressing room wall.
On the field Rangers continue their solid league form with a 2-1 over Motherwell at Ibrox.
14: Celtic thump Aberdeen 5-1 at Pittodrie.
15: Fergus McCann names British Aerospace boss Allan MacDonald as his successor at Parkhead.
16: Celtic pair Phil O'Donnell and Simon Donnelly announce they will sign for Sheffield Wednesday under freedom of contract at the end of the season. Dundee United set up a semi-final clash with Celtic in the Scottish Cup after beating Ayr in a Tannadice replay 2-1. Rangers will face St Johnstone in the other semi.
17: Rangers win the race to sign Dutch striker Michael Mols. The Utrecht hit-man will join the Ibrox club at the end of the season.
20: Rangers and Celtic announce a joint sponsorship deal with American cable giants NTL worth £13m. Rangers lose 1-0 to Dundee United at Ibrox, giving Celtic fresh hope in the title race.
21: Celtic can only draw 0-0 with Kilmarnock at Rugby Park and miss a golden chance to close the gap on Rangers. John Greig named Greatest Ever Ranger at a gala dinner in Glasgow.
25: Darren Jackson leaves Celtic to sign for Hearts in a £350,000 deal.
26: UEFA cancel Scotland's Euro qualifier against Bosnia at Ibrox over safety fears about NATO air strikes of Yugoslavia.
31: Scotland lose 2-1 to the Czech Republic in a vital Euro qualifier at Celtic Park. Skipper Gary McAllister is booed off the park as he is substituted after a lacklustre performance.

1998-99 REVIEW OF THE SEASON

April

2: Dick Advocaat signs American midfield star Claudio Reyna for £2m for Rangers' title run-in.
3: Celtic turn-over Dundee 5-0 at Parkhead to increase the pressure on championship favourites Rangers. Hearts stay rock-bottom after a 2-2 draw with Kilmarnock at Tynecastle.
4: Rangers lose 3-1 at St Johnwith new signing Craig Moore grabbing their goal as the gap at the top becomes just six points. Hibs clinch the First Division championship after a 2-0 win over Hamilton Accies.
7: Stephane Mahe claims he was ignored when he offered the hand of friendship to fellow-Frenchman Stephane Guivarc'h.
9: Jozef Venglos is given a clean bill of health by doctors in Slovakia after it was rumoured the Celtic boss would have to quit Parkhead due to ill health.
10: Celtic win through to the final of the Scottish Cup after a 2-0 win over Dundee United at Ibrox.
11: Rangers set up an Old Firm final as they demolish St Johnstone 4-0 at Parkhead.
13: Henrik Larsson brings months of speculation to an end by signing a new four-year deal at Celtic.
14: Celtic turn up the heat in the title race with a superb 4-2 win over Hearts at Tynecastle. Rangers keep their lead however, as they beat Dunfermline 1-0 in a nervy performance at Ibrox.
15: Jonas Thern effectively announces his retirement due to a knee injury.
16: Dr Jo Venglos announces he will be more than happy to have Kenny Dalglish at Parkhead as the club's Technical Director.
17: Celtic beat Motherwell 1-0 at Parkhead thanks to a Henrik Larsson penalty. 'Well keeper Andy Goram turns in an inspired performance to almost destroy Celtic's title dream.
18: Rangers again slip up in the championship with a 1-1 draw at Dundee. The result leaves rivals Celtic just four points behind. Henrik Larsson picks up the Player of the Year Award to cap a fine season at Parkhead.
19: Former Rangers boss Graeme Souness is sacked by Benfica after a string of bad results.
22: Manchester United reach the European Cup final after a magnificent 3-2 win over Juventus in Turin. They will face German side Bayern Munich in the final after they defeated Dynamo Kiev.
23: Celtic look set to steal Dariusz Adamczuk from under the noses of Rangers.
25: Celtic lose their grip on their title as they lose 1-0 at St Johnstone.
26: Rangers move seven points clear at the top as they come from a goal down to defeat Aberdeen 3-1 at Ibrox. The result means a win in the Old Firm game in a week's time will see Gers clinch the championship at the home of their greatest rivals.
28: Scotland stun Europe as they beat Germany 1-0 in a friendly in Bremen. Everton star Don Hutchieson fires the only goal of the game for a historic victory.
30: Motherwell are fined £5,250 for fielding Lee McCulloch in a game against Rangers while he was serving a ban.

1998-99 REVIEW OF THE SEASON

May

2: Rangers crush Celtic 3-0 at Parkhead to clinch the championship in stunning style.

Two goals from Neil McCann and a Jorg Albertz penalty seal a historic win for the Ibrox men.

However, the game is marred by crowd trouble before, after and during the game.

Referee Hugh Dallas orders Celt Stephane Mahe off for dissent with the score at 1-0 and is felled by a coin from the Celtic end. Shortly afterwards, he awards Rangers a penalty and Albertz nets to put Rangers home and dry.

In the second period Rangers' Rod Wallace is sent off for retaliation and Vidar Riseth joins him in an early bath four minutes later after a shocking attack on Claudio Reyna.

The jubilant Rangers players perform a huddle after the win, further enraging the already devasted Celts fans.

3: Kenny Dalglish denies he has already accepted the role of Technical Director at Celtic. Hearts are assured of a place in the Premier League next season after they beat Dunfermline 2-0 at Tynecastle .

5: Celtic Chief Executive Allan MacDonald denies rumours that he is set to quit the club over interference from the departed Fergus McCann.

6: Killie fans are riled after pictures reveal their players, Ally McCoist and Ian Durrant, in the Rangers end celebrating their old club's victory Celtic at Parkhead.

8: Jorg Albertz admits Rangers players were stupid to do a huddle after the Old Firm game.

9: Celtic are again in trouble after Mark Viduka is sent off for spitting at Marc Millar during their 2-1 victory over Dunfermline which relegates the Pars.

10: Rangers draw 0-0 with Hearts and pick up the Premier League trophy in front of 50,000 delighted fans at Ibrox.

11: Aberdeen announce that Paul Hegarty will step down as caretaker boss at the end of the season.

14: Dariusz Adamczuk turn his back on a move to Celtic because of the length of deal on offer.

15: Champions Rangers beat Motherwell 5-1 at Fir Park and Celtic beat Aberdeen 3-2 at Parkhead. In the battle for Europe, St Johnstone and Kilmarnock fight out a 1-1 draw at Rugby Park.

22: St Johnstone nick the last place in Europe after beating Dundee 1-0 at McDiarmid, Killie lose out on the last day as they draw 1-1 with champions Rangers at Ibrox.

In Division One, Hamilton and Stranraer are relegated with champs Livingston and runners-up Inverness Caley taking their place from Division Two.

East Fife and Forfar go down to the Third Division and Ross County come up as champs along with second-placed Stenhousemuir.

26: Manchester United win the European Cup courtesy of a stunning fightback to beat Bayern Munich 2-1 in Barcelona.

29: Rangers complete a magnificent treble by beating Celtic 1-0 to lift the Scottish Cup. Rod Wallace nets the winner.

ABERDEEN

Pittodrie Street, AB2 1QH
Phone: 01224 650400
Fax: 01224 644173

NICKNAME:	The Dons
COLOURS:	Red and white
GROUND	Pittodrie
CAPACITY:	21,634
RECORD ATT:	45,061 (v Hearts, 1954)
RECORD VICTORY	13-0 (v Peterhead, 1923)
RECORD DEFEAT	(0-8 v Celtic, 1965)
MANAGER:	Ebbe Skovdahl
CHAIRMAN:	Stewart Milne
MOST LEAGUE GOALS (1 SEASON)	38, Benny Yorston, 1929-30
GOALS (OVERALL)	199, Joe Harper

HONOURS

LEAGUE CHAMPIONSHIP (4): Division 1 – 1954-55. Premier Division – 1979-80, 1983-84, 1984-85. SCOTTISH CUP (7): 1947, 1970, 1982, 1983, 1984, 1986, 1990. LEAGUE CUP (5): 1955-56, 1976-77, 1985-86, S1989-90, 1995-96. EUROPEAN CUP-WINNERS CUP 1983. EUROPEAN SUPER CUP 1983-84.

LEAGUE RESULTS 1998-99

Dundee 0 Aberdeen 2
Aberdeen 3 Celtic 2
Hearts 2 Aberdeen 0
Dunfermline 1 Aberdeen 1
Aberdeen 1 Motherwell 1
St Johnstone 2 Aberdeen 0
Aberdeen 1 Rangers 1
Aberdeen 0, Kilmarnock 1
Dundee Utd 1 Aberdeen 0

Aberdeen 2 Dundee 2
Celtic 2 Aberdeen 0
Motherwell 2 Aberdeen 2
Aberdeen 2 Dunfermline 1
Rangers 2 Aberdeen 1
Aberdeen 0 St Johnstone 1
Aberdeen 0 Dundee Utd 3
Kilmarnock 4 Aberdeen 0
Aberdeen 2 Hearts 0

Dundee 1 Aberdeen 2
Dunfermline 1 Aberdeen 2
Aberdeen 1 Motherwell 1
St Johnstone 4 Aberdeen 1
Aberdeen 2 Rangers 4
Aberdeen 2 Kilmarnock 1
Dundee Utd 3 Aberdeen 0
Hearts 0, Aberdeen 2
Aberdeen 1 Celtic 5

Motherwell 1 Aberdeen 1
Aberdeen 3 Dunfermline 1
Kilmarnock 4 Aberdeen 2
Aberdeen 0 Dundee Utd 4
Rangers 3 Aberdeen 1
Aberdeen 1 St Johnstone 0
Aberdeen 1 Dundee 2
Celtic 3 Aberdeen 2
Aberdeen 2 Hearts 5

CELTIC

Celtic Park, Glasgow, G40 3RE
Phone: 0141 556 2611
Fax: 0141 551 8106

NICKNAME:	The Bhoys
COLOURS:	Green and white hoops, white shorts, white socks
GROUND	Celtic Park
CAPACITY:	60,294
RECORD ATT:	92,000 (v Rangers, 1954)
RECORD VICTORY	11-0 (v Dundee, 1895)
RECORD DEFEAT	(0-8 v Motherwell, 1937)
MANAGER:	Dr Jozef Venglos
CHIEF EXECUTIVE:	Allan MacDonald
MOST LEAGUE GOALS (1 SEASON)	50, Jimmy McGrory, 1935-36

HONOURS

LEAGUE CHAMPIONS (36): 1892-93, 1893-94, 1895-96, 1897-98, 1904-05, 1905-06, 1906-07, 1907-08, 1908-09, 1909-10, 1913-14, 1914-15, 1915-16, 1916-17, 1918-19, 1921-22, 1925-26, 1935-36, 1937-38, 1953-54, 1965-66, 1966-67, 1967-68, 1968-69, 1969-70, 1970-71, 1971-72, 1972-73, 1973-74, 1976-77, 1978-79, 1980-81, 1981-82, 1985-86, 1987-88, 97-98.

SCOTTISH CUP WINNERS (30): 1892, 1899, 1900, 1904, 1907, 1908, 1911, 1912, 1914, 1923, 1925, 1927, 1931, 1933, 1937, 1951, 1954, 1965, 1967, 1969, 1971, 1972, 1974, 1975, 1977, 1980, 1985, 1988, 1989, 1985.

LEAGUE CUP WINNERS (10): 1956-57, 1957-58, 1965-66, 1966-67, 1967-68, 1968-69, 1969-70, 1974-75, 1982-83, 1997-98.

EUROPEAN CUP WINNERS (1): 1966-67.

LEAGUE RESULTS 1998-99

Celtic 5 (Burley 3, Donnelly, MacKay), **Dunfermline 0**
Aberdeen 3 (Perry, Blinker og, Hignett), **Celtic 2** (Larsson 2, 1 pen).
Celtic 2 (Burley, Burchill), **Dundee United 1** (Winters)
Dundee 1 (Annand pen), **Celtic 1** (Burley)
Celtic 1 (Blinker), **Kilmarnock 1** (Varielle)
Rangers 0, Celtic 0
Celtic 0, St Johnstone 1 (Dassovic)
Celtic 1 (Donnelly), **Hearts 1** (Hamilton)
Motherwell 1 (Adams), **Celtic 2** (Brattbakk, Lambert)
Dunfermline 2 (Britton pen, French), **Celtic 2** (Larsson, Brattbakk)
Celtic 2 (Donnelly 2), **Aberdeen 0**
Kilmarnock 2 (Roberts, Mitchell) **Celtic 0**
Celtic 6 (Larsson 3, 2 pens, Burchill 2, Donnelly), **Dundee 1** (Annand).
St Johnstone 2 (Simao, McAnespie), **Celtic 1** (Larsson)
Celtic 5 (Moravcik 2, Larsson 2, Burchill), **Rangers 1** (Van Bronckhorst)
Celtic 2 (Larsson, O'Donnell), **Motherwell 0**
Hearts 2 (Adam 2) **Celtic** 1 (O'Donnell)
Dundee Utd 1 (Zetterlund), **Celtic** 1 (Larsson)
Celtic 5 (Larsson 2, 1 pen, Mjallby, Moravcik 2), **Dunfermline 0**
Dundee 0, Celtic 3 (O'Donnell, Riseth, Douglas og)
Rangers 2 (Amato, Wallace), **Celtic 2** (, Larsson)
Celtic 5 (Brattbakk 3, Moravcik, Larsson), **St Johnstone 0**
Celtic 3 (Larsson 3, 1 pen), **Hearts 0**
Celtic 1 (Riseth), **Kilmarnock 0**
Motherwell 1 (Brannan), **Celtic 7** (Larsson 4, 1 pen, Moravcik, Burley, Burchill)
Celtic 2 (Burley, Larsson), **Dundee Utd 1** (Dodds)
Aberdeen 1 (Winters), **Celtic 5** (Viduka 2, Larsson 2, Burley)
Kilmarnock 0, Celtic 0
Celtic 5 (Larsson 2, 1 pen, Burley, Viduka, Blinker), **Dundee 0**
Hearts 2 (Adam 2), **Celtic 4** (Riseth, Blinker, Viduka 2)
Celtic 1 (Larsson pen), **Motherwell 0**
St Johnstone 1 (O'Halloran), **Celtic 0**
Celtic 0, Rangers 3 (McCann 2, Albertz pen)
Dunfermline 1 (Coyle), **Celtic 2** (Johnson 2)
Celtic 3 (Blinker, Johnson, Burchill), **Aberdeen 2** (Mayer, Perry)
Dundee Utd 1 (Dodds pen), **Celtic 2** (Burchill 2)

LORENZO AMORUSO shows off the Premier League championship trophy

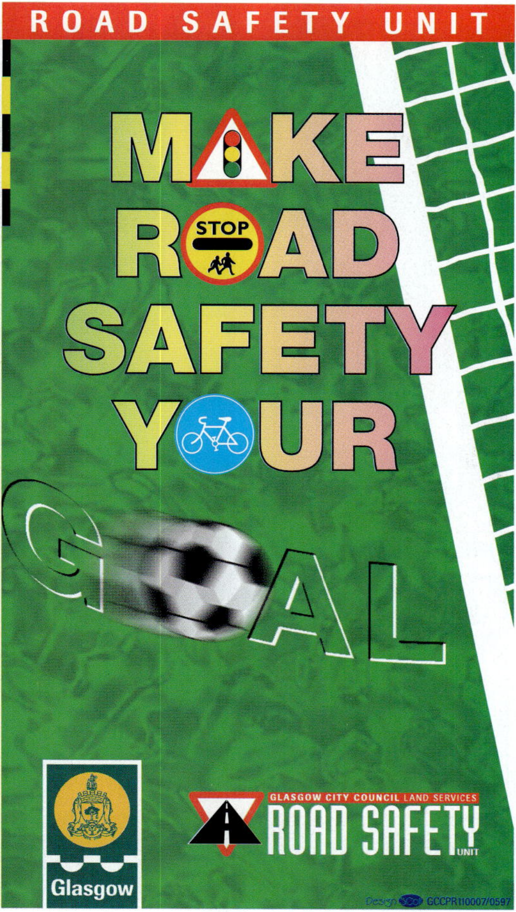
ROAD SAFETY UNIT
MAKE ROAD SAFETY YOUR GOAL
STOP
Glasgow
GLASGOW CITY COUNCIL LAND SERVICES
ROAD SAFETY UNIT
GCCPR110007/0597

KILMARNOCK F.C.

MOTHERWELL F.C.

DUNDEE

Sandeman Street, DD3 7JY
Phone: 01382 826104
Fax: 01382 832284

NICKNAME: The Dark Blues
COLOURS: Dark blue, red, and white
GROUND Dens Park
CAPACITY: 10,000
RECORD ATT: 43,024 v Rangers, 1953
RECORD VICTORY 10-0 v Alloa, 1957, and 10-0 v Dunfermline, 1957
RECORD DEFEAT 0-11 v Celtic 1895
MANAGER: Jocky Scott
CHAIRMAN: Jim Marr
MOST LEAGUE
GOALS (1 SEASON) 38, Dave Halliday, 1923-24
GOALS (OVERALL) 113, Alan Gilzean

HONOURS

LEAGUE CHAMPIONS (1): 1961-62. First Division (3): 1978-79, 1991-92, 1997-98. Division II (1): 1946-47. SCOTTISH CUP (1): 1910. LEAGUE CUP WINNERS (3): 1951-52, 1952-53, 1973-74.

LEAGUE RESULTS 1998-99

Dundee 0 Aberdeen 2
Dunfermline 2 Dundee 0
Dundee 0 St Johnstone 1
Dundee 1 Celtic 1
Hearts 0 Dundee 2
Dundee 2 Dundee Utd 2
Kilmarnock 2 Dundee 1
Dundee 1 Motherwell 0
Rangers 1 Dundee 0

Aberdeen 2 Dundee 2
Dundee 1 Dunfermline 0
Dundee 1 Hearts 0
Celtic 6 Dundee 1
Dundee 1 Kilmarnock 1
Dundee Utd 0 Dundee 1
St Johnstone 1 Dundee 1
Dundee 1 Aberdeen 2
Motherwell 2 Dundee 1

Dundee 0 Celtic 3
Hearts 1 Dundee 2
Dundee 1 Dundee Utd 3
Dundee 0 Rangers 4
Kilmarnock 0 Dundee 0
Dundee 1 Motherwell 0
Rangers 6 Dundee 1
Dundee 0 St Johnstone 1
Dunfermline 2 Dundee 0

Dundee 2 Hearts 0
Celtic 5 Dundee 0
Motherwell 1 Dundee 2
Dundee 1 Rangers 1
Dundee 2 Kilmarnock 1
Dundee Utd 0 Dundee 2
Aberdeen 1 Dundee 2
Dundee 3 Dunfermline 1
St Johnstone 1 Dundee 0

DUNDEE UNITED

Tannadice St, DD3 7JW
Phone: 01382 833166
Fax: 01382 889398

NICKNAME: **The Terrors**
COLOURS: **Tangerine and black**
GROUND **Tannadice Park**
CAPACITY: **14,209**
RECORD ATT: **28,000 v Barcelona, 1966**
RECORD VICTORY **14-0 v Nithsdale, 1931**
RECORD DEFEAT **1-12, v Motherwell, 1954**
MANAGER: **Paul Sturrock**
CHAIRMAN: **Jim McLean**
MOST LEAGUE
GOALS (1 SEASON) **41, John Coyle, 1955-56**
GOALS (OVERALL) **158, Peter Mackay**

HONOURS

LEAGUE CHAMPIONS (1): 1982-83. Division 2 (2): 1924-25, 1928-29. SCOTTISH CUP (1): 1994. LEAGUE CUP (2): 1979-80, 1980-81.

LEAGUE RESULTS 1998-99

Kilmarnock 2 Dundee Utd 0
Dundee Utd 0 Hearts 0
Celtic 2 Dundee Utd 1
Motherwell 1 Dundee Utd 0
Dundee Utd 0 Rangers 0
Dundee 2 Dundee Utd 2
Dundee Utd 1 Dunfermline 1
St Johnstone 1 Dundee Utd 3
Dundee Utd 1 Aberdeen 0

Dundee Utd 0 Kilmarnock 2
Hearts 0 Dundee Utd 1
Rangers 2 Dundee Utd 1
Dundee Utd 2 Motherwell 2
Dunfermline 2 Dundee Utd 1
Dundee Utd 0 Dundee 1
Aberdeen 0 Dundee Utd 3
Dundee Utd 1 St Johnstone 1
Dundee Utd 1 Celtic 1

Kilmarnock 2 Dundee Utd 0
Motherwell 2 Dundee Utd 0
Dundee Utd 1 Rangers 2
Dundee 1 Dundee Utd 3
Dundee Utd 1 Dunfermline 1
St Johnstone 1 Dundee Utd 0
Dundee Utd 3 Aberdeen 0
Celtic 2 Dundee Utd 1
Rangers 0 Dundee Utd 1

Dundee Utd 0 Motherwell 3
Dundee Utd 1 Hearts 3
Aberdeen 0 Dundee Utd 4
Dundee Utd 0 St Johnstone 1
Dunfermline 2 Dundee Utd 0
Dundee Utd 0 Dundee 2
Dundee Utd 0 Kilmarnock 0
Hearts 4 Dundee Utd 1
Dundee Utd 1 Celtic 2

HEART OF MIDLOTHIAN

Gorgie Road, Edinburgh, EH11 2NL
Telephone: 0131 337 6132
Fax: 0131 337 6132

NICKNAME: **The Jam Tarts**
COLOURS: **Maroon, white shorts, maroon and white socks**
GROUND: **Tynecastle Park**
CAPACITY: **18,000 (all seated)**
RECORD ATT: **53,396 (v Rangers, 1932)**
RECORD VICTORY **21-0 (v Anchor, 1880)**
RECORD DEFEAT **1-8 (v Vale of Leven, 1888)**
MANAGER: **Jim Jefferies**
CHAIRMAN: **Leslie G. Deans**
MOST LEAGUE
GOALS (1 SEASON) **44, Barney Battles**
GOALS (OVERALL) **214, John Robertson**

HONOURS

LEAGUE CHAMPIONSHIP (4): Division I – 1894-95, 1896-97, 1957-58, 1959-60. First Division – 1979-80. SCOTTISH CUP WINNERS (6): 1891, 1896, 1901, 1906, 1956, 1998. LEAGUE CUP WINNERS (4): 1954-55, 1958-59, 1959-60, 1962-63.

LEAGUE RESULTS 1998-99

Hearts 2 Rangers 1
Dundee Utd 0 Hearts 0
Hearts 2 Aberdeen 0
Kilmarnock 3 Hearts 0
Hearts 0 Dundee 2
Dunfermline 1 Hearts 1
Hearts 3 Motherwell 0
Celtic 1 Hearts 1
Hearts 1 St Johnstone 1

Rangers 3 Hearts 0
Hearts 0 Dundee Utd 1
Dundee 1 Hearts 0
Hearts 2 Kilmarnock 1
Motherwell 3 Hearts 2
Hearts 2 Dunfermline 1
Hearts 2 Celtic 1
St Johnstone 1 Hearts 1
Aberdeen 2 Hearts 0

Hearts 2 Rangers 3
Kilmarnock 1 Hearts 0
Hearts 1 Dundee 2
Dunfermline 0 Hearts 0
Hearts 0 Motherwell 2
Celtic 3 Hearts 0
Hearts 0 St Johnstone 2
Hearts 0 Aberdeen 2)
Dundee 2 Hearts 0

Hearts 2 Kilmarnock 2
Dundee United 1 Hearts 3
Hearts 2 Celtic 4
St Johnstone 0 Hearts 0
Motherwell 0 Hearts 4
Hearts 2 Dunfermline 0
Rangers 0 Hearts 0
Hearts 4 Dundee United 1
Aberdeen 2 Hearts 5

Isn't it time you got involved
in Men & Health Week?
A week of local and national events to promote
health and fitness. From 10th-17th September 1999.
MEN & HEALTH WEEK

HIBERNIAN

Albion Road, Edinburgh, EH7 5GQ
Telephone: 0131 661 2159
Fax: 0131 659 6488

NICKNAME: The Hibees
COLOURS: Green and white, white shorts, green and white socks
GROUND Easter Road
CAPACITY: 16,039 (all seated)
RECORD ATT: 65,860 (v Hearts, 1950)
RECORD VICTORY 22-1 (v 42nd Highlanders, 1881)
RECORD DEFEAT 0-10 (v Rangers, 1898)
MANAGER: Alex McLeish
CHAIRMAN: Thomas J. O'Malley
MOST LEAGUE GOALS (1 SEASON) 42, Joe Baker
GOALS (OVERALL) 364, Gordon Smith

HONOURS

LEAGUE CHAMPIONSHIP (4): Division I – 1902-03, 1947-48, 1950-51,1951-52. First Division – 1980-81, 1998-99. Division II 1893-94, 1894-94, 1932-33. SCOTTISH CUP (2): 1887, 1902. LEAGUE CUP (2): 1972-73, 1991-92.

LEAGUE RESULTS 1998-99

Morton 0 Hibs 1
Hibs 1 Stranraer 2
Falkirk 1 Hibs 1
Hibs 4 Ayr Utd 2
Clydebank 2 Hibs 2
St Mirren 2 Hibs 0
Hibs 3 Raith Rov 1
Hibs 0 Hamilton 0
Airdrie 1 Hibs 3

Stranraer 0 Hibs 1
Hibs 2 Morton 1
Ayr Utd 3 Hibs 3
Hibs 2 Clydebank 1
Raith 1 Hibs 3
Hamilton 2 Hibs 2
Hibs 4 St Mirren 1
Hibs 1 Airdrie 0
Morton 1 Hibs 3

Hibs 2 Falkirk 1
Hibs 3 Clydebank 0
Hibs 3 Ayr Utd 0
Hibs 5 Raith 1
St Mirren 1 Hibs 2
Hibs 4 Hamilton 0
Airdrie 1 Hibs 4
Hibs 2 Stranraer 0
Falkirk 1 Hibs 2

Ayr 1 Hibs 3
Clydebank 2 Hibs 0
Hibs 3 Airdrie 0
Hamilton 0 Hibs 2
Raith 1 Hibs 3
Hibs 2 St Mirren 1
Hibs 2 Morton 1
Stranraer 0 Hibs 4
Hibs 2 Falkirk 1

KILMARNOCK

Rugby Park, Kilmarnock, KA1 2DP
Telephone: 01563 525184
Fax: 01563 522181

NICKNAME: **Killie**
COLOURS: **Blue and white shirts, blue shorts and red socks**
GROUND **Rugby Park**
CAPACITY: **18,128 (all seated)**
RECORD ATT: **35,995 (v Rangers, 1962)**
RECORD VICTORY **11-1 (v Paisley Academical, 1930)**
RECORD DEFEAT **1-9 (v Celtic, 1938)**
MANAGER: **Bobby Williamson**
CHAIRMAN: **William Costley**
MOST LEAGUE
GOALS (1 SEASON) **34, Harry Cunningham, 1927-28**
GOALS (OVERALL) **148, W Culley, 1912-23**

HONOURS

LEAGUE CHAMPIONSHIP (1): Division I – 1964-65. Division II – 1897-98, 1898-99 SCOTTISH CUP (3): 1920, 1929, 1997.

LEAGUE RESULTS 1998-99

Kilmarnock 2 Dundee Utd 0
St Johnstone 0 Kilmarnock 0
Kilmarnock 1 Rangers 3
Kilmarnock 3 Hearts 0
Celtic 1 Kilmarnock 1
Motherwell 0 Kilmarnock 0
Kilmarnock 2 Dundee 1
Aberdeen 0 Kilmarnock 1
Kilmarnock 0 Dunfermline 0

Dundee Utd 0 Kilmarnock 2
Kilmarnock 2 St Johnstone 2
Kilmarnock 2 Celtic 0
Hearts 2 Kilmarnock 1
Dundee 1 Kilmarnock 1
Kilmarnock 0 Motherwell 0
Dunfermline 0 Kilmarnock 3
Kilmarnock 4 Aberdeen 0
Rangers 1 Kilmarnock 0

Kilmarnock 2 Dundee Utd 0
Kilmarnock 1 Hearts 0
Motherwell 1 Kilmarnock 2
Kilmarnock 0 Dundee 0
Aberdeen 2 Kilmarnock 1
Celtic 1 Kilmarnock 0
Kilmarnock 0 Rangers 5
Kilmarnock 0 Dunfermline 0
St Johnstone 0 Kilmarnock 1

Kilmarnock 0 Celtic 0
Hearts 2 Kilmarnock 2
Kilmarnock 4 Aberdeen 2
Dunfermline 0 Kilmarnock 6
Dundee 2 Kilmarnock 1
Kilmarnock 0 Motherwell 1
Dundee Utd 0 Kilmarnock 0
Kilmarnock 1 St Johnstone 1
Rangers 1 Kilmarnock 1

MOTHERWELL

Fir Park, Motherwell, ML12QN
Telephone: 01698 333333
Fax: 01698 276333

NICKNAME:	The Well
COLOURS:	Claret and amber shirts, white shorts
GROUND	Fir Park
CAPACITY:	13,742 (all seated)
RECORD ATT:	35,632 (v Rangers, 1952)
RECORD VICTORY	12-1 (v Dundee United, 1954)
RECORD DEFEAT	0-8 (v Aberdeen, 1979)
MANAGER:	Billy Davies
CHAIRMAN:	John Boyle
MOST LEAGUE GOALS (1 SEASON)	52, William McFadyen, 1931-32
GOALS (OVERALL)	283, Hugh Ferguson, 1916-25

HONOURS

LEAGUE CHAMPIONSHIP: Division I 1931-32. First Division 1981-82, 1984-85. Division II 1953-54, 1968-69. SCOTTISH CUP: 1952,1991. LEAGUE CUP: 1950-51

LEAGUE RESULTS 1998/99

Motherwell 1 St Johnstone 0
Rangers 2 Motherwell 1
Motherwell 0 Dunfermline 0
Motherwell 1 Dundee Utd 0
Aberdeen 1 Motherwell 1
Motherwell 0, Kilmarnock 0
Hearts 3 Motherwell 0
Dundee 1 Motherwell 0
Motherwell 1 Celtic 2

St Johnstone 5 Motherwell 0
Motherwell 1 Rangers 0
Motherwell 2 Aberdeen 2
Dundee Utd 2 Motherwell 2
Motherwell 3 Hearts 2
Kilmarnock 0, Motherwell 0
Celtic 2 Motherwell 0
Dunfermline 1 Motherwell 1
Motherwell 2 Dundee 1

Motherwell 1 St Johnstone 2
Motherwell 2 Dundee Utd 0
Aberdeen 1 Motherwell 1
Motherwell 1 Kilmarnock 2
Hearts 0, Motherwell 2
Dundee 1 Motherwell 0
Motherwell 1 Celtic 7
Motherwell 1 Dunfermline 1
Rangers 2 Motherwell 1

Motherwell 1 Aberdeen 1
Dundee Utd 0, Motherwell 3
Motherwell 1 Dundee 2
Celtic 1 Motherwell 0
Motherwell 0, Hearts 4
Kilmarnock 0, Motherwell 1
St Johnstone 0, Motherwell 0
Motherwell 1 Rangers 5
Dunfermline 1 Motherwell 2

RANGERS

Ibrox Stadium
150 Edmiston Drive, G51 2XD
Telephone: 0141 556 2611
Fax: 0141 4278504

NICKNAME:	The Gers
COLOURS:	Blue, red, and white
GROUND	Ibrox Stadium
CAPACITY:	50,411
RECORD ATT:	118,567 (v Celtic, 1939)
RECORD VICTORY	14-2 (v Blairgowrie, 1934)
RECORD DEFEAT	(2-10 v Airdrie, 1886)
MANAGER:	Dick Advocaat
SECRETARY:	Campbell Ogilvie
MOST LEAGUE GOALS (1 SEASON)	44, Sam English, 1931-32
GOALS (OVERALL)	250, Ally McCoist

HONOURS

LEAGUE CHAMPIONSHIP (48): 1890-91 (shared), 1898-99, 1899-1900, 1900-01, 1901-02, 1910-11, 1911-12, 1912-13, 1917-18, 1919-20, 1920-21, 1922-23, 1923-24, 1924-25, 1926-27, 1927-28, 1928-29, 1929-30, 1930-31, 1932-33, 1933-34, 1934-35, 1936-37, 1938-39, 1946-47, 1948-49, 1949-50, 1952-53, 1955-56, 1956-57, 1958-59, 1960-61, 1962-63, 1963-64, 1974-75, 1975-76, 1977-78, 1986-87, 1988-89, 1989-90, 1990-91, 1991-92, 1992-93, 1993-94, 1994-95, 1995-96, 1996-97, 1998-99.

SCOTTISH CUP (28): 1894, 1897, 1898, 1903, 1928, 1930, 1932, 1934, 1935, 1936, 1948, 1949, 1950, 1953, 1960, 1962, 1963, 1964, 1966, 1973, 1976, 1978, 1979, 1981, 1992, 1993, 1996, 1999.

LEAGUE CUP (21): 1946-47, 1948-49, 1960-61, 1961-62, 1963-64, 1964-65, 1970-71, 1975-76, 1977-78, 1978-79, 1981-82, 1983-84, 1984-85, 1986-87, 1987-88, 1988-89, 1990-91, 1992-93, 1993-94, 1996-97, 1998-99.

EUROPEAN CUP-WINNERS CUP: 1971-72

LEAGUE RESULTS 1998-99

Hearts 2 (Adam, Hamilton), **Rangers 1** (Wallace)
Rangers 2 (Wallace, Albertz), **Motherwell 1** (Coyle)
Kilmarnock 1 (Wright), **Rangers 3** (Wallace, Albertz, Miller)
Rangers 4 (Kanchelskis, Van Bronckhorst, Wallace, Albertz), **St Johnstone 0**
Dundee United 0, Rangers 0
Rangers 0, Celtic 0
Aberdeen 1 (Jess), **Rangers 1** (Wallace)
Dunfermline 0, Rangers 2 (Johansson, B Ferguson)
Rangers 1 (Albertz), **Dundee 0**
Rangers 3 (Johansson, Wallace), **Hearts 0**
Motherwell 1 (Spencer), **Rangers 0**
Rangers 2 (Wallace, Amoruso), **Dundee United 1** (Dodds)
St Johnstone 0, Rangers 7 (Wallace, Johansson, Albertz 2 pens, Kanchelskis, Guivarc'h)
Rangers 2 (Van Bronckhorst, Kanchelskis), **Aberdeen 1** (Jess)
Celtic 5 (Moravcik, Larsson, Burchill), **Rangers 1** (Van Bronckhorst)
Rangers 1 (Wallace), **Kilmarnock 0**
Hearts 2 (Locke, Hamilton), **Rangers 3** (Guivarc'h 2, Wallace)
Rangers 1 (Porrini), **St Johnstone 0**
Dundee United 1 (Dodds), **Rangers 2** (Wilson, Wallace)
Rangers 2 (Amato, Wallace), **Celtic 2** (Stubbs, Larsson)
Dundee 0, Rangers 4 (Miller, Guivar'ch, Johansson)
Aberdeen 2 (Newell, Jess), **Rangers 4** (Porrini, Wallace, Albertz pen, Kanchelskis)
Dunfermline 0, Rangers 3 (Kanchelskis, Johansson)
Rangers 6 (Albertz 2, McCann, Van Bronckhorst), **Dundee 1** (Adamczuk)
Kilmarnock 0, Rangers 5 (McCann, Wallace 3, Johansson)
Rangers 2 (Wallace, Johansson), **Motherwell 1** (Gower)
Rangers 0, Dundee Utd 1 (Olofsson)
St Johnstone 3 (Weir, Simao, McAnespie), **Rangers 1** (Moore)
Rangers 1 (Van Bronckhorst), **Dunfermline 0**
Dundee 1 (Anderson), **Rangers 1** (Vidmar)
Rangers 3 (Amato, Kanchelskis, Wallace), **Aberdeen 1** (Perry)
Celtic 0, Rangers 3 (McCann 2, Albertz pen)
Rangers 0, Hearts 0
Motherwell 1 (Nicolas), **Rangers 5** (Amato 3, Van Bronckhorst, Kanchelskis)
Rangers 1 (Amato), **Kilmarnock 1** (McGowne)

ST JOHNSTONE

Crieff Road, Perth, PH1 2SJ
Telephone: 01738 459 090
Fax: 01738 625771

NICKNAME: The Saints
COLOURS: Blue with white trim, white shorts, blue and white socks
GROUND McDiarmid Park
CAPACITY: 10,673 (all seated)
RECORD ATT: 10,504 (v Rangers, 1990)
RECORD VICTORY 9-0 (v Albion Rovers, 1946)
RECORD DEFEAT 1-10 (v Third Lanark, 1903)
MANAGER: Sandy Clark
CHAIRMAN: Geoffrey S. Brown
MOST LEAGUE GOALS (1 SEASON) 36, Jimmy Benson, 1931-32
GOALS (OVERALL) 140, John Brogan, 1977-83

HONOURS

LEAGUE CHAMPIONSHIP: First Division – 1982-83, 1989-90, 1996-97. Division II – 1923-24, 1959-60, 1962-63.

LEAGUE RESULTS 1998/99

Motherwell 1 St Johnstone 0
St Johnstone 0 Kilmarnock 0
Dundee 0 St Johnstone 1
Rangers 4 St Johnstone 0
St Johnstone 1 Dunfermline 1
St Johnstone 2 Aberdeen 0
Celtic 0 St Johnstone 1
St Johnstone 1 Dundee Utd 3
Hearts 1 St Johnstone 1

St Johnstone 5 Motherwell 0
Kilmarnock 2 St Johnstone 2
Dunfermline 1 St Johnstone 1
St Johnstone 0, Rangers 7
St Johnstone 2 Celtic 1
Aberdeen 0 St Johnstone 1
Dundee Utd 1 St Johnstone 1
St Johnstone 1 Hearts 1
St Johnstone 1 Dundee 1

Motherwell 1 St Johnstone 2
Rangers 1 St Johnstone 0
St Johnstone 1 Dunfermline 1
St Johnstone 4 Aberdeen 1
Celtic 5 St Johnstone 0
St Johnstone 1 Dundee Utd 0
Hearts 0 St Johnstone 2
Dundee 0 St Johnstone 1
St Johnstone 0 Kilmarnock 1

Dunfermline 1 St Johnstone 0
St Johnstone 3 Rangers 1
St Johnstone 0 Hearts 0
Dundee Utd 0, St Johnstone 1
St Johnstone 1 Celtic 0
Aberdeen 1 St Johnstone 0
St Johnstone 0, Motherwell 0
Kilmarnock 1 St Johnstone 1
St Johnstone 1 Dundee 0

AIRDRIEONIANS

NICKNAME:	The Diamonds
COLOURS:	White with red Diamond
GROUND	Shyberry Excelsior
TELEPHONE No:	01236 762067
CAPACITY:	10,215
RECORD ATT:	8,762 (v Celtic, 1998
SRECORD VICTORY	15-1 (v Dundee Wanderers,1894)
RECORD DEFEAT	(1-11 v Hibs, 1959)
MANAGER:	Gary Mackay
CHAIRMAN:	David W Smith
MOST LEAGUE GOALS (1 SEASON)	53, Hugh Baird, 1954-55

HONOURS

LEAGUE CHAMPIONS: Divison II – 1902-03, 1954-55, 1973-74.
SCOTTISH CUP: 1924.
B&Q CUP: 1994-95.

LEAGUE RESULTS 1998-99

Airdrie 0 Clydebank 0
Hamilton 1 Airdrie 1
Airdrie 1 St Mirren 0
Airdrie 0 Raith Rov 1
Stranraer 1 Airdrie 2
Airdrie 0 Morton 1
Falkirk 0 Airdrie 1
Ayr United 1 Airdrie 2
Airdrie 1 Hibernian 3

Airdrie 3 Hamilton 2
Clydebank 0 Airdrie 1
Airdrie 3 Stranraer 2
Raith Rov 1 Airdrie 3
Airdrie 0 Falkirk 3
Morton 0, Airdrie 0
Airdrie 0, Ayr 2
Hibernian 1, Airdrie 2
Airdrie 2 Clydebank 0

St Mirren 1 Airdrie 5
Stranraer 1 Airdrie 2
Airdrie 2 Raith Rov 2
Falkirk 1 Airdrie 1
Ayr 0, Airdrie 1
Airdrie 0 Morton 2
Airdrie 1 Hibernian 4
Hamilton 0 Airdrie 2
Airdrie 0, St Mirren 3

Raith Rov 0, Airdrie 1
Airdrie 2 Stranraer 0
Hibernian 3 Airdrie 0
Airdrie 0 Ayr 2
Airdrie 1 Falkirk 2
Morton 0 Airdrie 2
Clydebank 0 Airdrie 1
Airdrie 1 Hamilton 0
St Mirren 3 Airdrie 0

AYR UNITED

NICKNAME:	The Honest Men
COLOURS:	White with Black Trim
GROUND	Somerset Park
TELEPHONE No:	01292 263 435
CAPACITY:	12,128
RECORD ATT:	25,225 (v Rangers, 1969)
RECORD VICTORY	11-1 (v Dumbarton, 1952)
RECORD DEFEAT	0-9 v Rangers (1929), v Hearts (1931), Third Lanark (1954)
MANAGER:	Gordon Dalziel
CHAIRMAN:	William Barr
MOST LEAGUE GOALS (1 SEASON)	66, Jimmy Smith, 1927-28
GOALS (OVERALL)	213, Peter Price, 1955-61

HONOURS

LEAGUE CHAMPIONS: Division II – 1911-12, 1912-13, 1927-28, 1936-37, 1958-59, 1965-66. Second Division – 1987-88, 1996-97.

LEAGUE RESULTS 1998-99

Falkirk 1 Ayr United 0
Ayr United 1 Morton 0
Raith Rov 0 Ayr United 0
Hibernian 4 Ayr United 2
Ayr United 2 Hamilton 3
Clydebank 0 Ayr United 1
Ayr Utd 7 Stranraer 1
Ayr United 1 Airdrie 2
St Mirren 0 Ayr Utd

Morton 1 Ayr Utd 2
Ayr Utd 4 Falkirk 2
Ayr Utd 3 Hibernian 3
Hamilton 1 Ayr 3
Stranraer 0 Ayr 1
Ayr 4 Clydebank 1
Airdrie 0 Ayr 2
Ayr 1 St Mirren 1
Falkirk 3 Ayr 0

Ayr 0 Raith Rov 2
Ayr 5 Hamilton 0
Hibernian 3 Ayr 0
Ayr 4 Stranraer 0
Ayr 0 Airdrie 1
St Mirren 1 Ayr 0
Ayr 1 Morton 0
Raith Rov 2 Ayr 4
Ayr 1 Hibernian 3

Ayr 2 St Mirren 2
Hamilton 0 Ayr United 2
Airdrie 0 Ayr 2
Stranraer 0 Ayr 2
Ayr 0 Clydebank 0
Ayr 1 Falkirk 2
Clydebank 2 Ayr United 1
Morton 1 Ayr 4
Ayr 1 Raith Rov 0

CLYDEBANK

NICKNAME:	The Bankies
COLOURS:	Vertical red and white stripes, black shorts
GROUND	Ground sharing at Boghead
CAPACITY:	5,503
RECORD ATT:	14,900 (v Hibs, 1965)
RECORD VICTORY	8-1 (v Arbroath, 1977)
RECORD DEFEAT	(1-9 v Gala Fairydean, 1965)
MANAGER:	Ian McCall
CHAIRMAN:	Dr John Hall
MOST LEAGUE GOALS (1 SEASON)	29, Ken Eadie, 1990-91

HONOURS

LEAGUE CHAMPIONS: Second Division: 1975-76

LEAGUE RESULTS 1998-99

Airdrie 0 Clydebank 0
Clydebank 0 Falkirk 1
Stranraer 0 Clydebank
Morton 2 Clydebank 2
Clydebank 2 Hibernian 2
Clydebank 0 Ayr United 1
Hamilton 1 Clydebank 2
Clydebank 1 St Mirren 0
Raith Rov 0 Clydebank 1

Falkirk 2 Clydebank 2
Clydebank 0 Airdrie 1
Clydebank 2 Morton 1
Hibernian 2 Clydebank 1
Clydebank 0 Hamilton 0
Ayr United 4 Clydebank 1
St Mirren 0 Clydebank 0
Clydebank 1 Raith Rov 1
Airdrie 2 Clydebank 0
Clydebank 2 Stranraer 1

Hibernian 3 Clydebank 0
Morton 1 Clydebank 1
Hamilton 0 Clydebank 1
Clydebank 2 St Mirren 2
Raith Rov 2 Clydebank
Stranraer 0 Clydebank 2
Clydebank 1 Falkirk 2
Clydebank 2 Hibernian 0

Clydebank 0 Raith Rov 0
St Mirren 1 Clydebank 1
Clydebank 0 Hamilton 0
Ayr United 0 Clydebank 0
Clydebank 1 Morton 2
Clydebank 0 Airdrie 1
Clydebank 2 Ayr United 1
Falkirk 0 Clydebank 2
Clydebank 1 Stranraer 2

DUNFERMLINE

NICKNAME:	The Pars
COLOURS:	
GROUND:	East End Park
TELEPHONE:	01383 724295/ 721749
FAX:	01383 723468
CAPACITY:	12,509 (all seated
RECORD ATT:	27,816 (v Celtic, 1968)
RECORD VICTORY	11-2 (v Stenhousemuir, 1930)
RECORD DEFEAT	0-10 (v Dundee, 1947)
MANAGER:	Dick Campbell
CHAIRMAN:	C. Roy Woodrow
MOST LEAGUE GOALS (1 SEASON)	53, Bobby Skinner, 1925-26

HONOURS

LEAGUE CHAMPIONSHIP: First Division – 1988-89, 1995-96. Division II – 1925-26. Second Division – 1985-86. SCOTTISH CUP: 1961, 1968.

LEAGUE RESULTS 1998-99

Celtic 5 Dunfermline 0
Dunfermline 2 Dundee 0
Motherwell 0 Dunfermline 0
Dunfermline 1 Aberdeen 1
St Johnstone 1 Dunfermline 1
Dunfermline 1 Hearts 1
Dundee Utd 1 Dunfermline 1
Dunfermline 0 Rangers 2
Kilmarnock 0 Dunfermline 0

Dunfermline 2 Celtic 2
Dundee 1 Dunfermline 0
Dunfermline 1 St Johnstone 1
Aberdeen 2 Dunfermline 1
Dunfermline 2 Dundee Utd 1
Hearts 2 Dunfermline 1
Dunfermline 0, Kilmarnock 3
Rangers 1 Dunfermline 1
Dunfermline 1 Motherwell 1

Celtic 5 Dunfermline 0
Dunfermline 1 Aberdeen 2
St Johnstone 1 Dunfermline 1
Dunfermline 0 Hearts 0
Dundee Utd 1 Dunfermline 1
Dunfermline 0 Rangers 3
Motherwell 1 Dunfermline 1
Kilmarnock 0, Dunfermline 0
Dunfermline 2 Dundee 0

Dunfermline 1 St Johnstone 0
Aberdeen 3 Dunfermline 1
Rangers 1 Dunfermline 0
Dunfermline 0, Kilmarnock 6
Dunfermline 2 Dundee Utd 2
Hearts 2 Dunfermline 0
Dunfermline 1 Celtic 2
Dundee 3 Dunfermline 1
Dunfermline 1 Motherwell 2

FALKIRK

NICKNAME: The Bairns
COLOURS: Navy Blue, white shorts
GROUND Brockville Park
TELEPHONE No: 01324 624 121
CAPACITY: 9,706
RECORD ATT: 23,100 (v Celtic, 1953)
RECORD VICTORY 12-1 (v Laurieston, 1893)
RECORD DEFEAT (1-11 v Airdrie, 1951)
MANAGER: Alex Totten
CHAIRMAN: Douglas McIntyre
MOST LEAGUE
GOALS (1 SEASON) 43, Evelyn Morrison, 1928-29
GOALS (OVERALL) 86, Dougie Moran, 1957-61, 1964-67

HONOURS

LEAGUE CHAMPIONS: Division II – 1935-36, 1969-70, 1974-75. First Division – 1990-91, 1993-94. Second Division – 1979-80.
SCOTTISH CUP: 1913, 1957.
LEAGUE CHALLENGE CUP: 1997-98.
B&Q CUP: 1993-94.

LEAGUE RESULTS 1998-99

Falkirk 1 Ayr United 0
Clydebank 0 Falkirk 1
Falkirk 1 Hibernian 1
Falkirk 1 Stranraer 0
St Mirren 0 Falkirk 2
Raith Rov 1 Falkirk 1
Falkirk 0 Airdrie 1
Falkirk 2 Morton 1
Hamilton 2 Falkirk 1

Falkirk 2 Clydebank 2
Ayr United 4 Falkirk 2
Stranraer 1 Falkirk 2
Falkirk 1 St Mirren 1
Airdrie 0 Falkirk 3
Falkirk 1 Raith Rov 1
Morton 0 Falkirk 3
Falkirk 2 Hamilton 1
Falkirk 3 Ayr United 0

Hibernian 2 Falkirk 1
St Mirren 0 Falkirk 3
Falkirk 3 Stranraer 2
Falkirk 1 Airdrie 1
Raith Rov 2 Falkirk 1
Falkirk 1 Morton 2
Hamilton 0 Falkirk 2
Falkirk 1 Hibernian 2
Stranraer 0 Falkirk 1

Clydebank 1 Falkirk 2
Falkirk 1 St Mirren 0
Falkirk 6 Hamilton 1
Morton 3 Falkirk 2
Airdrie 1 Falkirk 2
Falkirk 1 Raith Rov 0
Ayr United 1 Falkirk 2
Falkirk 0 Clydebank 2
Hibernian 2 Falkirk 1

INVERNESS CT

NICKNAME: Caley
COLOURS: Blue and white stripes
GROUND: Caledonian Stadium
TELEPHONE: 01463 230274
CAPACITY: 5,600
RECORD ATT: 5,821 (v Dundee United, 1998)
RECORD VICTORY 8-1 (v Annan Athletic, 1998)
RECORD DEFEAT 0-4 (v Queen's Park 1937, Montrose, 1995)
MANAGER: Steve Paterson
PRESIDENT: Dugald McGilvray
MOST LEAGUE GOALS (1 SEASON) 27, Ian Stewart, 1996-97

HONOURS

LEAGUE CHAMPIONS: Third Division – 1996-97.

LEAGUE RESULTS 1998-99

Partick 0 Inverness 1
Inverness 2 Livingston 1
Alloa 1 Inverness 1
East Fife 1 Inverness 5
Inverness 2 Arbroath 1
Inverness 3 QOS 2
Stirling 0 Inverness 1
Clyde 4 Inverness CT
Inverness C T 2 Forfar 2

Livingston 2 Inverness 1
Inverness 3 Partick 2
Inverness 4 East Fife 2
Arbroath 0 Inverness 1
Inverness 3 Stirling 1
QOS 2 Inverness 2
Inverness 1 Clyde 1
Forfar 2 Inverness 2
Inverness 3 Alloa 2

Partick 2 Inverness 1
East Fife 3 Inverness 2
Inverness 2 Arbroath 0
Clyde 1 Inverness 1
Inverness 2 Forfar 0
Stirling 1 Inverness 5
Inverness 1 QOS 0
Alloa 1 Inverness 4
Inverness 3 Livingston 1

Arbroath 3 Inverness 1
Inverness 4 East Fife 0
Forfar 0 Inverness 3
Inverness 3 Clyde 0
Inverness 2 Stirling 2
QOS 1 Inverness 1
Inverness 3 Partick 2
Livingston 4 Inverness 3
Inverness 1 Alloa 1

LIVINGSTON

NICKNAME:	Livvy Lions
COLOURS:	Black with yellow trim
GROUND	Almondvale Stadium
TELEPHONE:	01506 417000
CAPACITY:	6,100
RECORD ATT:	4,100 (v East Stirling, 1996)
RECORD VICTORY	6-0 (v Raith Rovers, 1985)
RECORD DEFEAT	(0-8 v Hamilton Accies, 1974)
MANAGER:	Ray Stewart
CHAIRMAN:	Dominic Keene
MOST LEAGUE GOALS (1 SEASON)	21, John McGachie, 1986-87

HONOURS

LEAGUE CHAMPIONS: Second Division – 1986-87. Third Division: 1995-96. Second Division – 1998-99.

LEAGUE RESULTS 1997-98

Livingston 1 Stirling Alb 1
Inverness 2 Livingston 1
Livingston 1 Forfar 1
QOS 0 Livingston 1
Livingston 3 East Fife 1
Livingston 2 Arbroath 1
Clyde 1 Livingston 1
Alloa 3 Livingston 4
Livingston 1 Partick 0

Livingston 2 Inverness C
Stirling Alb 1 Livingston 3
Livingston 2 QOS 0
East Fife 2 Livingston 3
Livingston 2 Clyde 0
Arbroath 2 Livingston 2
Livingston 2 Alloa 1
Partick 1 Livingston 3
Forfar 1 Livingston 2

Livingston 0 Stirling Alb 0
QOS 2 Livingston 2
Alloa 1 Livingston 3
Livingston 1 East Fife 0
Livingston 1 Partick 1
Clyde 0 Livingston 3
Livingston 1 Arbroath 0
Livingston 5 Forfar 0
Inverness 3 Livingston 1

East Fife 1 Livingston 1
Livingston 1 QOS 2
Partick 1 Livingston 1
Livingston 1 Alloa 0
Livingston 2 Clyde 0
Arbroath 1 Livingston 1
Stirling 0 Livingston 0
Livingston 4 Inverness 3
Forfar 1 Livingston 2

MORTON

NICKNAME: **The Ton**
COLOURS: **Blue and white**
GROUND **Cappielow Park**
TELEPHONE: **01475 723571**
CAPACITY: **14,267**
RECORD ATT: **23,500 (v Celtic, 1922)**
RECORD VICTORY **11-0 (v Carfin Shamrock, 1886)**
RECORD DEFEAT **1-10 (v Port Glasgow Athletic 1894, St Bernard's 1933)**
MANAGER: **Billy Stark**
CHAIRMAN: **Hugh Scott**
MOST LEAGUE GOALS (1 SEASON) **58, Allan McGraw, 1963-64**

HONOURS

LEAGUE CHAMPIONS: First Division – 1977-78, 1983-84, 1986-87. Division II – 1949-50, 1963-64, 1966-67. Second Division – 1994-95.
SCOTTISH CUP: 1922.

LEAGUE RESULTS 1998-99

Morton 0 Hibernian 1
Ayr United 1 Morton 0
Morton 1 Hamilton 2
Morton 2 Clydebank 2
Raith Rov 0 Morton 0
Airdrie 0 Morton 1
Morton 0 St Mirren 1
Falkirk 2 Morton 1
Morton 3 Stranraer 0

Morton 1 Ayr Utd 2
Hibernian 2 Morton 1
Clydebank 2 Morton 1
Morton 2 Raith Rov 0
St Mirren 1 Morton 0
Morton 0 Airdrie 0
Morton 0 Falkirk 3
Stranraer 2 Morton 3
Morton 1 Hibernian 3

Hamilton 0 Morton 0
Raith Rov 1 Morton 3
Morton 1 Clydebank 1
Morton 0 St Mirren 0
Falkirk 1 Morton 2
Airdrie 0 Morton 2
Morton 1 Stranraer 0
Ayr 1 Morton 0
Morton 3 Hamilton 0

Morton 1 Raith Rov 1
Stranraer 0 Morton 1
Morton 3 Falkirk 2
St Mirren 1 Morton 5
Morton 0 Airdrie 2
Clydebank 1 Morton 2
Hibernian 2 Morton 1
Morton 1 Ayr 4
Hamilton 0 Morton 2

RAITH ROVERS

NICKNAME: The Rovers
COLOURS: Navy with white trim, white shorts
GROUND: Stark's Park
TELEPHONE: 01592 263 514
CAPACITY: 10,271 (all seated)
RECORD ATT: 31,306 (v Hearts, 1953)
RECORD VICTORY 10-1 (v Coldstream, 1954)
RECORD DEFEAT (2-11 v Morton, 1936)
MANAGER: Jimmy Nicholl
CHAIRMAN: Alan Kelly
MOST LEAGUE GOALS (1 SEASON) 38, Norman Haywood, 1937-38

HONOURS

LEAGUE CHAMPIONS: First Division – 1992-93, 1994-95. Division II – 1907-08, 1909-10 (shared), 1937-38, 1948-49. LEAGUE CUP – 1994-95.

LEAGUE RESULTS 1998-99

Raith Rov 0 Hamilton 2
St Mirren 2 Raith Rov 1
Raith Rov 0 Ayr United 0
Airdrie 0 Raith Rov 1
Raith Rov 0 Morton 0
Raith Rov 1 Falkirk 1
Hibernian 3 Raith Rov 1
Stranraer 2 Raith Rov 2
Raith Rov 0 Clydebank 1

Ayr 0 Raith Rov 2
Raith Rov 1 Morton 3
Airdrie 2 Raith Rov 2
Hibernian 5 Raith Rov 1
RaithRov 2 Falkirk 1
Stranraer 2 Raith Rov 0
Raith Rov 2 Clydebank 1
St Mirren 3 Raith Rov 1
Raith Rov 2 Ayr 4

Raith Rov 1 St Mirren 0
Hamilton 3 Raith Rov 2
Morton 2 Raith Rov 0
Raith Rov 1 Airdrie 3
Raith Rov 1 Hibernian 3
Falkirk 1 Raith Rov 1
RaithRov 2 Stranraer 0
Clydebank 1 Raith Rov 1
Raith Rov 1 Hamilton 1

Raith Rov 0 Airdrie 1
Morton 1 Raith Rov 1
Clydebank 0 Raith Rov 0
Raith Rov 3 Stranraer 2
Raith Rov 1 Hibernian 3
Falkirk 1 Raith Rov 0
Hamilton 1 Raith Rov 2
Raith Rov1 St Mirren 1
Ayr 1 Raith Rov 0

ST MIRREN

NICKNAME: The Buddies
COLOURS: Black and white vertical stripes
GROUND St Mirren Park
TELEPHONE: 0141 889 2558
CAPACITY: 15,410
RECORD ATT: 47,438 (v Celtic, 1925)
RECORD VICTORY 15-0 (v Glasgow University, 1960)
RECORD DEFEAT (0-9 v Rangers, 1897)
MANAGER: Tom Hendrie
CHAIRMAN: Stewart Gilmour
MOST LEAGUE
GOALS (1 SEASON) 45, Dunky Walker, 1921-22
GOALS (OVERALL) 221, David McCrae

HONOURS

LEAGUE CHAMPIONS: First Division – 1976-77, Division II – 1967-68.
SCOTTISH CUP: 1926, 1959, 1987.

LEAGUE RESULTS 1998-99

Stranraer 0 St Mirren 1
St Mirren 2 Raith Rovers 1
Airdrie 1 St Mirren 0
Hamilton 0 St Mirren 0
St Mirren 0 Falkirk 2
St Mirren 2 Hibernian 0
Morton 0 St Mirren 1
Clydebank 1 St Mirren 0
St Mirren 0 Ayr Utd 2

St Mirren 1 Airdrie 5
St Mirren 0 Falkirk 3
Hamilton 0 St Mirren 0
Morton 0 St Mirren 0
St Mirren 1 Hibernian 2
Clydebank 2 St Mirren 2
St Mirren 1 Ayr 0
St Mirren 3 Raith 1
Airdrie 0 St Mirren 3

Raith Rovers 1 St Mirren 0
St Mirren 1 Stranraer 0
St Mirren 3 Hamilton 2
Falkirk 1 St Mirren 1
St Mirren 1 Morton 0
St Mirren 0 Clydebank 0
Hibernian 4 St Mirren 1
Ayr 1 St Mirren 1
Stranraer 1 St Mirren 2

St Mirren 1 Hamilton 0
Falkirk 1 St Mirren 0
Ayr 2 St Mirren 2
St Mirren 1 Clydebank 1
St Mirren 1 Morton 5
Hibernian 2 St Mirren 1
St Mirren 5 Stranraer 1
Raith 1 St Mirren 1
St Mirren 3 Airdrie

ALLOA

NICKNAME: The Wasps
COLOURS: Gold with black trim, black shorts, black socks
GROUND: Recreation Park
TELEPHONE: 01259 722695
FAX: 01259 722695
CAPACITY: 931
RECORD ATT: 13,000 (v Dunfermline, 1939)
RECORD VICTORY 9-2 (v Forfar, 1933)
RECORD DEFEAT 0-10 v Dundee, 1937)
MANAGER: Terry Christie
CHAIRMAN: Robert Hopkins
MOST LEAGUE GOALS (1 SEASON) 49, William Crilley, 1921-22

HONOURS

LEAGUE CHAMPIONS: Division II – 1921-22. Third Division – 1997-98.

LEAGUE RESULTS 1998-99

Alloa 1 Forfar 2
East Fife 2 Alloa 2
Alloa 1 Inverness 1
Alloa 7 Stirling 0
Partick 1 Alloa 0
Alloa 3 Clyde 0
Arbroath 0, Alloa 2
Alloa 3 Livingston 4
QOS 2 Alloa 1

Alloa 5 East Fife 1
Forfar 1 Alloa 2
Stirling 4 Alloa 2
Alloa 3 Partick 1
Alloa 1 Arbroath 1
Clyde 2 Alloa 1
Livingston 2 Alloa 1
Alloa 2 QOS 1
Inverness 3, Alloa 2

Alloa 3 Forfar 1
Alloa 2 Stirling 2
Partick 2 Alloa 1
Alloa 1 Livingston 3
QOS 0, Alloa 0
Arbroath 1 Alloa 2
Alloa 1 Clyde 0
Alloa 1 Inverness 4
East Fife 0, Alloa 4

Alloa 0, Partick 1
Stirling 1 Alloa 1
Alloa 3 QOS 5
Livingston 1 Alloa 0
Alloa 1 Arbroath 2
Clyde 0, Alloa 1
Forfar 3 Alloa 1
Alloa 3 East Fife 1
Inverness 1 Alloa 1

ARBROATH

NICKNAME:	The Red Lichties
COLOURS:	Maroon with white and sky blue trim, white shorts, maroon with white and sky blue hooped topped socks
GROUND:	Gayfield Park
TELEPHONE:	01241 872157
FAX:	01241 872157
CAPACITY:	6,488
RECORD ATT:	13,510 (v Rangers, 1952)
RECORD VICTORY	36-0 (v Bon Accord, 1885)
RECORD DEFEAT	1-9 (v Celtic, 1993)
MANAGER:	David Baikie
PRESIDENT:	John D Christison
MOST LEAGUE GOALS (1 SEASON)	45, Dave Easson, 1958-59

LEAGUE RESULTS 1998-99

Arbroath 0 East Fife 2
QOS 0 Arbroath 0
Arbroath 0 Stirling 3
Arbroath 2 Forfar 1
Inverness Arbroath 1
Livingston 2 Arbroath 1
Arbroath 0 Alloa 2
Partick 2 Arbroath 0
Arbroath 0 Clyde 0

Arbroath 2 QOS 1
East Fife 0 Arbroath 3
Forfar 1 Arbroath 3
Arbroath 0 Inverness 1
Alloa 1 Arbroath 1
Arbroath 2 Livingston 2
Arbroath 1 Partick 0
Clyde 3 Arbroath 0
Stirling 0 Arbroath 1

Arbroath 2 East Fife 1
Inverness 2 Arbroath 0
Partick 0 Arbroath 0
Arbroath 2 Forfar 2
Arbroath 0 Clyde 3
Arbroath 1 Alloa 2
Livingston 1 Arbroath 0
Arbroath 1 Stirling 0
QOS 3 Arbroath 0

Arbroath 3 Inverness 1
Forfar 5 Arbroath 2
Clyde 1 Arbroath 1
Arbroath 2 Partick 1
Alloa 1 Arbroath 2
Arbroath 1 Livingston 1
East Fife 1 Arbroath 2
Arbroath 0 QOS 2
Stirling 2 Arbroath 1

CLYDE

NICKNAME:	The Bully Wee
COLOURS:	White with red and black trim
GROUND:	Broadwood Stadium
TELEPHONE:	01236 451511
CAPACITY:	8,200
RECORD ATT:	52,000 (v Rangers, 1908, at Shawfield)
RECORD VICTORY	11-1 (v Cowdenbeath, 1951)
RECORD DEFEAT	0-11 v Dumbarton 1879, Rangers, 1880)
MANAGER:	Ronnie McDonald
CHAIRMAN:	W. B. Carmichael
MOST LEAGUE GOALS (1 SEASON)	32, Bill Boyd, 1932-33

HONOURS

LEAGUE CHAMPIONS: Division II - 1904-05, 1951-52, 1956-57, 1961-62, 1972-73. Second Division - 1977-78, 1981-82, 1992,93.

SCOTTISH CUP: 1939, 1955, 1958.

LEAGUE RESULTS 1998-99

Clyde 2 QOS 0
Stirling 1 Clyde 2
Clyde 0 East Fife 0
Clyde 1 Partick 2
Forfar 2 Clyde 2
Alloa 3 Clyde 0
Clyde 1 Livingston 1
Clyde 4 Inverness
Arbroath 0 Clyde 0

Clyde 2 QOS 1
Clyde 0 Partick 1
Clyde 1 Inverness 1
Arbroath 0 Clyde 3
Forfar 3 Clyde 1
Clyde 0 Livingston 3
Alloa 1 Clyde 0
Clyde 1 East Fife 0
Stirling 2 Clyde 3

Clyde 2 Stirling 1
QOS 2 Clyde 1
Partick 0 Clyde 2
Clyde 3 Forfar 1
Livingston 2 Clyde 0
Clyde 2 Alloa 1
Inverness 1 Clyde 1
Clyde 3 Arbroath 0
East Fife 0 Clyde 0

Clyde 1 Forfar 0
Partick 0 Clyde 1
Clyde 1 Arbroath 1
Inverness 3 Clyde 0
Livingston 2 Clyde 0
Clyde 0 Alloa 1
QOS 2 Clyde 1
Clyde 4 Stirling 1
East Fife 2 Clyde 1

HAMILTON ACCIES

NICKNAME:	The Accies
COLOURS:	Red and white hoops
GROUND:	Ground sharing at Firhill
TELEPHONE:	01698 286103
MATCHDAYS:	0141 945 4811
CAPACITY:	20,876
RECORD ATT:	28,690 (v Hearts, 1937)
RECORD VICTORY	11-1 (v Chryston, 1885)
RECORD DEFEAT	(1-11 v Hibs, 1965)
MANAGER:	Colin Miller
CHIEF EXECUTIVE:	William Sherry
MOST LEAGUE GOALS (1 SEASON)	34, David Wilson, 1936-37

HONOURS

LEAGUE CHAMPIONS: First Division: 1985-86.
B&Q Cup; 1991-92, 1992-93.

LEAGUE RESULTS 1998-99

Raith Rov 0 Hamilton
Hamilton 1 Airdrie 1
Morton 1 Hamilton 2
Hamilton 0 St Mirren 0
Ayr United 2 Hamilton 3
Stranraer 2 Hamilton 1
Hamilton 1 Clydebank 2
Hibernian 0 Hamilton 0
Hamilton 2 Falkirk 1

Airdrie 3 Hamilton 2
Hamilton 3 Raith Rov 2
St Mirren 3 Hamilton 2
Hamilton 1 Ayr United 3
Clydebank 0 Hamilton 0
Hamilton 1 Stranraer 2
Hamilton 2 Hibernian 2
Falkirk 2 Hamilton 1
Raith Rov 1 Hamilton 1

Hamilton 0 Morton 0
Ayr United 5 Hamilton 0
Hamilton 0 St Mirren 0
Stranraer 2 Hamilton 2
Hamilton 0 Clydebank 1
Hibernian 4 Hamilton 0
Hamilton 0 Falkirk 2
Hamilton 0 Airdrie 2
Morton 3 Hamilton 0

St Mirren 1 Hamilton 0
Falkirk 6 Hamilton 1
Hamilton 0 Ayr United 2
Hamilton 0 Hibernian 2
Clydebank 0 Hamilton 0
Hamilton 1 Stranraer 0
Hamilton 1 Raith Rov 2
Airdrie 1 Hamilton 0
Hamilton 0 Morton 2

PARTICK THISTLE

NICKNAME: The Jags
COLOURS: Red and yellow hoops, black shorts, red and yellow socks
GROUND: Firhill Park
TELEPHONE: 0141 945 4811
FAX: 1041 945 1525
CAPACITY: 20,876
RECORD ATT: 49,838 (v Rangers, 1922)
RECORD VICTORY 16-0 (v Royal Albert, 1931)
RECORD DEFEAT 0-10 (v Queen's Park, 1881)
MANAGER: John Lambie
CHAIRMAN: T. Brown McMaster
MOST LEAGUE GOALS (1 SEASON) 41, Alec Hair, 1926-27

HONOURS

LEAGUE CHAMPIONSHIP: First Division 1975-76. Division II – 1896-97, 1899-1900, 1770-71.
SCOTTISH CUP: 1921
LEAGUE CUP: 1971-72

LEAGUE RESULTS 1998-99

Partick 0 Inverness 1
Forfar 0 Partick 1
Partick 2 QOS 2
Clyde 1 Partick 2
Partick 1 Alloa 0
Partick 1 Stirling 0
East Fife 1 Partick 3
Partick 2 Arbroath 0
Livingston 1 Partick 0

Partick 2 Forfar 0
Inverness 3 Partick 2
Partick 0 Clyde 2
Alloa 3 Partick 1
Partick 0 East Fife 1
Stirling 2 Partick 0
Arbroath 1 Partick 0
Partick 1 Livingston 3
QOS 0 Partick 0

Partick 2 Inverness 1
Clyde 0 Partick 1
Partick 2 Alloa 1
Partick 0 Arbroath 0
Livingston 1 Partick 1
East Fife 1 Partick 0
Partick 0 Stirling 1
Partick 1 QOS 3
Forfar 2 Partick 1

Alloa 0 Partick 1
Partick 0 Clyde 1
Partick 1 Livingston 1
Arbroath 2 Partick 1
Partick 2 East Fife 2
Stirling 3 Partick 0
Inverness 3 Partick 2
Partick 1 Forfar 0
QOS 2 Partick 2

QUEEN OF THE SOUTH

NICKNAME:	The Doonhamers
COLOURS:	Royal blue
GROUND	Palmerston Park
TELEPHONE:	01387 254853
CAPACITY:	8,352
RECORD ATT:	24,500 (v Hearts, 1952)
RECORD VICTORY	11-1 (v Stranraer, 1932)
RECORD DEFEAT	(2-10 v Dundee, 1962)
MANAGER:	George Rowe, Ken Eadie
CHAIRMAN:	Norman Blount
MOST LEAGUE GOALS (1 SEASON)	41, Jimmy Rutherford, 1931-32

HONOURS

LEAGUE CHAMPIONS: Division II.

LEAGUE RESULTS 1998-99

Clyde 2 QOS 0
QOS 0 Arbroath 0
Partick 2 QOS 2
QOS 0 Livingston 1
Stirling 1 QOS 0
Inverness 3 QOS 2
QOS 3 Forfar 0
East Fife 2 QOS 0
QOS 2 Alloa 1

Arbroath 2 QOS 1
QOS 2 Clyde 1
Livingston 2 QOS 0
QOS 2 Stirling 3
Forfar 1 QOS 0
QOS 2 Inverness 2
QOS 0 East Fife 0
Alloa 2 QOS 1
QOS 0 Partick 0

Clyde 2 QOS 1
QOS 2 Livingston 2
East Fife 0 QOS 1
Stirling 1 QOS 3
QOS 0 ALLOA 0
QOS 0 Forfar 3
Inverness 1 QOS 0
Partick 1 QOS 3
QOS 3 Arbroath 0

QOS 3 Stirling 0
Livingston 1 QOS 2
Alloa 3 QOS 5
QOS 2 East Fife 0
Forfar 2 QOS 1
QOS 1 Inverness 1
QOS 2 Clyde 1
Arbroath 0 QOS 2
QOS 2 Partick 2

ROSS COUNTY

NICKNAME:	The County
COLOURS:	Dark blue with white trim, white shorts, red socks
GROUND:	Victoria Park
TELEPHONE:	01349 860860
FAX:	01349 866277
CAPACITY:	5,400
RECORD ATT:	8,000 (v Rangers, 1966)
RECORD VICTORY	11-0 (v St Cuthbert's Wanderers, 1993)
RECORD DEFEAT	1-10 (v Inverness Thistle)
MANAGER:	Neale Cooper
CHAIRMAN:	Roy McGregor
MOST LEAGUE GOALS (1 SEASON)	22, D Adams

LEAGUE RESULTS 1998-99

Ross Co 1 E Stirling 0
Albion Rov 0 Ross Co 8
Ross Co 3 Montrose 1
Ross Co 2 Cow'beath 0
Berwick 0 Ross Co 2
Queen's Pk 4 Ross Co 2
Ross Co 0 Sten'muir 1
Ross Co 0 Brechin 1
Dumbarton 1 Ross Co 2

Ross Co 1 Albion Rov 2
Montrose 3 Ross Co 6
Cow'beath 1 Ross Co 2
Ross Co 3 Berwick 1
Stenmuir 2 Ross Co 4
Ross Co 5 Queen's Pk 1
Brechin 0 Ross Co 1
Ross Co 2 Dumbarton 0
E Stirling 2 Ross Co 2

Ross Co 3 Montrose 0
Ross Co 1 Cowdenbeath 0
Berwick 2 Ross Co 2
Dumbarton XXXX
Ross Co 2 Sten'muir 2
Queen's Pk 0 Ross Co 3
Albion Rov 3 Ross Co 3
Ross Co 4 E Stirling 2
Ross Co 6 Berwick 0

Ross Co 2 Brechin 1
Cow'beath 2 Ross Co 3
Ross Co 1 Dumbarton 2
Brechin 0 Ross Co 1
Sten'muir 3 Ross Co 2
Ross Co 1 Queen's Pk 2
Montrose 2 Ross Co 3
Ross Co 2 Albion Rov 0
E Stirling 1 Ross Co 2

STENHOUSEMUIR

NICKNAME:	The Warriors
COLOURS:	Maroon with silver stripe, white and maroon shorts, white socks
GROUND:	Ochilview Park
TELEPHONE:	01324 562992
FAX:	01324 562980
CAPACITY:	3,520
RECORD ATT:	12,500 (v East Fife, 1950)
RECORD VICTORY	9-2 (v Dundee United, 1937)
RECORD DEFEAT	2-11 (v Dunfermline, 1930)
MANAGER:	Graeme Armstrong
CHAIRMAN:	A. Terry Bulloch
MOST LEAGUE GOALS (1 SEASON)	32, Robert Taylor, 1995-96

HONOURS

LEAGUE CHALLENGE CUP: 1995-96

LEAGUE RESULTS 1998-99

Brechin 1 Sten'muir 0
Sten'muir 1 Cow'beath 2
Dumbarton 0 Sten'muir 2
Sten'muir 1 E Stirling 0
Queen's Pk 0 Sten'muir 0
Sten'muir 4 Montrose 0
Ross Co 0 Sten'muir 1
Berwick 1 Sten'muir 2
Sten'muir 4 Albion Rov 1

Cowdenb'th 0 Sten'muir 2
Sten'muir 0 Dumbarton 3
E Stirling 1 Sten'muir 1
Sten'muir 2 Queen's Pk 1
Sten'muir 2 Ross Co 4
Montrose 0 Sten'muir 0
Sten'muir 1 Berwick 2
Albion Rov 1 Sten'muir 3
Sten'muir 0 Brechin 1

Dumbarton 1 Sten'muir 4
Sten'muir 2 E Stirling 2
Berwick 2 Sten'muir 1
Queen's Pk 4 Sten'muir 1
Sten'muir 1 Albion Rov 2
Ross Co 2 Sten'muir 2
Brechin 0 Sten'muir 2
Sten'muir 3 Montrose 1
Sten'muir 4 Cowdenb'th 1

Sten'muir 4 Queen's Pk 1
E Stirling 1 Sten'muir 1
Albion 1 Sten'muir 2
Sten'muir 1 Berwick 1
Sten'muir 3 Ross Co 2
Montrose 1 Sten'muir 2
Sten'muir 0 Dumbarton 2
Cowdenb'th 0 Sten'muir 2
Sten'muir 1 Brechin 0

STIRLING ALBION

NICKNAME:	The Beanos
COLOURS:	Red and white halves, red and white shorts, red socks
GROUND:	Forthbank Stadium
TELEPHONE:	01786 450399
FAX:	01786 448592
CAPACITY:	3,808
RECORD ATT:	26,400 (v Celtic, 1959, at Annfield)
RECORD VICTORY	20-0 (v Selkirk, 1984)
RECORD DEFEAT	0-9 v Dundee United, 1967)
MANAGER:	John Philliben
CHAIRMAN:	Peter McKenzie
MOST LEAGUE GOALS (1 SEASON)	27, Joe Hughes, 1969-70

HONOURS

LEAGUE CHAMPIONSHIP: Division II – 1952-53, 1957-58, 1960-61, 1964-65. Second Division – 1976-77, 1990-91, 1995-96.

LEAGUE RESULTS 1998-99

Livingston 1 Stirling 1
Stirling 1 Clyde 2
Arbroath 0 Stirling 3
Alloa 7 Stirling 0
Stirling 1 QOS 0
Partick 1 Stirling 0
Stirling 0 Inverness 1
Forfar 1 Stirling 2
Stirling 3 East Fife 2

Livingston 0 Stirling 0
Alloa 2 Stirling 2
Forfar 3 Stirling 3
Stirling 1 QOS 3
Stirling 0 East Fife 1
Stirling 1 Inverness 5
Partick 0 Stirling 1
Arbroath 1 Stirling 0
Stirling 2 Clyde 3

Clyde 2 Stirling 1
Stirling 1 Livingston 3
Stirling 4 Alloa 2
QOS 2 Stirling 3
Inverness 3 Stirling 1
Stirling 2 Partick 0
Stirling 3 Forfar 1
East Fife 2 Stirling 3
Stirling 0 Arbroath 1

QOS 3 Stirling 0
Stirling 1 Alloa 1
East Fife 1 Stirling 0
Stirling 2 Forfar 2
Inverness 2 Stirling 2
Stirling 3 Partick 0
Stirling 0 Livingston 0
Clyde 4 Stirling 1
Stirling 2 Arbroath 1

STRANRAER

NICKNAME: The Blue
COLOURS: Blue and white
GROUND: Stair Park
TELEPHONE: 01776 703271
CAPACITY: 6,100
RECORD ATT: 6,500 (v Rangers, 1948)
RECORD VICTORY 7-0 (v Brechin, 1965)
RECORD DEFEAT (1-11 v Queen of the South, 1932)
MANAGER: Billy McLaren
CHIEF EXECUTIVE: Graham Rodgers
MOST LEAGUE GOALS (1 SEASON) 27, Derek Frye, 1997-98

HONOURS

LEAGUE CHAMPIONS: Second Division – 1993-94, 1997-98.
LEAGUE CHALLENGE CUP: 1996-97.

LEAGUE RESULTS 1998-99

Stranraer 0 St Mirren 1
Hibernian 1 Stranraer 2
Stranraer 0 Clydebank 2
Falkirk 1 Stranraer 0
Stranraer 1 Airdrie 2
Stranraer 2 Hamilton1
Ayr Utd 7 Stranraer 1
Stranraer 2 Raith Rov 2
Morton 3 Stranraer 0

Stranraer 0 Hibernian 1
St Mirren 1 Stranraer 0
Stranraer 1 Falkirk 2
Airdrie 3 Stranraer 2
Stranraer 0 Ayr 1
Hamilton 1 Stranraer 2
Raith Rov 2 Stranraer 0
Stranraer 2 Morton 3
Stranraer 1 St Mirren 2

Clydebank 2 Stranraer 1
Stranraer 1 Airdrie 2
Falkirk 3 Stranraer 2
Ayr 4 Stranraer 0
Stranraer 2 Hamilton 2
Stranraer 2 Raith Rov 0
Morton 1 Stranraer 0
Hibernian 2 Stranraer 0
Stranraer 0 Clydebank 2

Stranraer 0 Falkirk 1
Airdrie 2 Stranraer 0
Stranraer 0 Morton 1
Raith Rov 3 Stranraer 2
Stranraer 0 Ayr 2
Hamilton1 Stranraer 0
St Mirren 5 Stranraer 1
Stranraer 0 Hibernian 4
Clydebank 1 Stranraer 2

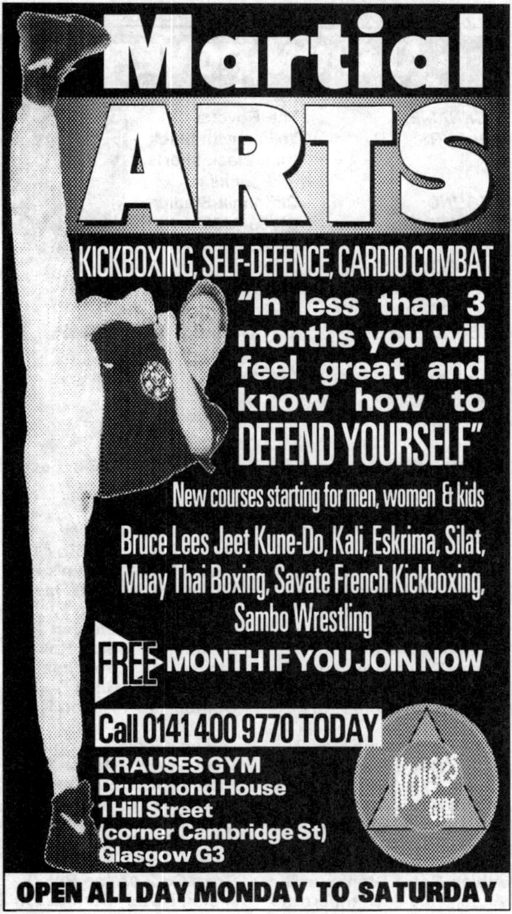
Martial
ARTS
KICKBOXING, SELF-DEFENCE, CARDIO COMBAT
"In less than 3 months you will feel great and know how to
DEFEND YOURSELF"
New courses starting for men, women & kids
Bruce Lees Jeet Kune-Do, Kali, Eskrima, Silat, Muay Thai Boxing, Savate French Kickboxing, Sambo Wrestling
FREE MONTH IF YOU JOIN NOW
Call 0141 400 9770 TODAY
KRAUSES GYM
Drummond House
1 Hill Street
(corner Cambridge St)
Glasgow G3
Krauses GYM
OPEN ALL DAY MONDAY TO SATURDAY

ALBION ROVERS

NICKNAME: The Rovers
COLOURS: Yellow with black trim, black shorts and socks
GROUND: Cliftonhill Stadium
TELEPHONE: 01236 606334
FAX: 01236 606334
CAPACITY: 2,496
RECORD ATT: 27,381 (v Rangers, 1936)
RECORD VICTORY 12-0 (v Airdriehill, 1887)
RECORD DEFEAT 1-11 (v Partick Thistle, 1993)
MANAGER: ——
CHAIRMAN: Andrew Dick
MOST LEAGUE GOALS (1 SEASON) 41, Jim Renwick, 1932-33

HONOURS

LEAGUE CHAMPIONSHIP: Division II – 1933-34. Second Division – 1988-89.

LEAGUE RESULTS 1998-99

Dumbarton 2 Albion Rov 0
Albion Rov 0, Ross Co 8
Berwick 2 Albion Rov 1
Albion Rov 2 Queen's Pk 1
Montrose 1 Albion Rov 2
E Stirling 0, Albion Rov 1
Albion Rov 1 Brechin 4
Albion Rov 0, Csow'beath 1
Sten'muir 4 Albion Rov 1

Ross Co 1 Albion Rov 2
Albion Rov 1 Berwick 1
Queen's Pk 0 Albion Rov 0
Albion Rov 4 Montrose 1
Brechin 1 Albion Rov 0
Albion 3 E Stirling 1
Cow'beath 2 Albion Rov 3
Albion Rov 1 Sten'muir 3
Albion Rov 0, Dumbarton 2

Berwick 1 Albion Rov 1
Albion Rov 1 Queen's Pk 0
Montrose 2 Albion Rov 3
Sten'muir 1 Albion Rov 2
Albion Rov 4 Brechin 1
E Stirling 4 Albion Rov 1
Albion Rov 1 Cow'beath 1
Albion Rov 3 Ross Co 3
Dumbarton 1 Albion Rov 1

Queen's Pk 0, Albion Rov 0
Queen's Pk 0 Albion Rov 0
Albion Rov 1 Sten'muir 2
Cow'beath 0, Albion Rov 2
Brechin 3 Albion Rov 1
Albion Rov 0, E Stirling 2
Albion Rov 0, Berwick 3
Ross Co 2 Albion Rov 0
Albion Rov 0, Dumbarton 2

BERWICK RANGERS

NICKNAME:	The Borderers
COLOURS:	Black with gold strripes, black and gold shorts and socks
GROUND:	Shielfield Park
TELEPHONE:	01289 307424
FAX:	01289 307424
CAPACITY:	4,131
RECORD ATT:	13,365 (v Rangers, 1967)
RECORD VICTORY	8-1 (v Forfar Athletic 1965, Vale of Leithen, 1966)
RECORD DEFEAT	1-9 (v Hamilton, 1980)
MANAGER:	Paul Smith
CHAIRMAN:	Tom Davidson
MOST LEAGUE GOALS (1 SEASON)	38, Ken Bowron, 1963-64

HONOURS

LEAGUE CHAMPIONSHIP: Second Division – 1978-79

LEAGUE RESULTS 1998-99

Berwick 0, Queen's Pk 3
Montrose 1 Berwick 1
Berwick 2 Albion Rov 1
Dumbarton 0, Berwick 0
Berwick 0, Ross Co 2
Cow'beath 1 Berwick 1
Berwick 1 E Stirling 2
Berwick 1 Sten'muir 2
Brechin 1 Berwick 1

Berwick 1 Albion Rov 1
Berwick 2 Sten'muir 1
Berwick 2 Ross Co 2
Brechin 0, Berwick 3
Dumbarton 1 Berwick 1
Berwick 1 E Stirling 2
Cow'beath 1 Berwick 2
Berwick 0, Queen's Pk 2
Montrose 0, Berwick 3

Berwick 1 Montrose 1
Albion Rov 1 Berwick 1
Berwick 3 Dumbarton 1
Ross Co 3 Berwick 1
E Stirling 0, Berwick 0
Berwick 3 Cow'beath 1
Sten'muir 1 Berwick 2
Berwick 3 Brechin 0
Queen's Pk 1 Berwick 1

Sten'muir 1 Berwick 1
Ross Co 6 Berwick 0
Berwick 0, Dumbarton 1
Berwick 2 Brechin 3
E Stirling 3 Berwick 3
Berwick 2 Cow'beath 1
Albion Rov 0, Berwick 3
Berwick 4 Montrose 1
Queen's Pk 1 Berwick 1

BRECHIN CITY

NICKNAME: The City
COLOURS: Red with white trimming for shirts, shorts, and socks
GROUND: Glebe Park
TELEPHONE: 01356 622856
FAX: 01356 625371
CAPACITY: 3,980
RECORD ATT: 8,122 (v Aberdeen, 1973)
RECORD VICTORY 12-1 (v Thornhill, 1926)
RECORD DEFEAT 0-10 (v Airdrie, Albion Rovers, Cowdenbeath, all 1937-38)
MANAGER: John Young
CHAIRMAN: David Birse
MOST LEAGUE GOALS (1 SEASON) 26, W McIntosh, 1959-60

HONOURS

LEAGUE CHAMPIONSHIP: Second Division – 1982-83, 1989-90. C Division – 1953-54.

LEAGUE RESULTS 1998-99

Brechin 1 Sten'muir 0
E Stirling1 Brechin 1
Brechin 2 Queen's Pk 2
Brechin 3 Montrose 0
Cow'beath 0, Brechin 1
Brechin 0, Dumbarton 0
Albion Rov 1 Brechin 4
Ross Co 0, Brechin 1
Brechin 1 Berwick 1

Brechin 0, E Stirling 0
Queens Pk 1 Brechin 1
Montrose 1 Brechin 2
Brechin 2 Cow'beath 1
Brechin 1 Albion Rov 0
Dumbarton 1 Brechin 2
Brechin 0, Ross Co 1
Berwick 3 Brechin 0
Sten'muir 0, Brechin 1

Brechin 1 Queen's Pk 0
Cow'beath 0, Brechin 2
Brechin 0, Berwick 3
Albion Rov 4 Brechin 1
Brechin 3 Dumbarton 3
Brechin 2 Montrose 3
Brechin 0, Sten'muir 2
E Stirling 4 Brechin 1
Brechin 1 Cow'beath 1

Ross Co 2 Brechin 1
Montrose 1 Brechin 3
Berwick 2 Brechin 3
Brechin 0, Ross Co 1
Brechin 3 Albion Rov 1
Dumbarton 2 Brechin 0
Queen's Pk 0, Brechin 2
Brechin 1 E Stirling 0
Sten'muir 1 Brechin 0

COWDENBEATH

NICKNAME: The Blue Brazil
COLOURS: Royal blue with red piping, white and blue shorts, royal blue socks
GROUND: Central Park
TELEPHONE: 01383 610166
FAX: 01383 512132
CAPACITY: 5,268
RECORD ATT: 25,586 (v Rangers, 1949)
RECORD VICTORY 12-0 (v Johnstone, 1928)
RECORD DEFEAT 1-11 (v Clyde, 1951)
MANAGER: Craig Levein
CHAIRMAN: Gordon McDougall
MOST LEAGUE GOALS (1 SEASON) 54, Rab Walls 1938-39

HONOURS

LEAGUE CHAMPIONSHIP: Division II – 1913-14, 1914-15, 1938-39.

LEAGUE RESULTS 1998-99

Cow'beath 4 Montrose 1
Sten'muir 1 Cow'beath 2
Cow'beath 2 E Stirling 1
Ross Co 2 Cow'beath 0
Cow'beath 0 Brechin 1
Cow'beath 1 Berwick 1
Dumbarton 5 Cow'beath 0
Albion Rov 0 Cow'beath 1
Cow'beath 0 Queen's Pk 3

Cow'beath 0 Sten'muir 2
E Stirling 1 Cow'beath 1
Cow'beath 1 Ross Co 2
Brechin 2 Cow'beath 1
Cow'beath 0 Dumbarton 2
Berwick 3 Cow'beath 1
Cow'beath 2 Albion Rov 3
Queen's Pk 2 Cow'beath 0
Montrose 1 Cow'beath 1

Cow'beath 3 E Stirling 2
Ross Co 1 Cow'beath 0
Cow'beath 0 Brechin 2
Cow'beath 0 Queen's Pk 0
Cow'beath 1 Berwick 2
Cow'beath 1 Montrose 0
Albion Rov 1 Cow'beath 1
Sten'muir 4 Cow'beath 1
Brechin 1 Cow'beath 1

Cow'beath 2 Ross Co 3
Queen's Pk 2 Cow'beath 1
Cow'beath 0 Albion Rov 2
Dumbarton 6 Cow'beath 1
Cow'beath 2 Dumbarton 1
Berwick 2 Cow'beath 1
East Stirling 0 Cow'beath 0
Cow'beath 0 Sten'muir 2
Montrose 1 Cow'beath 2

DUMBARTON

NICKNAME: The Sons
COLOURS: White with yellow horizontal band between two black bands, white shorts
GROUND: Boghead Park
TELEPHONE: *01389 762569*
FAX: *01389 762629*
CAPACITY: 5,503
RECORD ATT: 18,000 (v Raith Rovers, 1957)
RECORD VICTORY 13-1 (v Kirkintilloch, 1888)
RECORD DEFEAT 1-11 (v Albion Rovers 1926, Ayr United 1952)
MANAGER: Jimmy Brown
CHAIRMAN Douglas Dalgleish
GOALS (1 SEASON) 38, Kenny Wilson, 1971-72

HONOURS

LEAGUE CHAMPIONS: Division I – 1890-91 (shared with Rangers), 1891-92. Division II – 1910-11, 1971-72. Second Division – 1991-92.
SCOTTISH CUP: 1883.

LEAGUE RESULTS 1998-99

Dumbarton 2 Albion Rov 0
Queen's Pk 0, Dumbarton 1
Dumbarton 0 Sten'muir 2
Dumbarton 0, Berwick 0
E Stirling 1 Dumbarton 2
Brechin 0, Dumbarton 0
Dumbarton 5 Cowd'nb'th 0
Montrose 1 Dumbarton 1
Dumbarton 1 Ross Co 2

Dumbarton 1 Queen's Pk 0
Sten'muir 0 Dumbarton 3
Berwick 3 Dumbarton 1
Dumbarton 2 E Stirling 2
Cowd'nb'th 0 Dumbarton 2
Dumbarton 1 Brechin 2
Dumbarton 0 Montrose 2
Ross Co 2 Dumbarton 0
Albion Rov 0 Dumbarton 2

Dumbarton 1 Sten'muir 4
Montrose 4 Dumbarton 2
E Stirling 1 Dumbarton 2
Dumbarton 0, Ross Co 0
Dumbarton 1 Berwick 1
Brechin 3 Dumbarton 3
Queen's Pk 1 Dumbarton 1
Dumbarton 0 E Stirling 2
Dumbarton 1 Albion Rov 1

Berwick 0, Dumbarton 1
Ross Co 1 Dumbarton 2
Dumbarton 2 Montrose 1
Dumbarton 6 Cow'beath 1
Cowd'nb'th 2 Dumbarton 1
Dumbarton 2 Brechin 0
Sten'muir 0 Dumbarton 2
Dumbarton 0, Queen's Pk 1
Albion Rov 0 Dumbarton 2

EAST FIFE

NICKNAME: **The Fifers**
COLOURS: **Amber and black diamonds, black and amber shots, and socks**
GROUND: **New Bayview Park**
TELEPHONE: **01333 426323**
FAX: **01383 426376**
CAPACITY: **2,000**
RECORD ATT: **22,515 (v Raith Rovers,1950)**
RECORD VICTORY **13-2 (v Edinburgh City, 1937)**
RECORD DEFEAT **0-9 (v Hearts, 1957)**
MANAGER: **Steve Kirk**
CHAIRMAN:
MOST LEAGUE GOALS (1 SEASON) **41, Jock Wood, 1926-27, and Henry Morris 1947-48**

HONOURS

LEAGUE CHAMPIONSHIP: Division II – 1947-48.
SCOTTISH CUP: 1938
LEAGUE CUP: 1947-48, 1949-50, 1953-54.

LEAGUE RESULTS 1998-99

Arbroath 0 East Fife 2
East Fife 2 Alloa 2
Clyde 0 East Fife 0
East Fife 1 Inverness 5
Livingston 3 East Fife 1
Forfar 1 East Fife 2
East Fife 1 Partick 3
East Fife 2 QOS 0
Stirling 3 East Fife 2

Alloa 5 East Fife 1
East Fife 0 Arbroath 3
Inverness 4 East Fife 2
East Fife 2 Livingston 3
Partick 0 East Fife 1
East Fife 1 Forfar 0
QOS 0 East Fife 0
East Fife 2 Stirling 3
East Fife 0 Clyde 0

Arbroath 2 East Fife 1
East Fife 3 Inverness 2
East Fife 0 QOS 1
Livingston 1 East Fife 0
Stirling 0 East Fife 1
East Fife 1 Partick 0
Forfar 2 East Fife 4
Clyde 1 East Fife 0
East Fife 0 Alloa 4

East Fife 1 Livingston 1
Inverness 4 East Fife 0
East Fife 1 Stirling 0
QOS 2 East Fife 0
Partick 2 East Fife 2
East Fife 2 Forfar 1
East Fife 1 Arbroath 2
Alloa 3 East Fife 1
East Fife 2 Clyde 1

EAST STIRLINGSHIRE

NICKNAME: The Shire
COLOURS: Black and white, black and white shorts, black and tangerine socks
GROUND: Firs Park
TELEPHONE: 01324 623583
FAX: 01324 637862
CAPACITY: 1,880
RECORD ATT: 12,000 (v Partick Thistle, 1921)
RECORD VICTORY 11-2 (v Vale of Bannock, 1888)
RECORD DEFEAT 1-12 (v Dundee United, 1936)
MANAGER: Hugh McCann
CHAIRMAN: Leslie G. Thomson
MOST LEAGUE GOALS (1 SEASON) 36, Malcolm Morrison, 1938-39, and
Henry Morris 1947-48

HONOURS

LEAGUE CHAMPIONSHIP: Division II – 1931-32. C Division – 1947-48.

LEAGUE RESULTS 1998-99

Ross Co 1 E Stirling 0
E Stirling 1 Brechin 1
Cowdenbeath 2 E Stirling 1
Sten'muir 1 E Stirling 0
E Stirling 1 Dumbarton 2
E Stirling 0 Albion Rov 1
Berwick 1 E Stirling 2
Queen's Pk 0 E Stirling 4
E Stirling 3 Montrose 1

Brechin 0 E Stirling 0
E Stirling 1 Cow'beath 1
E Stirling 1 Sten'muir 1
Dumbarton 2 E Stirling 2
E Stirling 0 Berwick 0
Albion 3 E Stirling 1
E Stirling 1 Queen's Pk 1
Montrose 2 E Stirling 0
E Stirling 2 Ross Co 2

Cow'beath 3 E Stirling 2
Sten'muir 2 E Stirling 2
E Stirling 1 Queen's Pk 1
E Stirling 1 Dumbarton 2
E Stirling 2 Montrose 1
Berwick 1 E Stirling 2
E Stirling 4 Albion Rov 1
E Stirling 4 Brechin 1
Ross Co 4 E Stirling 2

Dumbarton 0 E Stirling 2
E Stirling 1 Sten'muir 1
Montrose 1 E Stirling 0
Queen's Pk 2 E Stirling 1
E Stirling 3 Berwick 3
Albion Rov 0 E Stirling 2
E Stirling 0 Cow'beath 0
Brechin 1 E Stirling 0
E Stirling 1 Ross Co 2

FORFAR ATHLETIC

NICKNAME: **The Loons**
COLOURS: **Sky blue with navy piping, navy shorts and socks**
GROUND: **Station Park**
TELEPHONE: **01307 463576/462259**
FAX: **01307 466956**
CAPACITY: **8,732**
RECORD ATT: **10,780 (v Rangers, 1970)**
RECORD VICTORY **14-1 (v Lindertis, 1988)**
RECORD DEFEAT **2-12 (v King's Park, 1930)**
MANAGER: **Ian McPhee**
CHAIRMAN: **David McGregor**
MOST LEAGUE GOALS (1 SEASON) **45, Dave Kilgour, 1929-30**

HONOURS

LEAGUE CHAMPIONSHIP: Second Division – 1983-84. Third Division – 1994-95.

LEAGUE RESULTS 1998-99

Alloa 1 Forfar 2
Forfar 0 Partick 1
Livingston 1 Forfar 1
Arbroath 2 Forfar 1
Forfar 2 Clyde 2
Forfar 1 East Fife 2
QOS 3 Forfar 0
Forfar 1 Stirling 2
Inverness 2 Forfar 2

Partick 2 Forfar 0
Forfar 1 Alloa 2
Forfar 1 Arbroath 3
Clyde 3 Forfar 1
Forfar 1 QOS 0
East Fife 1 Forfar 0
Stirling 3 Forfar 1
Forfar 2 Inverness 2
Forfar 1 Livingston 2

Alloa 3 Forfar 1
Forfar 3 Stirling 3
Arbroath 2 Forfar 2
Inverness 2 Forfar 0
Forfar 3 Clyde 1
QOS 0 Forfar 3
Forfar 2 East Fife 4
Livingston 5 Forfar 0
Forfar 2 Partick 1

Clyde 1 Forfar 0
Forfar 5 Arbroath 2
Forfar 0 Inverness 3
Stirling 2 Forfar 2
Forfar 2 QOS 1
East Fife 2 Forfar 1
Forfar 3 Alloa 1
Partick 1 Forfar 0
Forfar 1 Livingston 2

MONTROSE

NICKNAME:	The Gable Endies
COLOURS:	Royal blue, white sleeves, white shorts, royal blue socks
GROUND:	Links Park
TELEPHONE:	01674 673200
FAX:	01674 677311
CAPACITY:	4,338
RECORD ATT:	8,983 (v Dundee, 1973)
RECORD VICTORY	12-0 (v Vale of Leithen, 1975)
RECORD DEFEAT	0-13 (v Aberdeen, 1951)
MANAGER:	Kevin Drinkell
CHAIRMAN:	Michael Craig
MOST LEAGUE GOALS (1 SEASON)	28, Brian Third, 1972-73

HONOURS

LEAGUE CHAMPIONSHIP: Second Division – 1984-85

LEAGUE RESULTS 1998-99

Cow'beath 4 Montrose 1
Montrose 1 Berwick 1
Ross Co 3 Montrose 1
Brechin 3 Montrose 0
Montrose 1 Albion Rov 2
Sten'muir 4 Montrose 0
Montrose 1 Queen's Pk 0
Montrose 1 Dumbarton 1
E Stirling 3 Montrose 1

Berwick 1 Montrose 1
Montrose 3 Ross Co 6
Montrose 1 Brechin 2
Albion Rov 4 Montrose 1
Queen's Pk 3 Montrose 0
Montrose 0 Sten'muir 0
Dumbarton 0 Montrose 2
Montrose 2 E Stirling 0
Montrose 1 Cow'beath 1

Ross Co 3 Montrose 0
Montrose 2 Albion Rov 3
Montrose 4 Dumbarton 2
E Stirling 2 Montrose 1
Montrose 3 Queen's Pk 0
Brechin 2 Montrose 3
Cow'beath 1 Montrose 0
Sten'muir 3 Montrose 1
Montrose 0 Berwick 3

Albion Rov Montrose
Montrosse 1 Brechin 3
Montrose 1 E Stirling 0
Dumbarton 2 Montrose 1
Queen's Pk 1 Montrose 2
Montrose 1 Sten'muir 2
Montrose 2 Ross Co 3
Berwick 4 Montrose 1
Montrose 1 Cow'beath 2

QUEEN'S PARK

NICKNAME: The Spiders
COLOURS: White and black hoops, white shorts, black and white socks
GROUND: Hampden Park
TELEPHONE: 0141 632 1275
FAX: 0141 636 1612
CAPACITY: 52,046
RECORD ATT: 95,772 (v Rangers, 1930) (for ground 149,547 – Scotland v England, 1937)
RECORD VICTORY 16-0 (v St Peter's, 1885)
RECORD DEFEAT 0-9 (v Motherwell, 1930)
MANAGER: John McCormack
CHAIRMAN: H. Gordon Wilson
MOST LEAGUE GOALS (1 SEASON) 30, William Martin, 1937-38

LEAGUE RESULTS 1998-99

HONOURS

LEAGUE CHAMPIONSHIP: Division II – 1922-23. B Division – 1955-56. Second Division – 1980-81.
SCOTTISH CUP: 1874, 1875, 1876, 1880, 1881, 1882, 1884, 1886, 1890, 1893.

Berwick 0 Queen's Pk 3
Queen's Pk 0 Dumbarton
Brechin 2 Queen's Pk 2
Albion Rov 2 Queen's Pk 1
Queen's Pk 0 Sten'muir 0
Queen's Pk 4 Ross Co 2
Montrose 1 Queen Pk 0
Queen's Pk 0 E Stirling 4
Cow'beath 0 Queen's Pk 3

Dumbarton 1 Queen Pk 0
Queens Pk 1 Brechin 1
Queen's Pk 0 Albion Rov 0
Sten'muir 2 Queen's Pk 1
Queen's Pk 3 Montrose 0
Ross Co 5 Queen's Pk 1
E Stirling 1 Queen's Pk 1
Queen's Pk 2 Cow'beath 0
Queen's Pk 1 Berwick 1

Brechin 1 Queen's Pk 0
Albion Rov 1 Queen's Pk 0
E Stirling 1 Queen's Pk 1
Queen's Pk 4 Sten'muir1
Cow'beath 0 Queen's Pk 0
Montrose 3 Queen's Pk 0
Queen's Pk 0 Ross Co 3
Berwick 0 Queen's Pk 2
Queen's Pk 1 Dumbarton 1

Sten'muir 4 Queen's Pk 1
Queen's Pk 0 Albion 0
Queen's Pk 2 Cow'beath 1
Queen's Pk 2 E Stirling 1
Queen's Pk 1 Montrose 2
Ross Co 1 Queen's Pk 2
Queen's Pk 0 Brechin 2
Dumbarton 0 Queen's Pk 1
Queen's Pk 1 Berwick 1

LEAGUE CHAMPIONS

YEAR	WINNERS
1890-91	RANGERS/ DUMBARTON
1891-92	DUMBARTON
1892-93	CELTIC
1893-94	CELTIC
1894-95	HEARTS
1895-96	CELTIC
1896-97	HEARTS
1897-98	CELTIC
1898-99	RANGERS
1899-1900	RANGERS
1900-01	RANGERS
1901-02	RANGERS
1902-03	HIBERNIAN
1903-04	THIRD LANARK
1904-05	CELTIC
1905-06	CELTIC
1906-07	CELTIC
1907-08	CELTIC
1908-09	CELTIC
1909-10	CELTIC
1910-11	RANGERS
1911-12	RANGERS
1912-13	RANGERS
1913-14	CELTIC
1914-15	CELTIC
1915-16	CELTIC
1916-17	CELTIC
1917-18	RANGERS
1918-19	CELTIC
1919-20	RANGERS
1920-21	RANGERS
1921-22	CELTIC
1922-23	RANGERS
1923-24	RANGERS
1924-25	RANGERS
1925-26	CELTIC
1926-27	RANGERS
1927-28	RANGERS
1928-29	RANGERS
1929-30	RANGERS
1930-31	RANGERS
1931-32	MOTHERWELL
1932-33	RANGERS
1933-34	RANGERS
1934-35	RANGERS
1935-36	CELTIC
1936-37	RANGERS
1937-38	CELTIC
1938-39	RANGERS
NO LEAGUE CHAMPIONSHIP	
1946-47	RANGERS
1947-48	HIBERNIAN
1948-49	RANGERS
1949-50	RANGERS
1950-51	HIBERNIAN
1951-52	HIBERNIAN
1952-53	RANGERS
1953-54	CELTIC
1954-55	ABERDEEN
1955-56	RANGERS
1956-57	RANGERS
1957-58	HEARTS
1958-59	RANGERS
1959-60	HEARTS
1960-61	RANGERS
1961-62	DUNDEE
1962-63	RANGERS
1963-64	RANGERS
1964-65	KILMARNOCK
1965-66	CELTIC
1966-67	CELTIC
1967-68	CELTIC
1968-69	CELTIC

YEAR	WINNERS
1969-70	CELTIC
1970-71	CELTIC
1971-72	CELTIC
1972-73	CELTIC
1973-74	CELTIC
1974-75	RANGERS
1975-76	RANGERS
PREMIER DIVISION	
1976-77	CELTIC
1977-78	RANGERS
1978-79	CELTIC
1979-80	ABERDEEN
1980-81	CELTIC
1981-82	CELTIC
YEAR	**WINNERS**
1982-83	DUNDEE UNITED
1983-84	ABERDEEN
1984-85	ABERDEEN
1985-86	CELTIC
1986-87	RANGERS
1987-88	CELTIC
1988-89	RANGERS
1989-90	RANGERS
1990-91	RANGERS
1991-92	RANGERS
1992-93	RANGERS
1993-94	RANGERS
1994-95	RANGERS
1995-96	RANGERS
1996-97	RANGERS
1997-98	CELTIC
1998-99	RANGERS

DICK ADVOCAAT . . . led Rangers to the title at the first time of asking

PROMOTION/RELEGATION

1921-1922	**Promoted**	Alloa
	Relegated	Dumbarton, Queen's Park, Clydebank
1922-23	**Promoted**	Queen's Park, Clydebank
	Relegated	Albion Rovers, Alloa
1923-24	**Promoted**	St Johnstone, Cowdenbeath
	Relegated	Clyde, Clydebank
1924-25	**Promoted**	Dundee Utd, Clydebank
	Relegated	Ayr United, Third Lanark
1925-26	**Promoted**	Dunfermline, Clyde
	Relegated	Raith Rovers, Clydebank
1926-27	**Promoted**	Bo'ness, Raith Rovers
	Relegated	Morton, Dundee United
1927-28	**Promoted**	Ayr United, Third Lanark
	Relegated	Bo'ness, Dunfermline
1928-29	**Promoted**	Dundee United, Morton
	Relegated	Third Lanark, Raith Rovers
1929-30	**Promoted**	Leith Ath, East Fife
	Relegated	Dundee United, St Johnstone
1930-31	**Promoted**	Third Lanark, Dundee United
	Relegated	Hibernian, East Fife
1931-32	**Promoted**	East Stirling, St Johnstone
	Relegated	Dundee United, Leith Ath
1932-33	**Promoted**	Hibernian, Queen of the South
	Relegated	Morton, East Stirling
1933-34	**Promoted**	Albion Rovers, Dunfermline
	Relegated	Third Lanark, Cowdenbeath
1934-35	**Promoted**	Third Lanark, Arbroath
	Relegated	St Mirren, Falkirk
1935-36	**Promoted**	Falkirk, St Mirren
	Relegated	Airdrie, Ayr United
1936-37	**Promoted**	Ayr United, Morton
	Relegated	Dunfermline, Albion Rovers
1937-38	**Promoted**	Raith Rovers, Albion Rovers
	Relegated	Dundee, Morton
1938-39	**Promoted**	Cowdenbeath, Alloa
	Relegated	Queen's Park, Raith Rovers
1946-47	**Promoted**	Dundee, Airdrie
	Relegated	Kilmarnock, Hamilton
1947-48	**Promoted**	East Fife, Albion Rovers
	Relegated	Airdrie, Queen's Park
1948-49	**Promoted**	Raith Rovers, Stirling Albion
	Relegated	Morton, Albion Rovers

1949-50	**Promoted**	Morton, Airdrie
	Relegated	Queen of the South, Stirling Alb
1950-51	**Promoted**	Queen of the South, Stirling Alb
	Relegated	Clyde, Falkirk
1951-52	**Promoted**	Clyde, Falkirk
	Relegated	Morton, Stirling Albion
1952-53	**Promoted**	Stirling Albion, Hamilton Accies
	Relegated	Motherwell, Third Lanark
1953-54	**Promoted**	Motherwell, Kilmarnock
	Relegated	Airdrie, Hamilton Accies
1954-55	**Promoted**	Airdrie, Dunfermline
	Relegated	Motherwell, Stirling Albion
1955-56	**Promoted**	Queen's Park, Ayr United
	Relegated	Clyde, Stirling Albion
1956-57	**Promoted**	Clyde, Third Lanark
	Relegated	Dunfermline, Ayr United
1957-58	**Promoted**	Stirling Albion, Dunfermline
	Relegated	East Fife, Queen's Park
1958-59	**Promoted**	Ayr United, Arbroath
	Relegated	Falkirk, Queen of the South
1959-60	**Promoted**	St Johnstone, Dundee United
	Relegated	Stirling Albion, Arbroath
1960-61	**Promoted**	Stirling Albion, Falkirk
	Relegated	Clyde, Ayr United
1961-62	**Promoted**	Clyde, Queen of the South
	Relegated	St Johnstone, Stirling Albion
1962-63	**Promoted**	St Johnstone, East Stirling
	Relegated	Clyde, Raith Rovers
1963-64	**Promoted**	Morton, Clyde
	Relegated	Queen of the South, East Stirling
1964-65	**Promoted**	Stirling Albion, Hamilton Accies
	Relegated	Airdrie, Third Lanark
1965-66	**Promoted**	Ayr United, Airdrie
	Relegated	Morton, Hamilton Accies
1966-67	**Promoted**	Morton, Raith Rovers
	Relegated	St Mirren, Ayr United
1967-68	**Promoted**	St Mirren, Arbroath
	Relegated	Motherwell, Stirling Albion
1968-69	**Promoted**	Motherwell, Ayr United
	Relegated	Falkirk, Arbroath
1969-70	**Promoted**	Falkirk, Cowdenbeath
	Relegated	Raith Rovers, Partick Thistle
1970-71	**Promoted**	Partick Thistle, East Fife
	Relegated	St Mirren, Cowdenbeath
1971-72	**Promoted**	Dumbarton, Arbroath
	Relegated	Clyde, Dunfermline

1972-73	**Promoted**	Clyde, Dunfermline
	Relegated	Kilmarnock, Airdrie
1973-74	**Promoted**	Airdrie, Kilmarnock
	Relegated	East Fife, Falkirk

1974-75 Leagues reformed into Premier, First and Second Divisions

1975-76	**Promoted to Premier** – Kilmarnock, Partick Th
	Relegated to First – Dundee, St Johnstone
	Promoted to First – Clydebank, Raith Rovers
	Relegated to Second – Clyde, Dunfermline
1976-77	**Promoted to Premier** – Clydebank, St Mirren
	Relegated to First – Hearts, Kilmarnock
	Promoted to First – Alloa, Stirling Albion
	Relegated to Second – Falkirk, Raith Rovers
1977-78	**Promoted to Premier** – Morton, Hearts
	Relegated to First – Ayr United, Clydebank
	Promoted to First – Clyde, Raith Rovers
	Relegated to Second – Alloa Athletic, East Fife
1978-79	**Promoted to Premier** – Dundee, Kilmarnock
	Relegated to First – Hearts, Motherwell
	Promoted to First – Berwick Ran, Dunfermline
	Relegated to Second – Montrose, QOS
1979-80	**Promoted to Premier** – Hearts, Airdrie
	Relegated to First – Dundee, Hibernian
	Promoted to First – East Stirling, Falkirk
	Relegated to Second – Arbroath, Clyde
1980-81	**Promoted to Premier** – Dundee, Hibernian
	Relegated to First – Hearts, Kilmarnock
	Promoted to First – Queen's Park, QOS
	Relegated to Second – Berwick R, Stirling Alb
1981-82	**Promoted to Premier** – Motherwell, Kilmarnock
	Relegated to First – Airdrie, Partick Thistle
	Promoted to First – Clyde, Alloa Athletic
	Relegated to Second – QOS, East Stirling
1982-83	**Promoted to Premier** – St Johnstone, Hearts
	Relegated to First – Kilmarnock, Morton
	Promoted to First – Brechin, Meadowbank
	Relegated to Second – Queen's Pk, Dunf'line
1983-84	**Promoted to Premier** — Dumbarton, Morton
	Relegated to First — Motherwell, St Johnstone
	Promoted to First — East Fife, Forfar
	Relegated to Second — Alloa, Raith Rovers
1984-85	**Promoted to Premier** — Motherwell, Clydebank
	Relegated to First — Dumbarton, Morton
	Promoted to First — Montrose, Alloa Athletic
	Relegated to Second — M'dowbank, St Johnstone
1985-86	**Promoted to Premier** – Hamilton Accies, Falkirk
	No relegation to First – league reorganisation
	Promoted to First – Dunfermline, QOS
	Relegated to Second – Ayr United, Alloa Ath

1986-87 **Promoted to Premier** – Morton, Dunfermline Ath
Relegated to First – Clydebank, Hamilton Accies
Promoted to First – Meadowbank Th, Raith Rovers
Relegated to Second – Brechin, Montrose

1987-88 **Promoted to Premier** – Hamilton Accies
Relegated to First – Falkirk, Dunfermline, Morton
Promoted to First – Ayr United, St Johnstone
Relegated to Second – East Fife, Dumbarton

1988-89 **Promoted to Premier** – Dunfermline Ath
Relegated to First – Hamilton Accies
Promoted to First – Albion Rovers, Alloa Ath
Relegated to Second – QOS, Kilmarnock

1989-90 **Promoted to Premier** – St Johnstone
Relegated to First – Dundee
Promoted to First – Brechin, Kilmarnock
Relegated to Second – Alloa Ath, Albion Rovers

1990-91 **Promoted to Premier** – Falkirk, Airdrie
No relegation to First
Promoted to First – Stirling Albion, Montrose
Relegated to Second – Brechin, Clyde

1991-92 **Promoted to Premier** – Dundee, Partick Thistle
Relegated to First – Dunfermline Ath, St Mirren
Promoted to First – Dumbarton, Cowdenbeath
Relegated to Second – Montrose, Forfar

1992-93 **Promoted to Premier** – Raith Rov, Kilmarnock
Relegated to First – Airdrie, Falkirk
Promoted to First – Clyde, Brechin
Relegated to Second – Cowdenbeath, Meadowb'k

1993-94 **Promoted to Premier** – Falkirk
Relegated to First – St Johnstone, Raith Rov,
Dundee **Promoted to First** – Stranraer
Relegated to Second – Dumbarton, Stirling Al, Clyde, Morton, Brechin
Relegated to Third – Alloa, Forfar
East Stirling, Montrose, Queen's Park, Arbroath
Albion Rovers, Cowdenbeath

1994-95 **Promoted to Premier** — Raith Rovers
Relegated to First — Dundee United
Promoted to First — Morton, Dumbarton
Relegated to Second — Ayr United, Stranraer
Relegated to Third — Meadowbank, Brechin City

1995-96 **Promoted to Premier** — Dunfermline Ath, Dundee U
Relegated to First — Falkirk, Partick Thistle
Promoted to First — Stirling Albion, East Fife
Relegated to Second — Dumbarton, Hamilton
Promoted to Second — Livingston, Brechin C
Relegated to Third — Forfar, Montrose

1996-97	**Promoted to Premier** – St Johnstone **Relegated to First** – Raith Rovers **Promoted to First** – Ayr United, Hamilton Accies **Relegated to Second** –Clydebank, East Fife **Promoted to Second** – Inverness CT, Forfar **Relegated to Third** – Dumbarton, Berwick Rangers
1997-98	**Promoted to Premier** – Dundee **Relegated to First** – Hibs **Promoted to First** – Stranraer, Clydebank **Relegated to Second** –Partick Thistle, Stirling Alb **Promoted to Second** – Alloa, Arbroath **Relegated to Third** – Stenhousemuir, Brechin
1998-99	**Promoted to Premier** – Hibs **Relegated to First** – Dunfermline **Promoted to First** – Livingston, Inverness CT **Relegated to Second** – Hamilton, Stranraer **Promoted to Second** – Ross Co, Stenhousemuir **Relegated to Third** – East Fife, Forfar Athletic

JOHN ROBERTSON . . . his goals helped Livingston to the Second Division title

EOIN JESS heads Scotland's goal during the 2-1 defeat by the Czech Republic

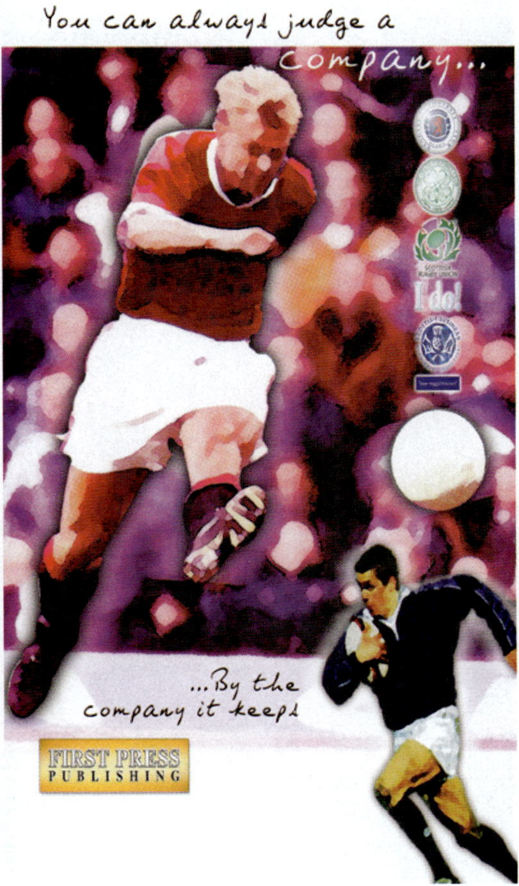
You can always judge a
company...
I do!
...By the
company it keeps
FIRST PRESS
PUBLISHING

CHEERS all round as the victorious Rangers team parade the Tennents Scottish Cup

RANGERS players celebrate after their 2-1 League Cup final win over St Johnstone

ST JOHNSTONE'S Nick Dasovic crashes home his side's goal in the League Cup final

DOUBLE Player of the Year winner Henrik Larsson

TOMMY BOYD in action for Scotland

TOMMY BOYD in action for Scotland

BILLY DODDS in action against Germany

JUBILANT Kilwinning Rangers following their OVD Scottish Junior Cup final triumph

SCOTTISH LEAGUE CUP 1998-99

FIRST ROUND

ARBROATH	0	CLYDEBANK	1
BRECHIN	2	HAMILTON	2
(aet, 90 mins 1-1) (Hamilton won 3-2 on penalties)			
CLYDE	1	BERWICK	1
(aet, 90 mins 1-1) (Berwick won 4-3 on penalties)			
COWDENBEATH	0	LIVINGSTON	2
DUMBARTON	0	ALLOA	4
EAST FIFE	3	PARTICK	2
(aet, 90 mins 2-2)			
FORFAR	0	STIRLING ALBION	1
QUEEN OF THE SOUTH	1	INVERNESS CALEY THISTLE	4
QUEEN'S PARK	1	AYR UNITED	3
ROSS COUNTY	4	MONTROSE	1
STENHOUSEMUIR	1	EAST STIRLING	0
STRANRAER	1	ALBION ROVERS	1
(aet, 90 mins 1-1) (Stranraer won 3-2 on penalties)			

SECOND ROUND

BERWICK	1	FALKIRK	5
DUNDEE	0	ALLOA	1
DUNDEE UNITED	2	STIRLING ALBION	2
(aet, 90 mins 2-2) (Dundee United won 3-0 on penalties)			
EAST FIFE	0	MOTHERWELL	1
GREENOCK MORTON	0	ROSS COUNTY	1
HAMILTON	1	HIBERNIAN	2
INVERNESS C	0	ABERDEEN	3
LIVINGSTON	1	DUNFERMLINE	0
(aet)			
RAITH	2	CLYDEBANK	0
ST JOHNSTONE	3	STRANRAER	0
ST MIRREN	1	AYR UNITED	3
STENHOUSEMUIR	0	AIRDRIE	2

THIRD ROUND

FALKIRK	0	ST JOHNSTONE	1
MOTHERWELL	0	AYR	2
RANGERS	4	ALLOA	0
KILMARNOCK	3	LIVINGSTON	1
(aet, 90 mins 1-1)			
AIRDRIE	1	CELTIC	0
HEARTS	4	RAITH	2
(aet, 90 mins 2-2)			
HIBERNIAN	1	ABERDEEN	0
ROSS COUNTY	2	DUNDEE UNITED	0
(aet, 90 mins 0-0)			

QUARTER-FINALS

AYR UNITED	0	RANGERS	2
KILMARNOCK	0	AIRDRIE	1
(aet)			
ST JOHNSTONE	4	HIBERNIAN	0
HEARTS	1	ROSS COUNTY	1
(aet, 90 mins, 1-1) (Hearts won 3-0 on penalties)			

SEMI-FINALS

RANGERS	5	AIRDRIE	0
ST JOHNSTONE	3	HEARTS	0

FINAL

RANGERS	2	ST JOHNSTONE	1

LEAGUE CUP WINNERS

1946-47	Rangers	4	Aberdeen	0
1947-48	East Fife	4	Falkirk	1
	(after 0-0 draw)			
1948-49	Rangers	2	Raith Rovers	0
1949-50	East Fife	3	Dunfermline	0
1950-51	Motherwell	3	Hibernian	0
1951-52	Dundee	3	Rangers	2
1952-53	Dundee	2	Kilmarnock	0
1953-54	East Fife	3	Partick Thistle	2
1954-55	Hearts	4	Motherwell	2
1955-56	Aberdeen	2	St Mirren	1
1956-57	Celtic	3	Partick Thistle	0
1957-58	Celtic	7	Rangers	1
1958-59	Hearts	5	Partick Thistle	1
1959-60	Hearts	2	Third Lanark	1
1960-61	Rangers	2	Kilmarnock	0
1961-62	Rangers	3	Hearts	1
	(after 1-1 draw)			
1962-63	Hearts	1	Kilmarnock	0
1963-64	Rangers	5	Morton	0
1964-65	Rangers	2	Celtic	1
1965-66	Celtic	2	Rangers	1
1966-67	Celtic	1	Rangers	0
1967-68	Celtic	5	Dundee	3
1968-69	Celtic	6	Hibs	2
1969-70	Celtic	1	St Johnstone	0
1970-71	Rangers	1	Celtic	0
1971-72	Partick Thistle	4	Celtic	1
1972-73	Hibs	2	Celtic	1
1973-74	Dundee	1	Celtic	0
1974-75	Celtic	6	Hibs	3
1975-76	Rangers	1	Celtic	0
1976-77	Aberdeen	2	Celtic	1
	(after extra time)			
1977-78	Celtic	1	Rangers	2
	(after extra time)			
1978-79	Rangers	2	Aberdeen	1
1979-80	Aberdeen	0	Dundee United	3
	(after 0-0 draw)			

1980-81	Dundee	0	Dundee United	3
1981-82	Rangers	2	Dundee United	1
1982-83	Celtic	2	Rangers	1
1983-84	Rangers	3	Celtic	2
	(after extra time)			
1984-85	Dundee United	0	Rangers	1
1985-86	Aberdeen	3	Hibernian	0
1986-87	Celtic	1	Rangers	2
1987-88	Rangers	3	Aberdeen	3
	(after extra time, Rangers won 5-3 on penalties)			
1988-89	Aberdeen	2	Rangers	3
1989-90	Aberdeen	2	Rangers	1
	(after extra time)			
1990-91	Rangers	2	Celtic	1
	(after extra time)			
1991-92	Hibernian	2	Dunfermline	0
1992-93	Rangers	2	Aberdeen	1
	(after extra time)			
1993-94	Rangers	2	Hibernian	1
1994-95	Celtic	2	Raith Rovers	2
	(After extra time, Raith Rovers won 6-5 on penalties)			
1995-96	Aberdeen	2	Dundee	0
1996-97	Rangers	4	Hearts	3
1997-98	Celtic	3	Dundee United	0
1998-99	Rangers	2	St Johnstone	1

FINAL SCORERS . . . Stephane Guivarc'h and Jorg Albertz

TENNENTS SCOTTISH CUP 1998-99

FIRST ROUND: Arbroath 1 Partick Th 2, Livingston 3, Dumbarton 0 (after 1-1 draw), Queen's Park 2 Berwick 0, Alloa 0 Stenhousemuir 2 (after 1-1 draw).

SECOND ROUND: Civil Service 0 Albion Rov 3, Dalbeattie 1 East Stirling 2, East Fife 0 Forfar 1 (after 2-2 draw), Huntly 3 Peterhead 0, Inverness Cal. 1 Livingston 2, Brechin 3 Keith 1 (after 0-0 draw), Stirling 2 Montrose 1 (after 0-0 draw), Partick 5 Cowdenbeath 2, Clyde 5 Spartans 0 (after 1-1 draw), Stenhousemuir 2 Whitehill 0 (after 1-1 draw) Queen of South 1 Ross County 3, Clachnacuddin 2 Queen's Park 3 (after 1-1 draw).

THIRD ROUND

Aberdeen	0	Livingston	1
Albion Rovers	3	Brechin City	1
(after 1-1 draw)			
Ayr United	3	Kilmarnock	0
Celtic	3	Airdrie	1
Dundee United	1	Queen's Park	0
(after 0-0 draw)			
Falkirk	3	Huntly	0
Greenock Morton	2	Dundee	1
Hamilton	1	St Mirren	0
(after 1-1 draw)			
Motherwell	3	Hearts	1
Partick Thistle	1	Dunfermline	2
Raith Rovers	0	Clyde	4
Rangers	2	Stenhousemuir	0
Ross County	2	Clydebank	3
(after 1-1 draw)			
St Johnstone	1	Forfar	0
Stirling Albion	2	Hibernian	1
(after 1-1 draw)			
Stranraer	1	East Stirling	0

FOURTH ROUND

Ayr United	1	Albion Rovers	0
Celtic	4	Dunfermline	0
Dundee United	3	Clydebank	0
(after 2-2 draw)			
Greenock Morton	6	Clyde	1
Hamilton	0	Rangers	5
Livingston	1	St Johnstone	3
Motherwell	2	Stirling Albion	0
Stranraer	1	Falkirk	2

QUARTER-FINAL

Motherwell	0	St Johnstone	2
Rangers	2	Falkirk	1
Greenock Morton	0	Celtic	3
Dundee United	2	Ayr United	1
(after 0-0 draw)			

SEMI-FINAL

Celtic	2	Dundee United	0
St Johnstone	0	Rangers	4

FINAL

Celtic	0	Rangers	1

PREVIOUS WINNERS

1873-74	QUEEN'S PARK	2	CLYDESDALE	0
1874-75	QUEEN'S PARK	3	RENTON	0
1875-76	QUEEN'S PARK	2	3RD LANARK RIFLES	0
	After 1-1 draw			
1876-77	VALE OF LEVEN	3	RANGERS	2
	After two replays 0-0, 1-1			
1877-78	VALE OF LEVEN	1	3RD LANARK RIFLES	0
1878-79	VALE OF LEVEN	1	RANGERS	1
	Vale of Leven awarded cup. Rangers failed to appear			
1879-80	QUEEN'S PARK	3	THORNLIEBANK	0
1880-81	QUEEN'S PARK	3	DUMBARTON	1
	After Dumbarton protested first game			
1881-82	QUEEN'S PARK	4	DUMBARTON	1
	After 2-2 draw			
1882-83	DUMBARTON	2	VALE OF LEVEN	1
	After 2-2 draw			
1883-84	QUEEN'S PARK	.wo	VALE OF LEVEN	
	Queen's Park awarded cup. Vale of Leven failed to appear.			
884-85	RENTON	3	VALE OF LEVEN	1
	After 0-0 draw			
1885-86	QUEEN'S PARK	3	RENTON	1
1886-87	HIBERNIAN	2	DUMBARTON	1
1887-88	RENTON	6	CAMBUSLANG	1
1888-89	THIRD LANARK	2	CELTIC	1
	After replay by order of Scottish FA because of playing conditions in first match			
1889-90	QUEEN'S PARK	2	VALE OF LEVEN	1
	After 1-1 draw			
1890-91	HEARTS	1	DUMBARTON	0
1891-92	CELTIC	5	QUEEN'S PARK	1
	After mutually protested first game			
1892-93	QUEEN'S PARK	2	CELTIC	1
	After 0-0 draw			
1893-94	RANGERS	3	CELTIC	1
1894-95	ST BERNARD'S	2	RENTON	1
1895-96	HEARTS	3	HIBS	1
1896-97	RANGERS	5	DUMBARTON	1
1897-98	RANGERS	2	KILMARNOCK	0
1898-99	CELTIC	2	RANGERS	0
1899-00	CELTIC	4	QUEEN'S PARK	3
1900-01	HEARTS	4	CELTIC	3
1901-02	HIBS	1	CELTIC	0

1902-03	RANGERS	2	HEARTS	0
	After two replays, 1-1, 0-0.			
1903-04	CELTIC	3	RANGERS	2
1904-05	THIRD LANARK	3	RANGERS	1
	After 0-0 draw			
1905-06	HEARTS	1	THIRD LANARK	0
1906-07	CELTIC	3	HEARTS	0
1907-08	CELTIC	5	ST MIRREN	1
1908-09	CELTIC	—	RANGERS	—
	Owing to riot, the cup was withheld after two drawn games.			
1909-10	DUNDEE	2	CLYDE	1
	After two draws, 2-2, 0-0			
1910-11	CELTIC	2	HAMILTON ACCIES	0
	After 0-0 draw			
1911-12	CELTIC	2	CLYDE	0
1912-13	FALKIRK	2	RAITH ROVERS	0
1913-14	CELTIC	4	HIBS	1
	After 0-0 draw			
1919-20	KILMARNOCK	3	ALBION ROVERS	2
1920-21	PARTICK THISTLE	1	RANGERS	0
1921-22	MORTON	1	RANGERS	0
1922-23	CELTIC	1	HIBS	0
1923-24	AIRDRIE	2	HIBS	0
1924-25	CELTIC	2	DUNDEE	1
1925-26	ST MIRREN	2	CELTIC	0
1926-27	CELTIC	3	EAST FIFE	1
1927-28	RANGERS	4	CELTIC	0
1928-29	KILMARNOCK	2	RANGERS	0
1929-30	RANGERS	2	PARTICK THISTLE	1
	After 0-0 draw			
1930-31	CELTIC	4	MOTHERWELL	2
	After 2-2 draw			
1931-32	RANGERS	3	KILMARNOCK	0
	After 1-1 draw			
1932-33	CELTIC	1	MOTHERWELL	0
1933-34	RANGERS	5	ST MIRREN	0
1934-35	RANGERS	2	HAMILTON ACCIES	1
1935-36	RANGERS	1	THIRD LANARK	0
1936-37	CELTIC	2	ABERDEEN	1
1937-38	EAST FIFE	4	KILMARNOCK	2
	After 1-1 draw			
1938-39	CLYDE	4	MOTHERWELL	0
1946-47	ABERDEEN	2	HIBS	1

1947-48 RANGERS . . . . . .1 MORTON 0
After extra time After 1-1 draw
1948-49 RANGERS . . . . . .4 CLYDE 1
1949-50 RANGERS . . . . . .3 EAST FIFE 0
1950-51 CELTIC . . . . .1 MOTHERWELL 0
1951-52 MOTHERWELL . .4 DUNDEE 0
1952-53 RANGERS . . . . . .1 ABERDEEN 0
After 1-1 draw
1953-54 CELTIC . . . . .2 ABERDEEN 1
1954-55 CLYDE . . . . .1 CELTIC 0
After 1-1 draw
1955-56 HEARTS . . . . .3 CELTIC 1
1956-57 FALKIRK . . . . . . .2 KILMARNOCK 1
After extra time After 1-1 draw
1957-58 CLYDE . . . . .1 HIBS 0
1958-59 ST MIRREN . . . .3 ABERDEEN 1
1959-60 RANGERS . . . . .2 KILMARNOCK 0
1960-61 DUNFERMLINE . .2 CELTIC 0
After 0-0 draw
1961-62 RANGERS . . . . .2 ST MIRREN 0
1962-63 RANGERS . . . . .3 CELTIC 0
After 1-1 draw
1963-64 RANGERS . . . . .3 DUNDEE 1
1964-65 CELTIC . . . . .3 DUNFERMLINE ATH. . . . 2
1965-66 RANGERS . . . . .1 CELTIC 0
After 0-0 draw
1966-67 CELTIC . . . . .2 ABERDEEN 0
1967-68 DUNFERMLINE . .3 HEARTS 1
1968-69 CELTIC . . . . .4 RANGERS 0
1969-70 ABERDEEN . . . . .3 CELTIC 1
1970-71 CELTIC . . . . .2 RANGERS 1
After 1-1 draw
1971-72 CELTIC . . . . .6 HIBS 1
1972-73 RANGERS . . . . .3 CELTIC 2
1973-74 CELTIC . . . . .3 DUNDEE UNITED 0
1974-75 CELTIC . . . . .3 AIRDRIE 1
1975-76 RANGERS . . . . .3 HEARTS 1
1976-77 CELTIC . . . . .1 RANGERS 0
1977-78 RANGERS . . . . .2 ABERDEEN 1
1978-79 RANGERS . . . . .3 HIBS 2
After two 0-0 draws, and extra time
1979-80 CELTIC . . . . .1 RANGERS 0
After extra time
1980-81 RANGERS . . . . .4 DUNDEE UNITED 1
After 0-0 draw

1981-82	ABERDEEN	4	RANGERS	1
	After extra time			
1982-83	ABERDEEN	1	RANGERS	0
	After extra time			
1983-84	ABERDEEN	2	CELTIC	1
	After extra time			
1984-85	CELTIC	2	DUNDEE UNITED	1
1985-86	ABERDEEN	3	HEARTS	0
1986-87	ST MIRREN	1	DUNDEE UNITED	0
	After extra time			
1987-88	CELTIC	2	DUNDEE UNITED	1
1988-89	CELTIC	1	RANGERS	0
1989-90	ABERDEEN	0	CELTIC	0
	After extra time. Aberdeen won 9-8 on penalties			
1990-91	MOTHERWELL	4	DUNDEE UNITED	3
	After extra time			
1991-92	RANGERS	2	AIRDRIE	1
1992-93	RANGERS	2	ABERDEEN	1
1993-94	DUNDEE UTD	1	RANGERS	0
1994-95	CELTIC	1	AIRDRIE	0
1995-96	RANGERS	5	HEARTS	1
1996-97	KILMARNOCK	1	FALKIRK	0
1998-99	RANGERS	1	CELTIC	0

CUP FINAL captains Tommy Boyd (Celtic) and Lorenzo Amoruso (Rangers)

SCOTTISH CUP WINNING TEAMS

1976-77 – CELTIC: Latchford, McGrain, Lynch, Stanton, McDonald, Aitken, Dalglish, Edvaldsson, Craig, Conn, Wilson.
1977-78 – RANGERS: McCloy, Jardine, Greig, Forsyth, Jackson, MacDonald, McLean, Russell, Johnstone, Smith, Cooper.
1978-79 – RANGERS: McCloy, Jardine, Dawson, Johnstone, Jackson, Watson, McLean, Russell, Parlane, McDonald, Cooper.
1979-80 – CELTIC: Latchford, Sneddon, McGrain, Aitken, Conroy, MacLeod, Provan, Doyle, McCluskey, Burns, McGarvey.
1980-81 – RANGERS: Stewart, Jardine, Dawson, Stevens, Forsyth, Bett, Cooper, Russell, D. Johnstone, Redford, MacDonald.
1981-82 – ABERDEEN: Leighton, Kennedy, Rougvie, McMaster, McLeish, Miller, Strachan, Cooper, McGhee, Simpson, Hewitt.
1982-83 – ABERDEEN: Leighton, Rougvie, McMaster, Cooper, McLeish, Miller, Strachan, Simpson, McGhee, Black, Weir.
1983-84 – ABERDEEN: Leighton, McKimmie, Rougvie, Cooper, McLeish, Miller, Strachan, Simpson, McGhee, Black, Weir.
1984-85 – CELTIC: Bonner, W. McStay, McGrain, Aitken, McAdam, MacLeod, Provan, P. McStay, Johnston, Burns, McGarvey.
1985-86 – ABERDEEN: Leighton, McKimmie, McQueen, McMaster, McLeish, Miller, Hewitt, Cooper, McDougall, Bett, Weir.
1986-87 – ST MIRREN: Money, Wilson, D. Hamilton, Abercromby, Winnie, Cooper, Ferguson, McGarvey, McDowall, B. Hamilton, Lambert.
1987-88 – CELTIC: McKnight, Morris, Rogan, Aitken, McCarthy, Whyte, Miller, McStay, McAvennie, Walker, Burns.
1988-89 – CELTIC: Bonner, Morris, Rogan, Aitken, McCarthy, Whyte, Grant, McStay, Miller, McGhee, Burns.
1989-90 – ABERDEEN: Snelders, McKimmie, Robertson, Grant, McLeish, Irvine, Nicholas, Bett, Mason, Connor, Gillhaus.
1990-91 – MOTHERWELL: Maxwell, Nijholt, Boyd, Griffin, Paterson, McCart, Arnott, Angus, Ferguson (Kirk), O'Donnell, Cooper (O'Neill).

1991-92 – RANGERS: Goram, Stevens, Robertson, Gough, Spackman, Brown, McCall, McCoist, Hateley, Mikhailitchenko, Durrant. Subs: Gordon, Rideout.
1992-93 – RANGERS: Goram, McPherson, Gough, Brown, Robertson, Murray, Ferguson, McCall, Durrant, Hateley, Huistra. Subs: Pressley, McSwegan.
1993-94 – DUNDEE UNITED: Van De Kamp, Cleland, Malpas, McInally, Petric, Welsh, Bowman, Hannah, McLaren, Brewster, Dailly. Subs: Nixon, Bollan.
1994-95 – CELTIC: Bonner, Boyd, McKinlay, Vata, McNally, Grant, McLaughlin, McStay, Van Hooijdonk (Falconer), Donnelly (O'Donnell), Collins,
1995-96 – RANGERS: Goram, Cleland, Robertson, Gough, McLaren, Brown, Durie, Gascoigne, Ferguson (Durrant), McCall, Laudrup. Subs (not used): Petric, Andersen.
1996-97 – KILMARNOCK: Lekovic, MacPherson, Kerr, Montgomerie, McGowne, Reilly, Bagan (Mitchell 88), Holt, Wright (Henry 77), McIntyre (Brown 83), Burke.
1997-98 – HEARTS: Rousett, McPherson, Naysmith, Weir, Salvatore, Ritchie, McCann, Fulton, Adam (Hamilton), Cameron, Flogel.
1998-99 – RANGERS: Klos, Porrini (Kanchelskis), Vidmar, Amoruso, Hendry, McCann (I Ferguson), McInnes, Wallace, van Bronckhorst, Amato (Wilson), Albertz.

For Skoda in Glasgow
ST ANDREWS
SKODA
AUTO
OF GLASGOW
• New Car Sales
• Service
• Parts
• Used Car Sales
• Corporate Sales
204 Maxwell Road, Glasgow
CALL NOW ON
0141 429 5999

PLAYER OF THE YEAR

AWARDED BY THE SCOTTISH FOOTBALL WRITERS' ASSOCIATION.

1965............BILLY McNEILL (Celtic)
1966............JOHN GREIG (Rangers)
1967............RONNIE SIMPSON (Celtic)
1968............GORDON WALLACE (Raith Rovers)
1969............BOBBY MURDOCH (Celtic)
1970............PAT STANTON (Hibernian)
1971............MARTIN BUCHAN (Aberdeen)
1972............DAVE SMITH (Rangers)
1973............GEORGE CONNELLY (Celtic)
1974............WORLD CUP SQUAD
1975............SANDY JARDINE (Rangers)
1976............JOHN GREIG (Rangers)
1977............DANNY McGRAIN (Celtic)
1978............DEREK JOHNSTONE (Rangers)
1979............ANDY RITCHIE (Morton)
1980............GORDON STRACHAN (Aberdeen)
1981............ALAN ROUGH (Partick Thistle)
1982............PAUL STURROCK (Dundee United)
1983............CHARLIE NICHOLAS (Celtic)
1984............WILLIE MILLER (Aberdeen)
1985............HAMISH McALPINE (Dundee United)
1986............SANDY JARDINE (Hearts)
1987............BRIAN McCLAIR (Celtic)
1988............PAUL McSTAY (Celtic)
1989............RICHARD GOUGH (Rangers)
1990............ALEX McLEISH (Aberdeen)
1991............MAURICE MALPAS (Dundee United)
1992............ALLY McCOIST (Rangers)
1993............ANDY GORAM (Rangers)
1994............MARK HATELEY (Rangers)
1995............BRIAN LAUDRUP (Rangers)
1996............PAUL GASCOIGNE (Rangers)
1997............BRIAN LAUDRUP (Rangers)
1998............CRAIG BURLEY (Celtic)
1999............HENRIK LARSSON (Celtic)

Indian Cuisine

25 HIGH St.
INDIAN RESTAURANT

Indian Cuisine

Monday : Closed
Tue, Wed, Thu: 12-2pm - 5-11pm
Friday , Saturday : 12-2pm - 5-11.30pm
Sunday : 5-11pm

Tel 0141 572 2001
0141 572 2125

---

3 Course Classic Lunch £3.95

3 Course Executive Lunch £5.95

3 Course Pre Theatre £5.95
(5pm - 6.30pm) Mon - Sat

A La Carte Mon - Sat

CARRY OUT MENU 10% DISCOUNT
PRIVATE FUNCTIONS CATERED FOR

PLAYER OF THE YEAR

PLAYER OF THE YEAR
Awarded by the
SCOTTISH PROFESSIONAL
FOOTBALLERS' ASSOCIATION

1977-78

Premier Division............................Derek Johnstone (Rangers)
First Division..Billy Pirie (Dundee)
Second Division.......................Dave Smith (Berwick Rangers)

Young Player of the Year
Graeme Payne (Dundee United)

1978-79

Premier Division.........................Paul Hegarty (Dundee United)
First Division ....Brian McLaughlin (Ayr United)
Second Division ....Michael Leonard (Dunfermline Ath)

Young Player of the Year
Raymond Stewart (Dundee United)

1979-80

Premier Division ....Davie Provan (Celtic)
First Division ....Sandy Clark (Airdrie)
Second Division ....Paul Leetion (Falkirk)

Young Player of the Year
John MacDonald (Rangers)

1980-81

Premier Division ....Mark McGhee (Aberdeen)
First Division..Eric Sinclair (Dundee)
Second Division.........Jimmy Robertson (Queen of the South)

Young Player of the Year
Charlie Nicholas (Celtic)

1981-82

Premier Division ....Sandy Clark (Airdrie)
First Division ....Brian McLaughlin (Motherwell)
Second Division...Pat Nevin (Clyde)

Young Player of the Year
Frank McAvennie (St Mirren)

1982-83

Premier Division ....Charlie Nicholas (Celtic)
First Division ....Gerry McCabe (Clydebank)
Second Division....................John Colquhoun (Stirling Albion)

Young Player of the Year
Paul McStay (Celtic)

1983-84

Premier Division ....Willie Miller (Aberdeen)
First Division ....Gerry McCabe (Clydebank)
Second Division ....Jim Liddle (Forfar Athletic)

Young Player of the Year
John Robertson (Hearts)

1984-85

Premier Division..Jim Duffy (Morton)
First Division ....Gerry McCabe (Clydebank)
Second Division..........................Bernie Slaven (Albion Rovers)

Young Player of the Year
Craig Levein (Hearts)

1985-86

Premier Division ....Richard Gough (Dundee United)
First Division.......................................John Brogan (Hamilton)
Second Division.............................Mark Smith (Queen's Park)

Young Player of the Year
Craig Levein (Hearts)

1986-87

Premier Division......................................Brian McClair (Celtic)
First Division ....Jim Holmes (Morton)
Second Division ....John Sludden (Ayr United)

Young Player of the Year
Robert Fleck (Rangers)

1987-88

Premier Division ....Paul McStay (Celtic)
First Division ....Alex Taylor (Hamilton)
Second Division ....Henry Templeton (Ayr United)

Young Player of the Year
John Collins (Hibernian)

1988-89

Premier Division..............................Theo Snelders (Aberdeen)
First Division.....................................Ross Jack (Dunfermline)
Second Division....................................Paul Hunter (East Fife)

Young Player of the Year
Billy McKinlay (Dundee United)

1989-90

Premier Division...Jim Bett (Aberdeen)
First Division ....Ken Eadie (Clydebank)
Second Division.............................Willie Watters (Kilmarnock)

Young Player of the Year
Scott Crabbe (Hearts)

1990-91

Premier Division....................Paul Elliott (Celtic)
First Division....................Simon Stainrod (Falkirk)
Second Division....................Kevin Todd (Berwick Rangers)

Young Player of the Year – Eoin Jess (Aberdeen)

1991-92

Premier Division....................Ally McCoist (Rangers)
First Division....................Gordon Dalziel (Raith Rovers)
Second Division....................Andy Thomson (Queen of the South)

Young Player of the Year – Phil O'Donnell (Motherwell)

1992-93

Premier Division....................Andy Goram (Rangers)
First Division....................Gordon Dalziel (Raith Rovers)
Second Division....................Sandy Ross (Brechin City)

Young Player of the Year – Eoin Jess (Aberdeen)

1993-94

Premier Division....................Mark Hateley (Rangers)
First Division....................Richard Cadette (Falkirk)
Second Division....................Andy Thomson (Queen of the South)

Young Player of the Year – Phil O'Donnell (Motherwell)

1994-95

Premier Division....................Brian Laudrup (Rangers)
First Division....................Stephen Crawford (Raith Rovers)
Second Division....................Derek McInnes (Morton)
Third Division....................David Bingham (Forfar Ath.)

Young Player of the Year – Charlie Miller (Rangers)

1995-96

Premier Division....................Paul Gascoigne (Rangers)
First Division....................George O'Boyle (St Johnstone)
Second Division....................Steven McCormick (Stirling A.)
Third Division....................Jason Young (Livingston)

Young Player of the Year – Jackie McNamara (Celtic)

1996-97

Premier Division....................Paolo di Canio (Celtic)
First Division....................Roddy Grant (St Johnstone)
Second Division....................Paul Ritchie (Hamilton)
Third Division....................Ian Stewart (Inverness CT)

Young Player of the Year – Robbie Winters (Dundee United)

1997-98

Premier Division....................Jackie McNamara (Celtic)
First Division....................James Grady (Dundee)
Second Division....................Paul Lovering (Clydebank)
Third Division....................Willie Irvine (Alloa)

Young Player of the Year – Gary Naysmith (Hearts)

1998-99

Premier Division....................Henrik Larsson (Celtic)
First Division....................Russell Latapy (Hibs)
Second Division....................David Bingham (Livingston)
Third Division....................Neil Tarrant (Ross County)

Young Player of the Year – Barry Ferguson (Rangers)

ENGLISH PLAYER OF THE YEAR

AWARDED BY THE ENGLISH FOOTBALL WRITERS' ASSOCIATION

1948 **Stanley Matthews** (Blackpool)
1949 **Johnny Carey** (Man Utd)
1950 **Joe Mercer** (Arsenal)
1951 **Harry Johnston** (Blackpool)
1952 **Billy Wright** (Wolves)
1953 **Nat Lofthouse** (Bolton W.)
1954 **Tom Finney** (Preston NE)
1955 **Don Revie** (Man City)
1956 **Bert Trautmann** (Man City)
1957 **Tom Finney** (Preston NE)
1958 **Danny Blanchflower** (Spurs)
1959 **Syd Owen** (Luton Town)
1960 **Bill Slater** (Wolves)
1961 **Danny Blanchflower** (Spurs)
1962 **Jimmy Adamson** (Burnley)
1963 **Stanley Matthews** (Stoke C)
1964 **Bobby Moore** (West Ham)
1965 **Bobby Collins** (Leeds Utd)
1966 **Bobby Charlton** (Man Utd)
1967 **Jackie Charlton** (Leeds Utd)
1968 **George Best** (Man Utd)
1969 **Dave Mackay** (Derby)/
Tony Book (Man City)
1970 **Billy Bremner** (Leeds Utd)
1971 **Frank McLintock** (Arsenal)
1972 **Gordon Banks** (Stoke City)
1973 **Pat Jennings** (Spurs)
1974 **Ian Callaghan** (Liverpool)
1975 **Alan Mullery** (Fulham)
1976 **Kevin Keegan** (Liverpool)
1977 **Emlyn Hughes** (Liverpool)
1978 **Kenny Burns** (Notts Forest)
1979 **Kenny Dalglish** (Liverpool)
1980 **Terry McDermott** (Liverpool)
1981 **Frans Thijssen** (Ipswich T)
1982 **Steve Perryman** (Spurs)
1983 **Kenny Dalglish** Liverpool)
1984 **Ian Rush** (Liverpool)
1985 **Neville Southall** (Everton)
1986 **Gary Lineker** (Everton)
1987 **Clive Allen** (Tottenham H.)
1988 **John Barnes** (Liverpool)
1989 **Steve Nicol** (Liverpool)
1990 **John Barnes** (Liverpool)
1991 **Gordon Strachan** (Leeds U)
1992 **Gary Lineker** (Spurs)
1993 **Chris Waddle** (Sheffield W)
1994 **Alan Shearer** (Blackburn R)
1995 **Jurgen Klinsmann** (Spurs)
1996 **Eric Cantona** (Man Utd)
1997 **Gianfranco Zola** (Chelsea)
1998 **Dennis Bergkamp** (Arsenal)
1999 **David Ginola** (Spurs)

Dennis Bergkamp

David Ginola

PFA PLAYER OF THE YEAR

AWARDED BY THE ENGLISH PROFESSIONAL FOOTBALLERS' ASSOCIATION

FULL AWARD

1974 **Norman Hunter** (Leeds Utd)
1975 **Colin Todd** (Derby County)
1976 **Pat Jennings** (Spurs)
1977 **Andy Gray** (Aston Villa)
1978 **Peter Shilton** (Notts F)
1979 **Liam Brady** (Arsenal)
1980 **Terry McDermott** (Liverpool)
1981 **John Wark** (Ipswich)
1982 **Kevin Keegan** (South'ton)
1983 **Kenny Dalglish** (Liverpool)
1984 **Ian Rush** (Liverpool)
1985 **Peter Reid** (Everton)
1986 **Gary Lineker** (Everton)
1987 **Clive Allen** (Spurs)
1988 **John Barnes** (Liverpool)
1989 **Mark Hughes** (Man Utd)
1990 **David Platt** (Aston Villa)
1991 **Mark Hughes** (Man Utd)
1992 **Gary Pallister** (Man Utd)
1993 **Paul McGrath** (Aston Villa)
1994 **Eric Cantona** (Man Utd)
1995 **Alan Shearer** (Blackburn R)
1996 **Les Ferdinand** (Newcastle)
1997 **Alan Shearer** (Newcastle)
1998 **Dennis Bergkamp** (Arsenal)
1999 **David Ginola** (Spurs)

YOUNG PLAYER

1974 **Kevin Beattie** (Ipswich)
1975 **Mervyn Day** (West Ham)
1976 **Peter Barnes** (Man City)
1977 **Andy Gray** (Aston Villa)
1978 **Tony Woodcock** (Notts F)
1979 **Cyrille Regis** (West Brom)
1980 **Glenn Hoddle** (Spurs)
1981 **Gary Shaw** (Aston Villa)
1982 **Steve Moran** (South'ton)
1983 **Ian Rush** (Liverpool)
1984 **Paul Walsh** (Luton Town)
1985 **Mark Hughes** (Man Utd)
1986 **Tony Cottee** (West Ham)
1987 **Tony Adams** (Arsenal)
1988 **Paul Gascoigne** (Spurs)
1989 **Paul Merson** (Arsenal)
1990 **Matt Le Tissier** (South'ton)
1991 **Lee Sharpe** (Man Utd)
1992 **Ryan Giggs** (Man Utd)
1993 **Ryan Giggs** (Man Utd)
1994 **Andy Cole** (Newcastle)
1995 **Robbie Fowler** (Liverpool)
1996 **Robbie Fowler** (Liverpool)
1997 **David Beckham** (Man Utd)
1998 **Michael Owen** (Liverpool)
1999 **Nicolas Anelka** (Arsenal

NICOLAS ANELKA . . . the young Frenchman showed some sublime skills during the season

EUROPEAN FOOTBALLER OF THE YEAR

1956 ..... STANLEY MATTHEWS (Blackpool)

1957 ..... ALFREDO DI STEFANO (Real Madrid)

1958 ..... RAYMOND KOPA (Real Madrid)

1959 ..... ALFREDO DI STEFANO (Real Madrid)

1960 ..... LUIS SUAREZ (Barcelona)

1961 ..... OMAR SIVORI (Juventus)

1962 ..... JOSEF MASOPUST (Dukla Prague)

1963 ..... LEV YASHIN (Moscow Dynamo)

1964 ..... DENIS LAW (Manchester United)

1965 ..... EUSEBIO (Benfica)

1966 ..... BOBBY CHARLTON (Manchester United)

1967 ..... FLORIAN ALBERT (Ferencvaros)

1968 ..... GEORGE BEST (Manchester United)

1969 ..... GIANNI RIVERA (AC Milan)

1970 ..... GERD MULLER (Bayern Munich)

1971 ..... JOHAN CRUYFF (Ajax Amsterdam)

1972 ..... FRANZ BECKENBAUER (Bayern Munich)

1973 ..... JOHAN CRUYFF (Barcelona)

1974 ..... JOHAN CRUYFF (Barcelona)

1975 ..... OLEG BLOKHIN (Dynamo Kiev)

1976 ..... FRANZ BECKENBAUER (Bayern Munich)

1977 ..... ALLAN SIMONSEN (Borussia Moenchengladbach)

1978 ..... KEVIN KEEGAN (SV Hamburg)

1979 ..... KEVIN KEEGAN (SV Hamburg)

1980 ..... KARL-HEINZ RUMMENIGGE (Bayern Munich)

1981 ..... KARL-HEINZ RUMMENIGGE (Bayern Munich)

1982 ..... PAOLO ROSSI (Juventus)

1983 ..... MICHEL PLATINI (Juventus)

1984 ..... MICHEL PLATINI (Juventus)

1985 ..... MICHEL PLATINI (Juventus)

1986 ..... IGOR BELANOV (Dynamo Kiev)

1987 ..... RUUD GULLIT (AC Milan)

1988 ..... MARCO VAN BASTEN (AC Milan)

1989 ..... MARCO VAN BASTEN (AC Milan)

1990 ..... LOTHAR MATTHAUS
(West Germany World Cup winning captain)

1991 ..... JEAN-PIERRE PAPIN (Marseilles)

1992 ..... MARCO VAN BASTEN (AC Milan)

1993 ..... MARCO VAN BASTEN (AC Milan)

1994 ..... ROBERTO BAGGIO (Juventus)

1995 ..... HIRSTO STOICHKOV (Barcelona)

1996 ..... GEORGE WEAH (AC Milan

1997 ..... MATTHIAS SAMMER (Borussia Dortmund)

1998 ..... RONALDO (Inter Milan)

SCOTLAND'S INTERNATIONAL RECORD

ENGLAND

1872	SCOTLAND	0	ENGLAND	0	Partick
1873	ENGLAND	4	SCOTLAND	2	The Oval
1874	SCOTLAND	2	ENGLAND	1	Partick
1875	ENGLAND	2	SCOTLAND	2	The Oval
1876	SCOTLAND	3	ENGLAND		0Partick
1877	ENGLAND	1	SCOTLAND	3	The Oval
1878	SCOTLAND	7	ENGLAND	2	Hampden
1879	ENGLAND	5	SCOTLAND	4	The Oval
1880	SCOTLAND	5	ENGLAND	4	Hampden
1881	ENGLAND	1	SCOTLAND	6	The Oval
1882	SCOTLAND	5	ENGLAND	1	Hampden
1883	ENGLAND	2	SCOTLAND	3	Sheffield
1884	SCOTLAND	1	ENGLAND	0	Cathkin
1885	ENGLAND	1	SCOTLAND	1	The Oval
1886	SCOTLAND	1	ENGLAND	1	Hampden
1887	ENGLAND	2	SCOTLAND	3	Blackburn
1888	SCOTLAND	0	ENGLAND	5	Hampden
1889	ENGLAND	2	SCOTLAND	3	The Oval
1890	SCOTLAND	1	ENGLAND	1	Hampden
1891	ENGLAND	2	SCOTLAND	1	Blackburn
1892	SCOTLAND	1	ENGLAND	4	Ibrox
1893	ENGLAND	5	SCOTLAND	2	Richmond
1894	SCOTLAND	2	ENGLAND	2	Celtic Park
1895	ENGLAND	3	SCOTLAND	0	Everton
1896	SCOTLAND	2	ENGLAND	1	Celtic Park
1897	ENGLAND	1	SCOTLAND	2	Crystal Pal
1898	SCOTLAND	1	ENGLAND	3	Celtic Park
1899	ENGLAND	2	SCOTLAND	1	Birmingham
1900	SCOTLAND	4	ENGLAND	1	Celtic Park
1901	ENGLAND	2	SCOTLAND	2	Crystal Pal
1902	ENGLAND	2	SCOTLAND	2	Birmingham
1903	ENGLAND	1	SCOTLAND	2	Sheffield
1904	SCOTLAND	0	ENGLAND	1	Celtic Park
1905	ENGLAND	1	SCOTLAND	0	Crystal Pal
1906	SCOTLAND	2	ENGLAND	1	Hampden
1907	ENGLAND	1	SCOTLAND	1	Newcastle
1908	SCOTLAND	1	ENGLAND	1	Hampden
1909	ENGLAND	2	SCOTLAND	0	Crystal Pal
1910	SCOTLAND	2	ENGLAND	0	Hampden
1911	ENGLAND	1	SCOTLAND	1	Liverpool
1912	SCOTLAND	1	ENGLAND	1	Hampden
1913	ENGLAND	1	SCOTLAND	0	Chelsea

1914	SCOTLAND 3	ENGLAND..........1	Hampden
1920	ENGLAND 5	SCOTLAND 4	Sheffield
1921	SCOTLAND 3	ENGLAND..........0	Hampden
1922	ENGLAND 0	SCOTLAND 1	Aston Villa
1923	SCOTLAND 2	ENGLAND..........2	Hampden
1924	ENGLAND 1	SCOTLAND 1	Wembley
1925	SCOTLAND 2	ENGLAND..........0	Hampden
1926	ENGLAND 0	SCOTLAND 1	Manchester
1927	SCOTLAND 1	ENGLAND..........2	Hampden
1928	ENGLAND 1	SCOTLAND 5	Wembley
1929	SCOTLAND 1	ENGLAND..........0	Hampden
1930	ENGLAND 5	SCOTLAND 2	Wembley
1931	SCOTLAND 2	ENGLAND..........0	Hampden
1932	ENGLAND 3	SCOTLAND 0	Wembley
1933	SCOTLAND 2	ENGLAND..........1	Hampden
1934	ENGLAND 3	SCOTLAND 0	Wembley
1935	SCOTLAND 2	ENGLAND..........0	Hampden
1936	ENGLAND 1	SCOTLAND 1	Wembley
1937	SCOTLAND 3	ENGLAND..........1	Hampden
1938	ENGLAND 0	SCOTLAND 1	Wembley
1939	SCOTLAND 1	ENGLAND..........2	Hampden
1947	ENGLAND 1	SCOTLAND 1	Wembley
1948	SCOTLAND 0	ENGLAND..........2	Hampden
1949	ENGLAND 1	SCOTLAND 3	Wembley
1950	SCOTLAND 0	ENGLAND..........1	Hampden
1951	ENGLAND 2	SCOTLAND 3	Wembley
1952	SCOTLAND 1	ENGLAND..........2	Hampden
1953	ENGLAND 2	SCOTLAND 2	Wembley
1954	SCOTLAND 2	ENGLAND..........4	Hampden
1955	ENGLAND 7	SCOTLAND 2	Wembley
1956	SCOTLAND 1	ENGLAND..........1	Hampden
1957	ENGLAND 2	SCOTLAND 1	Wembley
1958	SCOTLAND 0	ENGLAND..........4	Hampden
1959	ENGLAND 1	SCOTLAND 0	Wembley
1960	SCOTLAND 1	ENGLAND..........1	Hampden
1961	ENGLAND 9	SCOTLAND 3	Wembley
1962	SCOTLAND 2	ENGLAND..........0	Hampden
1963	ENGLAND 1	SCOTLAND 2	Wembley
1964	SCOTLAND 1	ENGLAND..........0	Hampden
1965	ENGLAND 2	SCOTLAND 2	Wembley

1966	SCOTLAND 3	ENGLAND 4	Hampden
1967	ENGLAND 2	SCOTLAND . . . 3	Wembley
1968	SCOTLAND 1	ENGLAND 1	Hampden
1969	ENGLAND 4	SCOTLAND . . . 1	Wembley
1970	SCOTLAND 0	ENGLAND 0	Hampden
1971	ENGLAND 3	SCOTLAND . . . 1	Wembley
1972	SCOTLAND 0	ENGLAND 1	Hampden
1973	ENGLAND 1	SCOTLAND . . . 0	Wembley
1973	SCOTLAND 0	ENGLAND 5	Hampden
1974	SCOTLAND 2	ENGLAND 0	Hampden

MAURICE MALPAS . . . played against England three times

1975	ENGLAND 5	SCOTLAND . . .1	Wembley
1976	SCOTLAND 2	ENGLAND 1	Hampden
1977	ENGLAND 1	SCOTLAND . . .2	Wembley
1978	SCOTLAND 0	ENGLAND 1	Hampden
1979	ENGLAND 3	SCOTLAND . . .1	Wembley
1980	SCOTLAND 0	ENGLAND 2	Hampden
1981	ENGLAND 0	SCOTLAND . . .1	Wembley
1982	SCOTLAND 0	ENGLAND 1	Hampden
1983	ENGLAND 2	SCOTLAND . . .0	Wembley
1984	SCOTLAND 1	ENGLAND 1	Hampden

SIR STANLEY ROUS CUP

1985	SCOTLAND 1	ENGLAND 0	Hampden
1986	ENGLAND 2	SCOTLAND . . .1	Wembley

BECAME A THREE-NATION COMPETITION

1987 SCOTLAND . . . . .0 ENGLAND . . . .0 Hampden

(Scotland 0 Brazil 2. England 1 Brazil 1; Winners – Brazil)

1988 ENGLAND . . . . .1 SCOTLAND . . .0 Wembley

(Scotland 0 Colombia 0; England 1 Colombia 1. Winners: England)

1989 SCOTLAND . . . . .0 ENGLAND . . . .2 Hampden

(Scotland 2 Chile 0; England 0 Chile 0. Winners – England)

1996 ENGLAND . . . . . .2 SCOTLAND . . .0 Wembley

NORTHERN IRELAND

1884	IRELAND	0	SCOTLAND	5	Belfast
1885	SCOTLAND	8	IRELAND	2	Glasgow
1886	IRELAND	2	SCOTLAND	7	Belfast
1887	SCOTLAND	4	IRELAND	1	Glasgow
1888	IRELAND	2	SCOTLAND	10	Belfast
1889	SCOTLAND	7	IRELAND	0	Glasgow
1890	IRELAND	1	SCOTLAND	4	Belfast
1891	SCOTLAND	2	IRELAND	1	Glasgow
1892	IRELAND	2	SCOTLAND	3	Belfast
1893	SCOTLAND	6	IRELAND	1	Glasgow
1894	IRELAND	1	SCOTLAND	2	Belfast
1895	SCOTLAND	3	IRELAND	1	Glasgow
1896	IRELAND	3	SCOTLAND	3	Belfast
1897	SCOTLAND	5	IRELAND	1	Glasgow
1898	IRELAND	0	SCOTLAND	3	Belfast
1899	SCOTLAND	9	IRELAND	1	Glasgow
1900	IRELAND	0	SCOTLAND	3	Belfast
1901	SCOTLAND	11	IRELAND	0	Glasgow
1902	IRELAND	1	SCOTLAND	5	Belfast
1903	SCOTLAND	0	IRELAND	2	Glasgow
1904	IRELAND	1	SCOTLAND	1	Dublin
1905	SCOTLAND	4	IRELAND	0	Glasgow
1906	IRELAND	0	SCOTLAND	1	Dublin
1907	SCOTLAND	3	IRELAND	0	Glasgow
1908	IRELAND	0	SCOTLAND	5	Dublin
1909	SCOTLAND	5	IRELAND	0	Glasgow
1910	IRELAND	1	SCOTLAND	0	Belfast
1911	SCOTLAND	2	IRELAND	0	Glasgow
1912	IRELAND	1	SCOTLAND	4	Belfast
1913	IRELAND	1	SCOTLAND	2	Dublin
1914	IRELAND	1	SCOTLAND	1	Belfast
1920	SCOTLAND	3	IRELAND	0	Glasgow
1921	IRELAND	0	SCOTLAND	2	Belfast
1922	SCOTLAND	2	IRELAND	1	Glasgow
1923	IRELAND	0	SCOTLAND	1	Belfast
1924	SCOTLAND	2	IRELAND	0	Glasgow
1925	IRELAND	0	SCOTLAND	3	Belfast
1926	SCOTLAND	4	IRELAND	0	Glasgow
1927	IRELAND	0	SCOTLAND	2	Belfast

1928	SCOTLAND 0	IRELAND............1	Glasgow
1929	IRELAND 3	SCOTLAND 7	Belfast
1930	SCOTLAND 3	IRELAND............1	Glasgow
1931	IRELAND 0	SCOTLAND 0	Belfast
1932	SCOTLAND 3	IRELAND............1	Glasgow
1933	IRELAND 0	SCOTLAND 4	Belfast
1934	SCOTLAND 1	IRELAND............2	Glasgow
1935	IRELAND 2	SCOTLAND 1	Belfast
1936	SCOTLAND 2	IRELAND............1	Edinburgh
1937	IRELAND 1	SCOTLAND 3	Belfast
1938	SCOTLAND 1	IRELAND............1	Aberdeen
1939	IRELAND 0	SCOTLAND 2	Belfast
1946	SCOTLAND 0	IRELAND............0	Glasgow
1947	IRELAND 2	SCOTLAND 0	Belfast
1948	SCOTLAND 3	IRELAND............2	Glasgow
1949	IRELAND 2	SCOTLAND 8	Belfast
1950	SCOTLAND 6	IRELAND............1	Glasgow
1951	IRELAND 0	SCOTLAND 3	Belfast
1952	SCOTLAND 1	IRELAND............1	Glasgow
1953	IRELAND 1	SCOTLAND 3	Belfast
1954	SCOTLAND 2	IRELAND............2	Glasgow
1955	IRELAND 2	SCOTLAND 1	Belfast
1956	SCOTLAND 1	IRELAND............0	Glasgow
1957	IRELAND 1	SCOTLAND 1	Belfast
1958	SCOTLAND 2	IRELAND............2	Glasgow
1959	IRELAND 0	SCOTLAND 4	Belfast
1960	SCOTLAND 5	IRELAND............2	Glasgow
1961	IRELAND 1	SCOTLAND 6	Belfast
1962	SCOTLAND 5	IRELAND............1	Glasgow
1963	IRELAND 2	SCOTLAND 1	Belfast
1964	SCOTLAND 3	IRELAND............2	Glasgow
1965	IRELAND 3	SCOTLAND 2	Belfast
1966	SCOTLAND 2	IRELAND............1	Glasgow
1967	IRELAND 1	SCOTLAND 0	Belfast
1969	SCOTLAND 1	IRELAND............1	Glasgow
1970	IRELAND 0	SCOTLAND 1	Belfast
1971	SCOTLAND 0	IRELAND............1	Glasgow
1972	IRELAND 0	SCOTLAND 2	Glasgow
1973	SCOTLAND 1	IRELAND............2	Glasgow
1974	SCOTLAND 0	IRELAND............1	Glasgow
1975	SCOTLAND 3	IRELAND............0	Glasgow

1976	SCOTLAND 3	IRELAND...........0	Glasgow
1977	SCOTLAND 3	IRELAND...........0	Glasgow
1978	SCOTLAND 1	IRELAND...........1	Glasgow
1979	SCOTLAND 1	IRELAND...........0	Glasgow
1980	IRELAND..............1	SCOTLAND 0	Belfast
1981	SCOTLAND 1	IRELAND...........1	Glasgow
1981	SCOTLAND 2	IRELAND...........0	Glasgow
1982	IRELAND..............0	SCOTLAND 0	Belfast
1982	IRELAND..............1	SCOTLAND 1	Belfast
1983	SCOTLAND 0	IRELAND...........0	Glasgow
1984	IRELAND..............2	SCOTLAND 0	Belfast
1992	SCOTLAND 1	IRELAND...........0	Glasgow

WALES

1876	SCOTLAND 4	WALES..............0	Glasgow
1877	WALES 0	SCOTLAND 2	Wrexham
1878	SCOTLAND 9	WALES..............0	Glasgow
1879	WALES 0	SCOTLAND 3	Wrexham
1880	SCOTLAND 5	WALES..............1	Glasgow
1881	WALES 1	SCOTLAND 5	Wrexham
1882	SCOTLAND 5	WALES..............0	Glasgow
1883	WALES 1	SCOTLAND 4	Wrexham
1884	SCOTLAND 4	WALES..............1	Glasgow
1885	WALES 1	SCOTLAND 8	Wrexham
1886	SCOTLAND 4	WALES..............1	Glasgow
1887	WALES 0	SCOTLAND 2	Wrexham
1888	SCOTLAND 5	WALES..............1	Edinburgh
1889	WALES 0	SCOTLAND 0	Wrexham
1890	SCOTLAND 5	WALES..............0	Paisley
1891	WALES 3	SCOTLAND 4	Wrexham
1892	SCOTLAND 6	WALES..............1	Edinburgh
1893	WALES 0	SCOTLAND 8	Wrexham
1894	SCOTLAND 5	WALES..............2	Kilmarnock
1895	WALES 2	SCOTLAND 2	Wrexham
1896	SCOTLAND 4	WALES..............0	Dundee
1897	WALES 2	SCOTLAND 2	Wrexham
1898	SCOTLAND 5	WALES..............2	Motherwell
1899	WALES 0	SCOTLAND 6	Wrexham
1900	SCOTLAND 5	WALES..............2	Aberdeen
1901	WALES 1	SCOTLAND 1	Wrexham
1902	SCOTLAND 5	WALES..............1	Greenock
1903	WALES 0	SCOTLAND 1	Cardiff
1904	SCOTLAND 1	WALES..............1	Dundee

1905	WALES 3	SCOTLAND 1	Wrexham
1906	SCOTLAND 0	WALES...............2	Edinburgh
1907	WALES 1	SCOTLAND 0	Wrexham
1908	SCOTLAND 2	WALES...............1	Dundee
1909	WALES 3	SCOTLAND 2	Wrexham
1910	SCOTLAND 1	WALES...............0	Kilmarnock
1911	WALES 2	SCOTLAND 2	Cardiff
1912	SCOTLAND 1	WALES...............0	Edinburgh
1913	WALES 0	SCOTLAND 0	Wrexham
1914	SCOTLAND 0	WALES...............0	Glasgow
1920	WALES 1	SCOTLAND 1	Cardiff
1921	SCOTLAND 2	WALES...............1	Aberdeen
1922	WALES 2	SCOTLAND 1	Wrexham
1923	SCOTLAND 2	WALES...............0	Paisley
1924	WALES 2	SCOTLAND 0	Cardiff
1925	SCOTLAND 3	WALES...............1	Edinburgh
1926	WALES 0	SCOTLAND 3	Cardiff
1927	SCOTLAND 3	WALES...............0	Glasgow
1928	WALES 2	SCOTLAND 2	Wrexham
1929	SCOTLAND 4	WALES...............2	Glasgow
1930	WALES 2	SCOTLAND 4	Cardiff
1931	SCOTLAND 1	WALES...............1	Glasgow
1932	WALES 2	SCOTLAND 3	Wrexham
1933	SCOTLAND 2	WALES...............5	Edinburgh
1934	WALES 3	SCOTLAND 2	Cardiff
1935	SCOTLAND 3	WALES...............2	Aberdeen
1936	WALES 1	SCOTLAND 1	Cardiff
1937	SCOTLAND 1	WALES...............2	Dundee
1938	WALES 2	SCOTLAND 1	Cardiff
1939	SCOTLAND 3	WALES...............2	Edinburgh
1946	WALES 3	SCOTLAND 1	Wrexham
1947	SCOTLAND 1	WALES...............2	Glasgow
1948	WALES 1	SCOTLAND 3	Cardiff
1949	SCOTLAND 2	WALES...............0	Glasgow
1950	WALES 1	SCOTLAND 3	Cardiff
1951	SCOTLAND 0	WALES...............1	Glasgow
1952	WALES 1	SCOTLAND 2	Cardiff
1953	SCOTLAND 3	WALES...............3	Glasgow
1954	WALES 0	SCOTLAND 1	Cardiff
1955	SCOTLAND 2	WALES...............0	Glasgow
1956	WALES 2	SCOTLAND 2	Cardiff

1957	SCOTLAND	1	WALES	1	Glasgow
1958	WALES	0	SCOTLAND	3	Cardiff
1959	SCOTLAND	1	WALES	1	Glasgow
1960	WALES	2	SCOTLAND	0	Cardiff
1961	SCOTLAND	2	WALES	0	Glasgow
1962	WALES	2	SCOTLAND	3	Cardiff
1963	SCOTLAND	2	WALES	1	Glasgow
1964	WALES	3	SCOTLAND	2	Cardiff
1965	SCOTLAND	4	WALES	1	Glasgow
1966	WALES	1	SCOTLAND	1	Cardiff
1967	SCOTLAND	3	WALES	2	Glasgow
1969	WALES	3	SCOTLAND	5	Wrexham
1970	SCOTLAND	0	WALES	0	Glasgow
1971	WALES	0	SCOTLAND	0	Cardiff
1972	SCOTLAND	1	WALES	0	Glasgow
1973	WALES	0	SCOTLAND	2	Wrexham
1974	SCOTLAND	2	WALES	0	Glasgow
1975	WALES	2	SCOTLAND	2	Cardiff
1976	SCOTLAND	3	WALES	1	Glasgow
1977	WALES	0	SCOTLAND	0	Wrexham
1977	SCOTLAND	1	WALES	0	Glasgow
1977	WALES	0	SCOTLAND	2	Liverpool
1978	SCOTLAND	1	WALES	1	Glasgow
1979	WALES	3	SCOTLAND	0	Cardiff
1980	SCOTLAND	1	WALES	0	Glasgow
1981	WALES	2	SCOTLAND	0	Swansea
1982	SCOTLAND	1	WALES	0	Glasgow
1983	WALES	0	SCOTLAND	2	Cardiff
1984	SCOTLAND	2	WALES	1	Glasgow
1985	SCOTLAND	0	WALES	1	Glasgow
1985	WALES	1	SCOTLAND	1	Cardiff
1997	SCOTLAND	0	WALES	1	Kilmarnock

JOHN TOSHACK . . . the giant Welsh striker was a constant threat to defences

AMERICA

1952	SCOTLAND 6	AMERICA...........0	Glasgow
1992	AMERICA 0	SCOTLAND 1	Denver
1996	AMERICA 2	SCOTLAND 1	Hartford
1998	AMERICA 0	SCOTLAND 0	Washington

ARGENTINA

1977	ARGENTINA 1	SCOTLAND 1	Buenos Aires
1979	SCOTLAND 1	ARGENTINA 3	Glasgow
1990	SCOTLAND 1	ARGENTINA 0	Glasgow

AUSTRALIA

1985	SCOTLAND 2	AUSTRALIA 0	Glasgow
1985	AUSTRALIA 0	SCOTLAND 0	Melbourne
1996	SCOTLAND 1	AUSTRALIA 0	Glasgow

AUSTRIA

1931	AUSTRIA 5	SCOTLAND 0	Vienna
1933	SCOTLAND 2	AUSTRIA............2	Glasgow
1937	AUSTRIA 1	SCOTLAND 1	Vienna
1950	SCOTLAND 0	AUSTRIA............1	Glasgow
1951	AUSTRIA 4	SCOTLAND 0	Vienna
1954	AUSTRIA 1	SCOTLAND 0	Zurich
1955	AUSTRIA 1	SCOTLAND 4	Vienna
1956	SCOTLAND 1	AUSTRIA............1	Glasgow
1960	AUSTRIA 4	SCOTLAND 1	Vienna
1963	SCOTLAND 4	AUSTRIA............1	Glasgow
	(Referee abandoned match after 79 minutes)		
1968	SCOTLAND 2	AUSTRIA............1	Glasgow
1969	AUSTRIA 2	SCOTLAND 0	Vienna
1978	AUSTRIA 3	SCOTLAND 2	Vienna
1979	SCOTLAND 1	AUSTRIA............1	Glasgow
1994	AUSTRIA 1	SCOTLAND 2	Vienna
1996	AUSTRIA 0	SCOTLAND 0	Vienna
1997	SCOTLAND 2	AUSTRIA............0	Glasgow

BELARUS

1997	BELARUS 0	SCOTLAND 1	Minsk
1997	SCOTLAND 4	BELARUS 1	Aberdeen

BELGIUM

1946	SCOTLAND 2	BELGIUM...........2	Glasgow
1947	BELGIUM..............2	SCOTLAND 1	Brussels
1948	SCOTLAND 2	BELGIUM...........0	Glasgow
1951	BELGIUM..............0	SCOTLAND 5	Brussels
1971	BELGIUM..............3	SCOTLAND 0	Liege
1971	SCOTLAND 1	BELGIUM...........0	Aberdeen
1974	BELGIUM..............2	SCOTLAND 1	Bruges
1979	BELGIUM..............2	SCOTLAND 0	Brussels
1979	SCOTLAND 1	BELGIUM...........3	Glasgow
1982	BELGIUM..............3	SCOTLAND 2	Brussels
1983	SCOTLAND 1	BELGIUM...........1	Glasgow
1987	BELGIUM..............4	SCOTLAND 1	Brussels
1987	SCOTLAND 2	BELGIUM...........0	Glasgow

BRAZIL

1966	SCOTLAND 1	BRAZIL 1	Glasgow
1972	BRAZIL 1	SCOTLAND 0	Rio
1973	SCOTLAND 0	BRAZIL 1	Glasgow
1974	SCOTLAND 0	BRAZIL 0	Frankfurt
1977	BRAZIL 2	SCOTLAND 0	Rio
1982	SCOTLAND 1	BRAZIL 4	Seville
1987	SCOTLAND 0	BRAZIL 2	Glasgow
1990	BRAZIL 1	SCOTLAND 0	Turin
1998	BRAZIL 2	SCOTLAND 1	Paris

BULGARIA

1978	SCOTLAND 2	BULGARIA.........1	Glasgow
1986	SCOTLAND 0	BULGARIA.........0	Glasgow
1987	BULGARIA............0	SCOTLAND 1	Sofia
1990	BULGARIA............1	SCOTLAND 1	Sofia
1991	SCOTLAND 1	BULGARIA.........1	Glasgow

CANADA

1983	CANADA...............0	SCOTLAND 2	Vancouver
1983	CANADA...............0	SCOTLAND 3	Edmonton
1983	CANADA...............0	SCOTLAND 2	Toronto
1992	CANADA...............1	SCOTLAND 3	Toronto

CHILE

1977	CHILE 2	SCOTLAND 4	Santiago
1989	SCOTLAND 2	CHILE 0	Glasgow

C.I.S.

1992	SCOTLAND 3	CIS....................0	Sweden

COLOMBIA

1988	SCOTLAND 0	COLOMBIA........0	Glasgow
1996	COLOMBIA 1	SCOTLAND 0	Miami
1998	COLOMBIA 2	SCOTLAND 2	New Jersey

COSTA RICA

1990	SCOTLAND 0	COSTA RICA......1	Genoa

CYPRUS

1968	CYPRUS 0	SCOTLAND 5	Nicosia
1969	SCOTLAND 8	CYPRUS............0	Glasgow
1989	CYPRUS 2	SCOTLAND 3	Limassol
1989	SCOTLAND 2	CYPRUS............1	Glasgow

CZECHOSLOVAKIA

1937	CZECH 1	SCOTLAND 3	Prague
1938	SCOTLAND 5	CZECH 0	Glasgow
1961	CZECH 4	SCOTLAND 0	Bratislava
1961	SCOTLAND 3	CZECH 2	Glasgow
1961	SCOTLAND 2	CZECH 4	Brussels
1972	SCOTLAND 0	CZECH 0	Porto Alegre
1973	SCOTLAND 2	CZECH 1	Glasgow
1973	CZECH 1	SCOTLAND 0	Bratislava
1976	CZECH 2	SCOTLAND 0	Prague
1977	SCOTLAND 3	CZECH 1	Glasgow

CZECH REPUBLIC

1999	SCOTLAND 1	CZECH REP......2	Glasgow
1999	CZECH REP 3	SCOTLAND.......2	Prague

DENMARK

1951	SCOTLAND 3	DENMARK 1	Glasgow
1952	DENMARK. 1	SCOTLAND.......2	Copenhagen
1968	DENMARK. 0	SCOTLAND.......1	Copenhagen
1970	SCOTLAND 1	DENMARK 0	Glasgow
1971	DENMARK. 1	SCOTLAND.......0	Copenhagen
1972	DENMARK. 1	SCOTLAND.......4	Copenhagen
1972	SCOTLAND 2	DENMARK 0	Glasgow
1975	DENMARK. 0	SCOTLAND.......1	Copenhagen
1975	SCOTLAND 3	DENMARK 1	Glasgow

DENMARK (continued)

1986	SCOTLAND	0	DENMARK	1	Neza
1996	DENMARK	2	SCOTLAND	0	Copenhagen
1998	SCOTLAND	0	DENMARK	1	Glasgow

EAST GERMANY

1974	SCOTLAND	3	E. GERMANY	0	Glasgow
1977	E. GERMANY	1	SCOTLAND	0	East Berlin
1982	SCOTLAND	2	E. GERMANY	0	Glasgow
1983	E. GERMANY	2	SCOTLAND	1	Halle
1986	SCOTLAND	0	E. GERMANY	0	Glasgow
1990	SCOTLAND	0	E. GERMANY	1	Glasgow

ECUADOR

1995	ECUADOR	1	SCOTLAND	2	Toyama

EGYPT

1990	SCOTLAND	1	EGYPT	3	Aberdeen

EIRE

1961	SCOTLAND	4	EIRE	1	Glasgow
1961	EIRE	0	SCOTLAND	3	Dublin
1963	EIRE	1	SCOTLAND	0	Dublin
1969	EIRE	1	SCOTLAND	1	Dublin
1986	EIRE	0	SCOTLAND	0	Dublin
1987	SCOTLAND	0	EIRE	1	Glasgow

ESTONIA

1993	ESTONIA	0	SCOTLAND	3	Tallinn
1993	SCOTLAND	3	ESTONIA	1	Aberdeen
1996	ESTONIA	0	SCOTLAND	0	Tallinn
	(abandoned after 3 seconds, replay ordered in Monaco)				
1997	ESTONIA	0	SCOTLAND	0	Monaco
1997	SCOTLAND	0	ESTONIA	0	Kilmarnock

FAROE ISLANDS

1994	SCOTLAND	5	FAROE ISLANDS	1	Glasgow
1995	FAROE ISLANDS	0	SCOTLAND	2	Torshavn
1999	FAROE ISLANDS	1	SCOTLAND	1	Toftir

FINLAND

1954	FINLAND	1	SCOTLAND	2	Helsinki
1964	SCOTLAND	3	FINLAND	1	Glasgow
1965	FINLAND	1	SCOTLAND	2	Helsinki
1976	SCOTLAND	6	FINLAND	0	Glasgow
1992	SCOTLAND	1	FINLAND	1	Glasgow
1994	FINLAND	0	SCOTLAND	2	Helsinki
1995	SCOTLAND	1	FINLAND	0	Glasgow

FRANCE

1930	FRANCE	0	SCOTLAND	2	Paris
1932	FRANCE	1	SCOTLAND	3	Paris
1948	FRANCE	3	SCOTLAND	0	Paris
1949	SCOTLAND	2	FRANCE	0	Glasgow
1950	FRANCE	0	SCOTLAND	1	Paris
1951	SCOTLAND	1	FRANCE	0	Glasgow
1958	FRANCE	2	SCOTLAND	1	Obrero
1984	FRANCE	2	SCOTLAND	0	Marseilles
1989	SCOTLAND	2	FRANCE	0	Glasgow
1989	FRANCE	3	SCOTLAND	0	Paris
1997	FRANCE	2	SCOTLAND	1	St Etienne

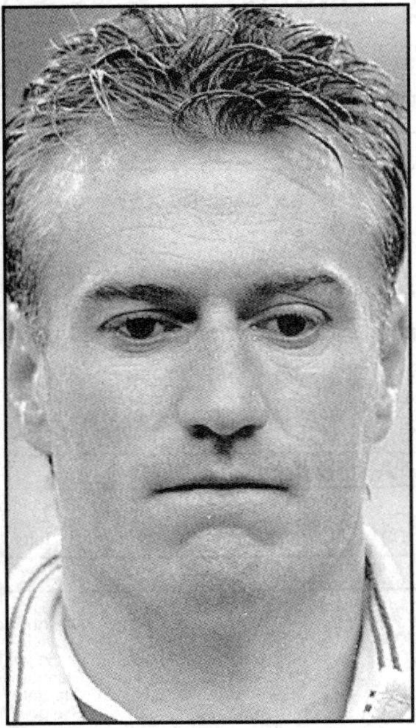

DIDIER DESCHAMPS . . . top French midfielder was a World Cup winner in 1998

COULDN'T WAIT

KILMARNOCK'S Jim Lauchlan had a good season

GERMANY

1936	SCOTLAND	2	GERMANY	0	Glasgow
1992	SCOTLAND	0	GERMANY	2	Sweden
1993	SCOTLAND	0	GERMANY	1	Glasgow
1999	GERMANY	0	SCOTLAND	1	Bremen

GREECE

1994	GREECE	1	SCOTLAND	0	Athens
1995	SCOTLAND	1	GREECE	0	Glasgow

HOLLAND

1929	HOLLAND	0	SCOTLAND	2	Amsterdam
1938	HOLLAND	1	SCOTLAND	3	Amsterdam
1959	HOLLAND	1	SCOTLAND	2	Amsterdam
1966	SCOTLAND	0	HOLLAND	3	Glasgow
1968	HOLLAND	0	SCOTLAND	0	Amsterdam
1971	HOLLAND	2	SCOTLAND	1	Amsterdam
1978	SCOTLAND	3	HOLLAND	2	Argentina
1982	SCOTLAND	2	HOLLAND	1	Glasgow
1986	HOLLAND	0	SCOTLAND	0	Eindhoven
1992	SCOTLAND	0	HOLLAND	1	Sweden
1994	SCOTLAND	0	HOLLAND	1	Glasgow
1994	HOLLAND	3	SCOTLAND	1	Utrecht
1996	HOLLAND	0	SCOTLAND	0	Birmingham

HUNGARY

1938	SCOTLAND	3	HUNGARY	1	Glasgow
1955	SCOTLAND	2	HUNGARY	4	Glasgow
1955	HUNGARY	3	SCOTLAND	1	Budapest
1958	SCOTLAND	1	HUNGARY	1	Glasgow
1960	HUNGARY	3	SCOTLAND	3	Budapest
1980	HUNGARY	3	SCOTLAND	1	Budapest
1987	SCOTLAND	2	HUNGARY	0	Glasgow

ICELAND

1984	SCOTLAND	3	ICELAND	0	Glasgow
1985	ICELAND	0	SCOTLAND	1	Reykjavik

IRAN

1978	SCOTLAND	1	IRAN	1	Cordoba

ISRAEL

1981	ISRAEL 0	SCOTLAND 1	Tel Aviv
1981	SCOTLAND 3	ISRAEL 1	Glasgow
1986	ISRAEL 0	SCOTLAND 1	Tel Aviv

ITALY

1931	ITALY 3	SCOTLAND 0	Rome
1965	SCOTLAND 1	ITALY.......................0	Glasgow
1965	ITALY 3	SCOTLAND 0	Naples
1988	ITALY 2	SCOTLAND 0	Perugia
1992	SCOTLAND 0	ITALY.......................0	Ibrox
1993	ITALY 3	SCOTLAND 1	Rome

JAPAN

1995	JAPAN 0	SCOTLAND 0	Hiroshima

LATVIA

1996	LATVIA 0	SCOTLAND 2	Riga
1997	SCOTLAND 2	LATVIA.....................0	Celtic Park

LUXEMBOURG

1947	LUXEMBOURG. 0	SCOTLAND 6	Luxembourg
1986	SCOTLAND 3	LUXEMBOURG 0	Glasgow
1987	LUXEMBOURG. 0	SCOTLAND 0	Luxembourg

MALTA

1988	MALTA 1	SCOTLAND 1	Valetta
1990	MALTA 1	SCOTLAND 2	Valetta
1993	SCOTLAND 3	MALTA 0	Glasgow
1993	MALTA 0	SCOTLAND 2	Valetta
1997	MALTA 2	SCOTLAND 3	Valetta

MOROCCO

1998	SCOTLAND 0	MOROCCO.............3	St Etienne

NEW ZEALAND

1982	SCOTLAND 5	NEW ZEALAND 2	Malaga

NORWAY

1929	NORWAY 3	SCOTLAND 7	Bergen
1954	SCOTLAND 1	NORWAY.................0	Glasgow
1954	NORWAY 1	SCOTLAND 1	Oslo
1963	NORWAY 4	SCOTLAND 3	Bergen
1963	SCOTLAND 6	NORWAY.................1	Glasgow
1974	NORWAY 1	SCOTLAND 2	Oslo
1978	SCOTLAND 3	NORWAY.................2	Glasgow
1979	NORWAY 0	SCOTLAND 4	Oslo
1988	NORWAY 1	SCOTLAND 2	Oslo

NORWAY (continued)

1989	SCOTLAND	1	NORWAY	1	Glasgow
1992	NORWAY	0	SCOTLAND	0	Oslo
1998	SCOTLAND	1	NORWAY	1	Bordeaux

PARAGUAY

1958	SCOTLAND	2	PARAGUAY	3	Norrkoping

PERU

1972	SCOTLAND	2	PERU	0	Glasgow
1978	SCOTLAND	1	PERU	3	Cardoba
1979	SCOTLAND	1	PERU	1	Glasgow

PORTUGAL

1950	PORTUGAL	2	SCOTLAND	2	Lisbon
1955	SCOTLAND	3	PORTUGAL	0	Glasgow
1959	PORTUGAL	1	SCOTLAND	0	Lisbon
1966	SCOTLAND	0	PORTUGAL	1	Glasgow
1971	PORTUGAL	2	SCOTLAND	0	Lisbon
1971	SCOTLAND	2	PORTUGAL	1	Glasgow
1975	SCOTLAND	1	PORTUGAL	0	Glasgow
1978	PORTUGAL	1	SCOTLAND	0	Lisbon
1980	SCOTLAND	4	PORTUGAL	1	Glasgow
1980	SCOTLAND	0	PORTUGAL	0	Glasgow
1981	PORTUGAL	2	SCOTLAND	1	Lisbon
1992	SCOTLAND	0	PORTUGAL	0	Glasgow
1993	PORTUGAL	5	SCOTLAND	0	Lisbon

POLAND

1958	POLAND	1	SCOTLAND	2	Warsaw
1960	SCOTLAND	2	POLAND	3	Glasgow
1965	POLAND	1	SCOTLAND	1	Chorzow
1965	SCOTLAND	1	POLAND	2	Glasgow
1980	POLAND	1	SCOTLAND	0	Poznan
1990	SCOTLAND	1	POLAND	1	Glasgow

ROMANIA

1975	ROMANIA	1	SCOTLAND	1	Bucharest
1975	SCOTLAND	1	ROMANIA	1	Glasgow
1986	SCOTLAND	3	ROMANIA	0	Glasgow
1990	SCOTLAND	2	ROMANIA	1	Glasgow
1991	ROMANIA	1	SCOTLAND	0	Bucharest

RUSSIA

1995	SCOTLAND	1	RUSSIA	1	Glasgow
1995	RUSSIA	0	SCOTLAND	0	Moscow

SAN MARINO

1991	SAN MARINO 0	SCOTLAND 2	Serraville
1991	SCOTLAND 4	SAN MARINO 0	Glasgow
1995	SAN MARINO 0	SCOTLAND 2	Serraville
1995	SCOTLAND 5	SAN MARINO 0	Glasgow

SAUDI ARABIA

1988	SAUDI ARABIA 2	SCOTLAND 2	Riyadh

SOVIET UNION

1967	SCOTLAND 0	SOVIET UNION.......2	Glasgow
1971	SOVIET UNION. 1	SCOTLAND 0	Moscow
1982	SCOTLAND 2	SOVIET UNION.......2	Malaga
1991	SCOTLAND 0	SOVIET UNION.......1	Glasgow

SPAIN

1957	SCOTLAND 4	SPAIN 2	Glasgow
1957	SPAIN. 4	SCOTLAND 1	Madrid
1963	SPAIN. 2	SCOTLAND 6	Madrid
1965	SCOTLAND 0	SPAIN 0	Glasgow
1974	SCOTLAND 1	SPAIN 2	Glasgow
1975	SPAIN. 1	SCOTLAND 1	Valencia
1982	SPAIN. 3	SCOTLAND 0	Valencia
1984	SCOTLAND 3	SPAIN 1	Glasgow
1985	SPAIN. 1	SCOTLAND 0	Seville
1988	SPAIN. 0	SCOTLAND 0	Madrid

SWEDEN

1952	SWEDEN 3	SCOTLAND 1	Stockholm
1953	SCOTLAND 1	SWEDEN 2	Glasgow
1975	SWEDEN 1	SCOTLAND 1	Gothenburg
1977	SCOTLAND 3	SWEDEN 1	Glasgow
1980	SWEDEN 0	SCOTLAND 1	Stockholm
1981	SCOTLAND 2	SWEDEN 0	Glasgow
1990	SCOTLAND 2	SWEDEN 1	Genoa
1995	SWEDEN 2	SCOTLAND 0	Stockholm
1996	SCOTLAND 1	SWEDEN 0	Glasgow
1997	SWEDEN 2	SCOTLAND 0	Gothenburg

SWITZERLAND

1931	SWITZERLAND..........2	SCOTLAND 3	Geneva
1946	SCOTLAND................3	SWITZERLAND.......1	Glasgow
1948	SWITZERLAND..........2	SCOTLAND 1	Berne
1950	SCOTLAND................3	SWITZERLAND.......1	Glasgow
1957	SWITZERLAND..........1	SCOTLAND 2	Basle
1957	SCOTLAND................3	SWITZERLAND.......2	Glasgow
1973	SWITZERLAND..........1	SCOTLAND 0	Berne
1976	SCOTLAND................1	SWITZERLAND.......0	Glasgow
1982	SWITZERLAND..........2	SCOTLAND 0	Berne
1983	SCOTLAND................2	SWITZERLAND.......2	Glasgow
1990	SCOTLAND................2	SWITZERLAND.......1	Glasgow
1991	SWITZERLAND..........2	SCOTLAND 2	Berne
1992	SWITZERLAND..........3	SCOTLAND 1	Berne
1993	SCOTLAND................1	SWITZERLAND.......1	Aberdeen
1996	SWITZERLAND..........0	SCOTLAND 1	Birmingham

TURKEY

1960	TURKEY......................4	SCOTLAND 2	Ankara

URUGUAY

1954	SCOTLAND................0	URUGUAY 7	Switzerland
1962	SCOTLAND................2	URUGUAY 3	Glasgow
1983	SCOTLAND................2	URUGUAY 0	Glasgow
1986	SCOTLAND................0	URUGUAY 0	Neza

WEST GERMANY

1957	W. GERMANY............1	SCOTLAND 3	Stuttgart
1959	SCOTLAND................3	W. GERMANY.........2	Glasgow
1964	W. GERMANY............2	SCOTLAND 2	Hanover
1969	SCOTLAND................1	W. GERMANY.........1	Glasgow
1969	W. GERMANY............3	SCOTLAND 2	Hamburg
1973	SCOTLAND................1	W. GERMANY.........1	Glasgow
1974	W. GERMANY............2	SCOTLAND 1	Frankfurt
1986	SCOTLAND................1	W. GERMANY.........2	Queretaro

GERMAN superstars Franz Beckenbauer (left) and Gerd Muller

YUGOSLAVIA

1955	YUGOSLAVIA.............2	SCOTLAND 2	Belgrade
1956	SCOTLAND................2	YUGOSLAVIA 0	Glasgow
1958	SCOTLAND................1	YUGOSLAVIA 1	Vaasteras
1972	SCOTLAND................2	YUGOSLAVIA 2	Belo Horizonte
1974	SCOTLAND................1	YUGOSLAVIA 1	Frankfurt
1984	SCOTLAND................6	YUGOSLAVIA 1	Glasgow
1988	SCOTLAND................1	YUGOSLAVIA 1	Glasgow
1989	YUGOSLAVIA.............3	SCOTLAND 1	Zagreb

ZAIRE

1974	SCOTLAND................2	ZAIRE 0	Dortmund

JOE JORDAN . . . scored against Zaire

ANNIESLAND
College
Make the
champion's choice
Call today
for your colour
prospectus

LIST OF PLAYERS HONOURED

This is a list of full international appearances by Scots in matches against the Home Countries and against foreign nations.

The code for countries is as follows

A, Austria; Arg, Argentina; Aus, Australia; Bel, Belgium; Blr, Belarus; Br, Brazil; Bul, Bulgaria; Ca, Canada; Ch, Chile; C.I.S. Commonwealth of Independent States; Co, Columbia; Cr, Costa Rica; Cy, Cyprus; Cz, Czechoslovakia; CzR, Czech Republic; D, Denmark; E, England; Ec, Ecquador; Ei, Eire; EG, East Germany; Eg, Egypt; Est, Estonia; Fr, France; Fin, Finland; Fi, Faroe Islands; G, Germany; Gr, Greece; H, Hungary; Holl, Holland; I, Italy; Ice, Iceland; Ir, Iran; Is, Israel; J, Japan; L, Luxembourg; La, Latvia; Lth, Lithuania; M, Morocco; Ma, Malta; N, Norway; Ni, Northern Ireland; Nz, New Zealand; Por, Portugal; Pe, Peru; Pol, Poland; R, Romania; Ru, Russia; S.Ar, Saudi Arabia; Se, Sweden; Sm, San Marino; Sp, Spain; Sw, Switzerland; T, Turkey; U, Uruguay; US, United States of America; USSR, Soviet Union; W, Wales; WG, West Germany; Y, Yugoslavia; Z, Zaire.

The year refers to the season. For example, 1989 is the 1988-89 season

ADAMS, J. (Hearts) (3): 1889 v Ni; 1892 v W; 1893 v Ni.
AGNEW, W. B. (Kilmarnock) (3): 1907 v Ni; 1908 v W, Ni.
AIRD, J. (Burnley) (4): 1954 v N (2); A, U.
AITKEN A. (Newcastle Utd, Middlesbrough, Leicester Fosse) (14): 1901 v E; 1902 v E; 1903 v E, W; 1904 v E; 1905 v E, W; 1906 v E; 1907 v E, W; 1908 v E; 1910 v E; 1911 v E, Ni.
AITKEN, G, G. (East Fife, Sunderland) (8): 1949 v E, Fr; 1950 v W, Ni, Sw; 1953 v W, Ni; 1954 v E.
AITKEN, R. (Dumbarton) (2): 1886 v E: 1888 v Ni.
AITKEN, R. (Celtic, Newcastle Utd, St Mirren) (57): 1980 v Pe, Bel, W, E, Pol; 1983 v Bel, Ca (2); 1984 v Bel, Ni, W; 1985 v E, Ice; 1986 v W, EG, Aus (2), Is, R, E, D, WG, U; 1987 v Bul, Ei (2), L, Bel, E, Br; 1988 v H, Bel, Bul, L, S.Ar., Ma, Sp, Co, E; 1989 v N, Y, I, Cy, (2), Fr, E, Ch; 1990 v Y, Fr, N, Arg, Pol, Ma, Cr, Se, Br; 1992 v R.
AITKENHEAD, W. A. C. (Blackburn R.) (1): 1912 v Ni.
ALBISTON, A. (Manchester Utd) (14): 1982 v Ni; 1984 v U, Bel, EG, W, E; 1985 v Y, Ice, Sp (2), W; 1986 v EG, Holl, U.
ALEXANDER, D. (East Stirlingshire) (2): 1894 v W, Ni.
ALLAN, D. S. (Queen's Park) (3): 1885 v E, W; 1886 v W.
ALLAN, G. (Liverpool) (1): 1897 v E.
ALLAN, H. (Hearts, b) (1): 1902 v W.
ALLAN, J. (Queen's Park) (2): 1887 v E, W.
ALLAN, T. (Dundee) (2): 1974 v WG, N.
ANCELL, R. F. D. (Newcastle Utd) (2): 1937 v W, Ni.
ANDERSON, A. (Hearts) (23): 1933 v E; 1934 v A, E, W, Ni; 1935 v E, W, Ni; 1936 v E, W, Ni; 1937 v G, E, W, Ni, A; 1938 v E, W, Ni, Cz, Holl; 1939 v W, H.
ANDERSON, F. (Clydesdale) (1): 1874 v E.
ANDERSON, G. (Kilmarnock) (1): 1901 v Ni.
ANDERSON, H. A. (Raith Rovers) (1): 1914 v W.
ANDERSON, J. (Leicester City) (1): 1954 v Fin.
ANDERSON, K. (Queen's Park) (3): 1896 v Ni; 1898 v E, Ni.
ANDERSON, W. (Queen's Park) (6): 1882 v E: 1883 v E, W; 1884 v E; 1885 v E, W.
ANDREWS, P. (Eastern) (1): 1875 v E.
ARCHIBALD, A. (Rangers) (8): 1921 v W; 1922 v W, E; 1923 v Ni; 1924 v E, W; 1931 v E; 1932 v E.
ARCHIBALD, S. (Aberdeen, Tottenham H., Barcelona) (27): 1980 v Por, Ni, Pol, H; 1981 v Se, Is (2), Ni (2), E; 1982 v Ni, Por, Sp, Holl, Nz, Br, USSR; 1983 v EG, Sw, Bel; 1984 v EG, E, Fr; 1985 v Sp, E, Ice; 1986 v WG.
ARMSTRONG, M. W. (Aberdeen) (3): 1936 v W, Ni; 1937 v G.

ARNOTT, W. (Queen's Park) (14): 1883 v W; 1884 v E, Ni; 1885 v E, W; 1886 v E; 1887 v E, W; 1888 v E; 1889 v E; 1890 v E; 1891 v E; 1892 v E; 1893 v E.
AULD, J. R. (Third Lanark) (3): 1887 v E, W; 1889 v W.
AULD, R. (Celtic) (3): 1959 v H, Por; 1960 W.
BAIRD, A. (Queen's Park) (2): 1892 v Ni; 1894 v W.
BAIRD, D. (Hearts) (3): 1890 v Ni; 1891 v E; 1892 v W.
BAIRD, H. (Airdrie) (1): 1956 v A.
BAIRD, J. C. (Vale of Leven) (3): 1876 v E; 1878 v W; 1880 v E.
BAIRD, S. (Rangers) (7): 1957 v Y, Sp (2), Sw, WG: 1958 v Fr, Ni.
BAIRD, W. U. (St Bernard) (1): 1897 v Ni.
BANNON , E. (Dundee Utd) (11): 1980 v Bel; 1983 v Ni, W, E, Ca; 1984 v EG; 1986 v Is, R, E, D, WG.
BARBOUR, A. (Renton) (1): 1885 v Ni.
BARKER, J. B. (Rangers) (2): 1893 v W: 1894 v W.
BARRETT, F. (Dundee) (2): 1894 v Ni; 1895 v W.
BATTLES, B. (Celtic) (3): 1901 v E, W, Ni.
BATTLES, B. (Hearts) (1): 1931 v W.
BAULD, W. (Hearts) (3): 1950 v E, Sw, Por.
BAXTER, J. C. (Rangers, Sunderland) (34): 1961 v Ni, Ei (2), Cz; 1962 v Ni, W, E, Cz (2), U; 1963 v W, Ni, E, A, N, Ei, Sp; 1964 v W, E, N, WG; 1965 v W, Ni, Fin; 1966 v Por, Br, Ni, W, E, I; 1967 v W, E, USSR; 1968 v W.
BAXTER, R. D. (Middlesbrough) (3): 1939 v E, W, H.
BEATTIE, A. (Preston NE) (7): 1937 v E, A, Cz; 1938 v E; 1939 v W, Ni, H.
BEATTIE, R. (Preston NE) (1): 1939 v W.
BEGBIE, I. (Hearts) (4): 1890 v Ni; 1891 v E; 1892 v W; 1894 v E.
BELL, A. (Manchester Utd) (1): 1912 v Ni.
BELL, J. (Dumbarton, Everton, Celtic) (10): 1890 v Ni; 1892 v E; 1896 v E; 1897 v E; 1898 v E; 1899 v E, W, Ni; 1900 v E, W.
BELL, M. (Hearts) (1): 1901 v W.
BELL, W. J. (Leeds Utd) (2): 1966 v Por, Br.
BENNETT, A. (Celtic, Rangers) (11): 1904 v W; 1907 v Ni; 1908 v W: 1909 v W, Ni, E; 1910 v E, W; 1911 E, W; 1913 v Ni.
BENNIE, R. (Airdrie) (3): 1925 v W, Ni; 1926 v Ni.
BERNARD, P. (Oldham Ath.) (2): 1995 v J, Ec.
BERRY, D. (Queen's Park) (3): 1894 v W; 1899 v W, Ni.
BERRY, W. H. (Queen's Park) (4): 1888 v E; 1889 v E; 1890 v E; 1891 v E.
BETT, J. (Rangers, Lokeren, Aberdeen) (25): 1982 v Holl; 1983 v Bel; 1984 v Bel, W, E, Fr; 1985 v Y, Ice, (2), Sp (2), W, E; 1986 v W, Is, Holl; 1987 v Bel; 1988 v H; 1989 v Y; 1990 v Fr, N, Arg, Eg, Ma, Cr.

BEVERIDGE, W. W. (Glasgow University) (3): 1879 v E, W; 1880 v W.
BLACK, A (Hearts) (3): 1938 v Cz, Holl; 1939 v H.
BLACK, D. (Hurlford) (1): 1889 v Ni.
BLACK, E. (Metz) (2): 1988 v H, L.
BLACK, I. H. (Southampton) (1): 1948 v E.
BLACKBURN, J. E. (Royal Engineers) (1): 1873 v E.
BLACKLAW, A. S. (Burnley) (3): 1963 v N, Sp; 1966 v I.
BLACKLEY, J. (Hibernian) (7): 1974 v Cz, E, Bel, Z; 1976 v Sw; 1977 v W, Se.
BLAIR, D. (Clyde, Aston Villa) (8): 1929 v W, Ni; 1931 v E, A, I; 1932 v W, Ni; 1933 v W.
BLAIR, J. (Sheffield W., Cardiff City) (8): 1920 v E, Ni; 1921 v E; 1922 v E; 1923 v E, W, Ni; 1924 v W.
BLAIR, J. (Motherwell) (1): 1934 v W.
BLAIR, J. A. (Blackpool) (1): 1947 v W.
BLAIR, W. (Third Lanark) (1): 1896 v W.
BLESSINGTON, J. (Celtic) (4): 1894 v E, Ni; 1896 v E, Ni.
BLYTH, J. A. (Coventry City) (2): 1978 v Bul, W.
BOWMAN, D. (Dundee United) (6): 1992 v Fin, US; 1993 v G, Est; 1994 v Sw, I.
BONE, J. (Norwich City) (2): 1972 v Y; 1973 v D.
BOOTH, S. (Aberdeen, Utrecht) (17): 1993 v G, Est (2); 1994 v Sw, Ma; 1995 v Fi, Ru; 1996 v Fin, Sm, Aus, US, Holl, Sw; 1998 D, Fin, Co, M.
BOWIE, J. (Rangers) (2): 1920 v E, Ni.
BOWIE, W. (Linthouse) (1): 1891 v Ni.
BOWMAN, G. A. (Montrose) (1): 1892 v Ni.
BOYD, J. M. (Newcastle Utd) (1): 1934 v Ni.
BOYD, R. (Mossend Swifts) (2): 1889 v Ni; 1891 v W.
BOYD, T. (Motherwell, Chelsea, Celtic) (65): 1991 v R (2), Sw, Bul, USSR; 1992 Sw, Fin, Ca, N, CIS; 1993 v Sw, Por, I, Ma, G, Est (2); 1994 v I, Ma, Holl, A; 1995 v Fin, Fi, Ru (2), Gr, Sm. 1996 v Gr, Fin, Se, Sm, Aus, D, US, U, Holl, E, Sw; 1997 v A (2), La, Se (2), Est (2), W, Ma, Blr; 1998 v Blr, La, Fr, D, Fin, Co, US, Br, N, M. 1999 v Lth, Est, Fi, CzR (2), G, Fi.
BOYD, W. G. (Clyde) (2): 1931 v I, Sw, Fin.
BRACKENBRIDGE, T. (Hearts) (1): 1888 v Ni.
BRADSHAW, T. (Bury) (1): 1928 v E.
BRAND, R. (Rangers) (8): 1961 v Ni, Cz, Ei. (2); 1962 v Ni, W, Cz, U.
BRANDEN, T. (Blackburn R.) (1): 1896 v E.
BRAZIL, A. (Ipswich Town) (13): 1980 v Pol, H; 1982 v Sp, Holl, Ni, W, E, Nz, USSR; 1983 v EG, Sw, W, E.
BREMNER, D. (Hibernian) (1): 1976 v Sw.
BREMNER, W. J. (Leeds Utd) (54): 1965 v Sp; 1966 v E, Pol, P, Br, I (2); 1967 v W, Ni, E; 1968 v W, E; 1969 v W, E, Ni, D, A, WG, Cy (2); 1970 v Ei, WG, A; 1971 v W, E; 1972 v Por, Bel, Holl, Ni, W, E, Y, Cz, Br; 1973 v D (2), E (2), Ni, Sw, Br; 1974 v Cz, WG, Ni, W, E, Bel, N, Z, Br, Y; 1975 v Sp (2); 1976 v D.
BRENNAN, F. (Newcastle Utd) (7): 1947 v W, Ni; 1953 v W, Ni, E; 1954 v Ni, E.
BRESLIN, B. (Hibernian) (1): 1897 v W.

BREWSTER, G. (Everton) (1): 1921 v E.
BROGAN, J. (Celtic) (4): 1971 v W, Ni, Por, E.
BROWN, A. (Middlesbrough) (1): 1904 v E.
BROWN, A. (St Mirren) (2): 1890 v W; 1891 v W.
BROWN, A. D. (East Fife, Blackpool) (14): 1950 v Sw, Por, Fr; 1952 v USA, D, Se; 1953 v W; 1954 v W, E, N (2), Fin, A, U.
BROWN, G. C. P. (Rangers) (19): 1931 v W; 1932 v E, W, Ni; 1933 v E; 1935 v A, E, W; 1936 v E, W; 1937 v G, E, W, Ni, Cz; 1938 v E, W, Cz, Holl.
BROWN, H. (Partick Th.) (3): 1947 v W, Bel, L.
BROWN, J. (Cambuslang) (1): 1890 v W.
BROWN, J. B. (Clyde) (1): 1939 v W.
BROWN, J. G. (Sheffield U.) (1): 1975 v R.
BROWN, R. (Dumbarton) (2): 1884 v W, Ni.
BROWN, R. (Rangers) (3): 1947 v Ni; 1949 v Ni; 1952 v E.
BROWN, R. (Dumbarton) (1): 1885 v W.
BROWN, W. D. F. (Dundee, Tottenham H.) (28): 1958 v Fr; 1959 v E, W, Ni; 1960 v W, Ni, Pol, A, H, T; 1962 v Ni, W, E, Cz; 1963 v W, Ni, E, A; 1964 v Ni, W, N; 1965 v E, Fin, Pol, Sp; 1966 v Ni, Pol, I.
BROWNING, J. (Celtic) (1): 1914 v W.
BROWNLIE, J. (Hibernian) (7): 1971 v USSR; 1972 v Pe, Ni, E; 1973 v D (2); 1976 v R.
BROWNLIE, J. (Third Lanark) (16): 1909 v E, Ni; 1910 v E, W, Ni; 1911 v W, Ni; 1912 v W, Ni, E; 1913 v W, Ni, E; 1914 v W, Ni, E.
BRUCE, D. (Vale of Leven) (1): 1890 v W.
BRUCE, R. F. (Middlesbrough) (1): 1934 v A.
BUCHAN, M. M. (Aberdeen, Manchester Utd.) (34): 1972 v Por, Bel, W, Y, Cz, Br; 1973 v D (2), E; 1974 v WG, Ni, W, N, Br, Y; 1975 v EG, Sp, Por; 1976 v D, R; 1977 v Fin, Cz, Ch, Arg, Br; 1978 v EG, W, Ni, Pe, Ir, Holl; 1979 v A, N, Por.
BUCHANAN, J. (Cambuslang) (1): 1889 v Ni.
BUCHANAN, J. (Rangers) (2): 1929 v E; 1930 v E.
BUCHANAN, P. S. (Chelsea) (1): 1938 v Cz.
BUCHANAN, R. (Abercorn) (1): 1891 v W.
BUCKLEY, P. (Aberdeen) (3): 1954 v N; 1955 v W, Ni.
BUICK, A. (Hearts) (2): 1902 v W, Ni.
BURLEY C. (Chelsea, Celtic) (30): 1995 v J, Ec, Fi. 1996 v Gr, Se, Aus, D, US, Co, Ho, E, Sw; 1997 v A (2), La, Se (2), Est, Ma, Blr 1998 v Blr, La, Fr, Co, US, Br, N, M. 1999 v Fi, CzR.
BURLEY, G. (Ipswich Town) (11): 1979 v W, Ni, E, Arg, N; 1980 v Por, Ni, E, Pol; 1982 v W, E.
BURNS, F. (Manchester Utd) (1): 1970 v A.
BURNS, K. (Birmingham City, Nottingham F.) (20): 1974 v WG; 1975 v EG, Sp (2); 1977 v Cz, W, (2), Se; 1978 v Ni, W, E, Pe, Ir; 1979 v N; 1980 v Pe, A, Bel; 1981 v Is, Ni, W.

BURNS, T. (Celtic) (8): 1981 v Ni; 1982 v Holl, W; 1983 v Bel, Ni, Ca (2); 1988 v E.
BUSBY, M. W. (Manchester City) (1): 1934 v W.
CAIRNS, T. (Rangers) (8): 1920 v W; 1922 v E; 1923 v E, W; 1924 v Ni; 1925 v W, E, Ni.
CALDERHEAD, D. (Q.O.S. Wanderers) (1): 1889 v Ni.
CALDERWOOD, C. (Tottenham Hotspur) (34): 1995 v Ru, Sm, J, Ec, Fi. 1996 v Gr, Fin, Se, Sm, US, U, Holl, E, Sw; 1997 A (2), La, Se (2), Est (2); 1998 v Blr, La, Fr, D, Fin, Co, US, Br, N. 1999 v Lth, Est, Fi, CzR.
CALDERWOOD, R. (Cartvale) (3): 1885 v Ni, E, W.
CALDOW, E. (Rangers) (40): 1957 Sp (2), Sw, WG, E; 1958 v Ni, W, Sw, Par, H, Pol, Y, Fr; 1959 v E, W, Ni, WG, Holl, Por; 1960 v E, W, Ni, A, H, T; 1961 v E, W, Ni, Ei (2), Cz; 1962 v Ni, W, E, Cz (2), U; 1963 v W, Ni, E.
CALLAGHAN, P. (Hibernian) (1): 1900 v Ni.
CALLAGHAN, W. C. Dunfermline Ath.) (2): 1970 v Ei, W.
CAMERON, C. (Hearts) (2): v1999 v G, Fi.
CAMERON, J. (Rangers) (1): 1886 v NI.
CAMERON, J. (Queen's Park) (1): 1896 v Ni.
CAMERON, J. (St Mirren, Chelsea) (2): 1904 v Ni; 1909 v E.
CAMPBELL, C. (Queen's Park) (13): 1874 v E; 1876 v W; 1877 v E, W; 1878 v E; 1879 v E; 1880 v E; 1881 v E; 1882 v E, W; 1884 v E; 1885 v E; 1886 v E.
CAMPBELL, H. (Renton) (1): 1889 v W.
CAMPBELL, J. (Sheffield W.) (1): 1913 v W.
CAMPBELL, J. (South Western) (1): 1880 v W.
CAMPBELL, J. (Kilmarnock) (2): 1891 v Ni; 1892 v W.
CAMPBELL, J. (Celtic) (12): 1893 v E, Ni; 1898 v E, Ni; 1900 v E, Ni; 1901 v E, W, Ni; 1902 v W, Ni; 1903 v W.
CAMPBELL, J. (Rangers) (4): 1899 v E, W, Ni; 1901 v Ni.
CAMPBELL, K. (Liverpool, Partick Th.) (8): 1920 v E, W, Ni; 1921 v W, Ni; 1922 v W. Ni, E.
CAMPBELL, P. (Rangers) (2): 1878 v W; 1879 v W.
CAMPBELL, P. (Morton) (1): 1898 v W.
CAMPBELL, R. (Falkirk, Chelsea) (5): 1947 v Bel, L; 1950 v Sw, Por, Fr.
CAMPBELL, W. (Morton) (5): 1947 v Ni; 1948 v E, Bel, Sw, Fr.
CARABINE, J. (Third Lanark) (3): 1938 v Holl; 1939 v E, Ni.
CARR, W. M. (Coventry City) (6): 1970 v Ni, W, E; 1971 v D; 1972 v Pe; 1973 v D.
CASSIDY, J. (Celtic) (4): 1921 v W, Ni; 1923 v Ni; 1924 v W.
CHALMERS, S. (Celtic) (5): 1965 v W, Fin; 1966 v Por, Br; 1967 v Ni.
CHALMERS, W. (Rangers) (1): 1885 v Ni.
CHALMERS, W. S. (Queen's Park) (1): 1929 v Ni.

CHEYNE, A. G. (Aberdeen) (5): 1929 v E, N, G, Holl; 1930 v Fr.
CHRISTIE, A. J. (Queen's Park) (3): 1898 v W; 1899 v E, Ni.
CHRISTIE, R. M. (Queen's Park) (1): 1884 v E.
CLARK, J. (Celtic) (4): 1966 v Br; 1967 v W, Ni, USSR.
CLARK, R. B. (Aberdeen) (17): 1968 v W, Holl; 1970 v Ni; 1971 v W, Ni, E, D, Por, USSR; 1972 v Bel, Ni, W, E, Cz, Br; 1973 v D, E.
CLARKE, S. (Chelsea) (6): 1988 v H, Bel, Bul, S.Ar, Ma; 1984 v Holl.
CLELAND, J. (Royal Albert) (1): 1891 v Ni.
CLEMENTS, R. (Leith Ath.) (1): 1891 v Ni.
CLUNAS, W. L. (Sunderland) (2): 1924 v E; 1926 v W.
COLLIER, W. (Raith R.) (1): 1922 v W.
COLLINS, J. (Hibs, Celtic, Monaco) (53): 1988 v S.Ar; 1990 v EG, Pol, Ma; 1991 v Sw, Bul, Ni, Fin; 1993 v Por (2), Ma, G, Est (2); 1994 v Sw, Holl (2), A; 1995 v Fin, Fi (2), Ru (2), Gr, Sm. 1996 v Gr, Fin, Se, Sm, Aus, D, US, U, Holl, E, Sw; 1997 v A (2), La, Se (2), Est, Ma; 1998 v Blr, La, Fr, Fin, Co, US, Br, M, N. 1999 v Lth.
COLLINS, R. Y. (Celtic, Everton, Leeds Utd) (31): 1951 v W, Ni, A; 1955 v Y, A, H; 1956 v Ni, W; 1957 v E, W, Sp (2), Sw, WG; 1958 v Ni, W, Sw, H, Pol, Y, Fr, Par; 1959 v E, W, Ni, WG, Holl, Por; 1965 v E, Pol, Sp.
COLLINS, T. (Hearts) (1): 1909 v W.
COLMAN, D. (Aberdeen) (4): 1911 v E, W, Ni; 1913 v Ni.
COLQUHOUN, E. P. (Sheffield Utd) (9): 1972 v Por, Holl, Pe, Y, Cz, Br; 1973 v D (2), E.
COLQUHOUN, J. (Hearts) (1): 1988 v S.Ar.
COMBE, J. R. (Hibernian) (3): 1948 v E, Bel, Sw.
CONN, A. (Hearts) (1): 1956 v A.
CONN, A. (Tottenham H.) (2): 1975 v Ni, E.
CONNACHAN, E. D. (Dunfermline Ath.) (2): 1962 v Cz, U.
CONNELLY, G. (Celtic) (2): 1974 v Cz, WG.
CONNOLLY, J. (Everton) (1): 1973 v Sw.
CONNOR, J. (Airdrie) (1): 1886 v Ni.
CONNOR, J. (Sunderland) (4): 1930 v Fr; 1932 v Ni; 1934 v E; 1935 v Ni.
CONNOR, R. (Dundee, Aberdeen) (4): 1986 v Holl; 1988 v S.Ar; 1989 v E; 1991 v R.
COOK, W. L. (Bolton W.) (3): 1934 v E; 1935 v W, Ni.
COOKE, C. (Dundee, Chelsea) (16): 1966 v W, I, Por, Br; 1968 v E, Holl; 1969 v W, Ni, A, WG, Cy (2); 1970 v A; 1971 v Bel; 1975 v Sp, Por.
COOPER, D. (Rangers, Motherwell) (22): 1980 v Pe, A; 1984 v W, E; 1985 v Y, Ice, Sp (2), W; 1986 v W, EG, Aus (2), Holl, WG, U; 1987 v Bul, L, Ei, Br; 1990 v N, Eg.
CORMACK, P. B. (Hibernian, Nottingham F.) (9): 1966 v Br; 1969 v D; 1970 v Ei, WG; 1971 v D, W, Por, E; 1972 v Holl.
COWAN, J. (Aston Villa) (3): 1896 v E; 1897 v E; 1898 v E.

COWAN, J. (Morton) (25): 1948 v Bel, Sw, Fr; 1949 v E, W, Fr; 1950 v E, W, Ni, Sw, Por, Fr; 1951 v E, W, Ni, A (2), D, Fr, Bel; 1952 v Ni, W, USA, D, Se.
COWAN, W. D. (Newcastle Utd) (1): 1924 v E.
COWIE, D. (Dundee) (20): 1953 v E, Se; 1954 v Ni, W, Fin, N, A, U; 1955 v W, Ni, A, H; 1956 v W, A; 1957 v Ni, W; 1958 v H, Pol, Y, Par.
COX, S. (Rangers) (25): 1948 v Fr; 1949 v E, Fr; 1950 v E, Fr, W, Ni, Sw, Por; 1951 v E, D, Fr, Bel, A; 1952 v Ni, W, USA, D, Se; 1953 v W, Ni, E; 1954 v W, Ni, E.
CRAIG, A. (Motherwell) (3): 1929 v Ni, Holl; 1932 v E.
CRAIG, J. (Celtic) (1): 1977 v Se.
CRAIG, J. P. (Celtic) (1): 1968 v W.
CRAIG, T. (Rangers) (8): 1927 v Ni; 1928 v Ni; 1929 v N, G, Holl; 1930 v Ni, E, W.
CRAIG, T. B. (Newcastle Utd) (1): 1976 v Sw.
CRAPNELL, J. (Airdrie) (9): 1929 v E, N, G; 1930 v Fr; 1931 v Ni, Sw; 1932 v E, Fr; 1933 v Ni.
CRAWFORD, D. (St Mirren) (3): 1894 v W, Ni; 1900 v W.
CRAWFORD, J. (Queen's Park) (5): 1932 v Fr, Ni; 1933 v E, W, Ni.
CRAWFORD, S. (Raith R.) (1): 1995 v Ec.
CRERAND, P. T. (Celtic, Manchester Utd) (16): 1961 v Ei (2), Cz; 1962 v Ni, W, E, Cz (2), U; 1963 v W, Ni; 1964 v Ni; 1965 v E, Pol, Fin; 1966 v Pol.
CRINGAN, W. (Celtic) (5): 1920 v W; 1922 v E, Ni; 1923 v W, E.
CROSBIE, J. A. (Ayr Utd, Birmingham City) (2): 1920 v W; 1922 v E.
CROAL, J. A. (Falkirk) (3): 1913 v Ni; 1914 v E, W.
CROPLEY, A. J. (Hibernian) (2): 1972 v Por, Bel.
CROSS, J. H. (Third Lanark) (1): 1903 v Ni.
CRUICKSHANK, J. (Hearts) (6): 1964 v WG; 1970 v W, E; 1971 v D, Bel; 1976 v R.
CRUM, J. (Celtic) (2): 1936 v E; 1939 v Ni.
CULLEN, M. J. (Luton Town) (1): 1956 v A.
CUMMING, D. S. (Middlesbrough) (1): 1938 v E.
CUMMING, J. (Hearts) (9): 1955 v E, H, Por, Y; 1960 v E, Pol, A, H, T.
CUMMINGS, G. (Partick Th., Aston Villa) (9): 1935 v E; 1936 v W, Ni, E; 1937 v G; 1938 v W, Ni, Cz; 1939 v E.
CUNNINGHAM, A. N. (Rangers) (12): 1920 v Ni; 1921 v W, E; 1922 v Ni; 1923 v E, W; 1924 v E, Ni; 1926 v E, Ni; 1927 v E, W.
CUNNINGHAM, W. C. (Preston NE) (8): 1954 v N (2), U, Fin, A; 1955 v W, E, H.

CURRAN, H. P. (Wolves) (5): 1970 v A; 1971 v Ni, E, D, USSR.
DAILLY, C. (Derby Co.) (13): 1997 v W, Ma, Blr; 1998 v Blr, La, D, Fin, Co, US, Br, N, M. 1999 v Lth.
DALGLISH, K. (Celtic, Liverpool) (102): 1972 v Bel, Holl; 1973 v D (2), E (2), W, Ni, Sw, Br; 1974 v Cz (2), WG (2), Ni, W, E, Bel, N, Z, Br, Y; 1975 v EG, Sp (2), Se, Por, W, Ni, E, R; 1976 v D (2), R, Sw, Ni, E; 1977 v Fin, Cz, W (2), Se, Ni, E, Ch, Arg, Br; 1978 v EG, Cz, W, Bul, Ni, W, E, Pe, Ir, Holl; 1979 v A, N, Por, W, Ni, E, Arg, N; 1980 v Pe, A, Bel (2), Por, Ni, W, E, Pol, H; 1981 v Se, Por, Is; 1982 v Se, Ni, Por, Sp, Holl, Ni, W, E, Nz, Br; 1983 v Bel, Sw; 1984 v U, Bel, EG; 1985 v Y, Ice, Sp, W; 1986 v EG, Aus, R; 1987 v Bul, L.
DAVIDSON, C. (Blackburn Rovers) (7): 1999 v Lth, Est, Fi, CzR (2), G, Fi.
DAVIDSON, D. (Queen's Park) (5): 1878 v W; 1879 v W; 1880 v W; 1881 v E, W.
DAVIDSON, J. A. (Partick Th.) (8): 1954 v N (2), A, U; 1955 v W, Ni, E, H.
DAVIDSON, S. (Middlesbrough) (1): 1921 v E.
DAWSON, A. (Rangers) (5): 1980 v Pol, H; 1983 v Ni, Ca (2).
DAWSON, J. (Rangers) (14): 1935 v Ni; 1936 v E; 1937 v G, E, W, Ni, A, Cz; 1938 v W, Holl, Ni; 1939 v E, Ni, H.
DEANS, J. (Celtic) (2): 1975 v EG, Sp.
DELANEY, J. (Celtic, Manchester Utd) (13): 1936 v W, Ni; 1937 v G, E, A, Cz; 1938 v Ni; 1939 v W, Ni; 1947 v E; 1948 v E, W, Ni.
DEVINE, A. (Falkirk) (1): 1910 v W.
DEWAR, G. (Dumbarton) (2): 1888 v Ni; 1889 v E.
DEWAR, N. (Third Lanark) (3): 1932 v E, Fr; 1933 v W.
DICK, J. (West Ham Utd) (1): 1959 v E.
DICKIE, M. (Rangers) (3): 1897 v Ni; 1899 v Ni; 1900 v W.
DICKSON, W. (Dumbarton) (1): 1888 v Ni.
DICKSON, W. (Kilmarnock) (5): 1970 v Ni, W, E; 1971 v D, USSR.
DIVERS, J. (Celtic) (1): 1895 v W.
DIVERS, J. (Celtic) (1): 1939 v Ni.
DOCHERTY, T. H. (Preston NE, Arsenal) (25): 1952 v W; 1953 v E, Se; 1954 v N (2), A, U; 1955 v W, E, H (2), A; 1957 v E, Y, Sp (2), Sw, WG; 1958 v Ni, W, E, Sw; 1959 v W, E, Ni.
DODDS, D. (Dundee Utd) (2): 1984 v U, Ni.
DODDS, J. (Celtic) (3): 1914 v E, W, Ni.
DODDS, W. (Aberdeen, Dundee United) (9): 1997 v La, W, Blr; 1998 v Blr. 1999 v Est, Fi, G, Fi, CzR.
DOIG, J. E. (Arbroath, Sunderland) (5): 1887 v Ni; 1889 v Ni; 1896 v E; 1899 v E; 1903 v E.
DONACHIE, W. (Manchester City) (35): 1972 v Pe, Ni, E, Y, Cz, Br; 1973 v D, E, W, Ni; 1974 v Ni; 1976 v R, Ni, W, E,; 1977 v Fin, Cz, W (2), Se, Ni, E, Ch, Arg, Br; 1978 v EG, W (2), Bul, E, Ir, Holl; 1979 v A, N, Por.

DONALDSON, A. (Bolton) (6): 1914 v E, Ni, W; 1920 v E, Ni; 1922 v Ni.
DONNACHIE, J. (Oldham Ath.) (3): 1913 v E; 1914 v E, Ni.
DONNELLY, S. (Celtic) (10): 1997 v W, Ma; 1998 La, Fr, D, Fin, Co, US. 1999 v Est. Fi.
DOUGALL, C. (Birmingham City) (1): 1947 v W.
DOUGALL, J. (Preston NE) (1): 1939 v E.
DOUGAN, R. (Hearts) (1): 1950 v Sw.
DOUGLAS, A. (Chelsea) (1): 1911 v Ni.
DOUGLAS, J. (Renfrew) (1): 1880 v W.
DOWDS, P. (Celtic) (1): 1892 v Ni.
DOWNIE, R. (Third Lanark) (1): 1892 v W.
DOYLE, D. (Celtic) (8): 1892 v E; 1893 v W; 1894 v E; 1895 v E, Ni; 1897 v E; 1898 v E, Ni.
DOYLE, J. (Ayr Utd) (1): 1976 v R.
DRUMMOND, J. (Falkirk, Rangers) (14): 1892 v Ni; 1894 v Ni; 1895 v Ni, E; 1896 v E, Ni; 1897 v Ni; 1898 v E; 1900 v E; 1901 v E; 1902 v E, W, Ni; 1903 v Ni.
DUNBAR, M. (Cartvale) (1): 1886 v Ni.
DUNCAN, A. (Hibernian) (6): 1975 v Por, W, Ni, E, R; 1976 v D.
DUNCAN, D. (Derby Co.) (14): 1933 v E, W; 1934 v A, W; 1935 v E, W; 1936 v E, W, Ni; 1937 v G, E, W, Ni; 1938 v W.
DUNCAN, D. M. (East Fife) (3): 1948 v Bel, Sw, Fr.
DUNCAN, J. (Alexandra Ath.) (2): 1878 v W; 1882 v W.
DUNCAN, J. (Leicester City) (1): 1926 v W.
DUNCANSON, J. (Rangers) (1): 1947 v Ni.
DUNLOP, J. (St Mirren) (1): 1890 v W.
DUNLOP, W. (Liverpool) (1): 1906 v E.
DUNN, J. (Hibernian, Everton) (6): 1925 v W, Ni; 1927 v Ni; 1928 v Ni, E; 1929 v W.
DURIE, G. S. (Chelsea, Tottenham, Rangers) (43): 1988 v Bul; 1989 v I, Cy; 1990 v Y, EG, Eg, Se; 1991 v Sw, Bul (2), USSR, Sm (2), 1992 v Sw, R, Ni, Fin, Ca, N, Holl, G; 1993 v Sw, I; 1994 v Sw, I, Holl (2). 1996 US, Holl, E, Sw; 1997 v A, Se, Ma, Blr; 1998 Blr, La, Fr, Fin, Co, Br, N, M.
DURRANT, I. (Rangers, Kilmarnock) (16): 1988 v H, Bel, Ma, Sp; 1989 v N; 1993 v Sw, Por (2), I; 1994 v I, Ma. 1999 v Est, Fi, G, Fi, CzR.
DYKES, J. (Hearts) (2): 1938 v Holl; 1939 v Ni.
EASSON, J. F. (Portsmouth) (3): 1931 v A, Sw; 1934 v W.
ELLIOTT, M. (Leicester City) (7): 1998 v Fr, D, Fin. 1999, v Lth, Fi, CzR, Fi.
ELLIS, J. (Mossend Swifts) (1): 1892 v Ni.
EVANS, A. (Aston Villa) (4): 1982 v Holl, Ni, E, Nz.
EVANS, R. (Celtic, Chelsea) (48): 1949 v E, W, Ni, Fr; 1950 v W, Ni, Sw, Por; 1951 v E, A; 1952 v Ni; 1953 v Se; 1954 v Ni, W, E, N, Fin; 1955 v Ni, Por, Y, A, H; 1956 v E, Ni, W, A; 1957 v WG, Sp; 1958 v Ni, W, E, Sw, H, Pol, Y, Par, Fr; 1959 v E, WG, Holl, Por; 1960 v E, Ni, W, Pol; 1960 v A, H, T.
EWART, J. (Bradford City) (1): 1921 v E.

EWING, T. (Partick Th.) (2): 1958 v W, E.
FARM, G. N. (Blackpool) (10): 1953 v W, Ni, E, Se; 1954 v Ni, W, E; 1959 v WG, Holl, Por.
FERGUSON, B. (Rangers) (1): 1999 v Lth.
FERGUSON, D. (Rangers) (2): 1988 v Ma, Co.
FERGUSON, D. (Dundee United, Everton) (7): 1992 v US, Ca, Holl; 1993 v G; 1995 v Gr; 1997 v A, Est.
FERGUSON, I. (Rangers) (9): 1989 v I, Cy, Fr; 1993 v Ma, Est; 1994 v Ma, A, Holl; 1997 v Est.
FERGUSON, J. (Vale of Leven) (6): 1874 v E; 1876 v E, W; 1877 v E, W; 1878 v W.
FERGUSON, R. (Kilmarnock) (7): 1966 v W, E, Holl, Por, Br; 1967 v W, Ni.
FERNIE, W. (Celtic) (12): 1954 v Fin, A, U; 1955 v W, Ni; 1957 v E, Ni, W, Y; 1958 v W, Sw, Par.
FINDLAY, R. (Kilmarnock) (1): 1898 v W.
FITCHIE, T. T. (Woolwich Arsenal, Queen's Park) (4): 1905 v W: 1906 v W, Ni; 1907 v W.
FLAVEL, R. (Airdrie) (2): 1947 v Bel, L.
FLECK, R. (Norwich City) (4): 1990 v Arg, Se, Br; 1991 v USSR.
FLEMING, C. (East Fife) (1): 1954 v Ni.
FLEMING, J. W. (Rangers) (3): 1929 v G, Holl; 1930 v E.
FLEMING, R. (Morton): 1886 v Ni.
FORBES, A. R. (Sheffield Utd, Arsenal) (14): 1947 v Bel, L, E; 1948 v W, Ni; 1950 v E, Por, Fr; 1951 v W, Ni, A; 1952 v W, D, Se.
FORBES, J. (Vale of Leven) (5): 1884 v E, W, Ni; 1887 v W, E.
FORD, D. (Hearts) (3): 1974 v Cz, WG, W.
FORREST, J. (Rangers, Aberdeen) (5): 1966 v W, I; 1971 v Bel, D, USSR.
FORREST, J. (Motherwell) (1): 1958 v E.
FORSYTH, A. (Partick Th., Manchester Utd) (10): 1972 v Y, Cz, Br; 1973 v D, E; 1975 v Sp, Ni, R, EG; 1976 v D.
FORSYTH, C. (Kilmarnock) (4): 1964 v E; 1965 v W, Ni, Fin.
FORSYTH, T. (Motherwell, Rangers) (22): 1971 v D; 1974 v Cz; 1976 v Sw, Ni, W, E; 1977 v Fin, Se, W, Ni, E, Ch, Arg, Br; 1978 v Cz, W, Ni, W, E, Pe, Ir, Holl.
FOYERS, R. (St Bernards) (2): 1893 v W; 1894 v W.
FRASER, D. M. (WBA) (2): 1968 v Holl; 1969 v Cy.
FRASER, J. (Moffat) (1): 1891 v Ni.
FRASER, M. J. E. (Queen's Park) (5): 1880 v W; 1882 v W, E; 1883 v W, E.
FRASER, J. (Dundee) (1): 1907 v Ni.
FRASER, W. (Sunderland) (2): 1955 v W, Ni.
FULTON, W. (Abercorn) (1): 1884 v Ni.
FYFE, J. H. (Third Lanark) (1): 1895 v W.
GABRIEL, J. (Everton) (2): 1961 v W; 1964 v N.

GALLACHER, K. W. (Dundee Utd, Coventry, Blackburn R.) (43): 1988 v Co, E; 1989 v N; I; 1991 v Sm (2); 1992 v R, Ni, N, Holl, G, CIS; 1993 v Sw, Por (2), Est (2); 1994 v I, Ma; 1996 v Aus, D, U, Holl; 1997 v Se (2), Est (2), A, W, Ma, Blr; 1998 v Blr, La, Fr, Fin, US, Br, N, M. 1999 v Lth, Est, Fi, CzR.
GALLACHER, P. (Sunderland) (1): 1935 v Ni.
GALLAGHER, H. K. (Airdrie, Newcastle Utd, Chelsea, Derby C.) (20): 1924 v Ni; 1925 v E, W, Ni; 1926 v W, E, Ni; 1927 v E, W, Ni; 1928 v E, W; 1929 v E, W, Ni; 1930 v W, Ni, Fr; 1934 v E; 1935 v E.
GALLOWAY, M. (Celtic) (1): 1992 v R.
GALT, J. H. (Rangers) (2): 1908 v W, Ni.
GARDINER, I. (Motherwell) (1): 1958 v W.
GARDNER, D. R. (Third Lanark) (1): 1897 v W.
GARDNER, R. (Queen's Park, Clydesdale) (5): 1872 v E; 1873 v E; 1874 v E; 1875 v E; 1878 v E.
GEMMELL, T. (St Mirren) (2): 1955 v Por, Y.
GEMMELL, T. (Celtic) (18): 1966 v E; 1967 v W, Ni, E, USSR; 1968 v Ni, E; 1969 v W, Ni, E, D, A, WG, Cy; 1970 v E, Ei, WG; 1971 v Bel.
GEMMILL, A. (Derby Co., Nottingham F., Birmingham City) (43): 1971 v Bel; 1972 v Por, Holl, Pe, Ni, W, E; 1976 v D, R, Ni, W, E; 1977 v Fin, Cz, W (2), Ni, E, Ch, Arg, Br; 1978 v EG, Bul, Ni, W, E, Pe, Ir, Holl; 1979 v A, N. Por, N; 1980 v A, Por, Ni, W, E, H; 1981 v Se, Por, Is, Ni.
GEMMILL, S. (Nottingham F, Everton) (15): 1995 v J, Ec, Fi; 1996 v Sm, D, US; 1997 v Est, Se, W, Ma, Blr; 1998 v D, Fin; 1999 v G, Fi.
GIBB, W. (Clydesdale) (1): 1873 v E.
GIBSON, D. W. (Leicester City) (7): 1963 v A, N, Ei, Sp; 1964 v Ni; 1965 v W, Fin.
GIBSON, J. D. (Partick Th., Aston Villa) (8): 1926 v E; 1927 v E, W, Ni; 1928 v E, W; 1930 v W. Ni.
GIBSON, N. (Rangers, Partick Th.) (14): 1895 v E, Ni; 1896 v E, Ni; 1897 v E, Ni; 1898 v E; 1899 v E, W, Ni; 1900 v E, Ni; 1901 v W; 1905 v Ni.
GILCHRIST, J. E. (Celtic) (1): 1922 v E.
GILHOOLEY, M. (Hull City) (1): 1922 v W.
GILLESPIE, G. (Rangers, Queen's Park) (7): 1880 v E, W; 1882 v E; 1886 v W; 1890 v W; 1891 v Ni.
GILLESPIE, G. T. (Liverpool) (13): 1988 v Bel, Bul, Sp; 1989 v N, Fr, Ch; 1990 v Y, EG, Eg, Pol, Ma, Br; 1991 v Bul.
GILLESPIE, Jas. (Third Lanark) (1): 1898 v W.
GILLESPIE, John (Queen's Park) (1): 1896 v W.
GILLESPIE, R. (Queen's Park) (4): 1927 v W; 1931 v W; 1932 v Fr; 1933 v E.
GILLICK, T. (Everton) (5): 1937 v A, Cz; 1939 v W, Ni, H.
GILMOUR, J. (Dundee) (1): 1931 v W.

GILZEAN, A. J. (Dundee, Tottenham H.) (22): 1964 v W, E, N, WG; 1965 v Ni, Sp; 1966 v Ni, W, Pol, I; 1968 v W; 1969 v W, E, WG, Cy (2), A; 1970 v Ni, E, WG, A; 1971 v Por.
GLAVIN, R. (Celtic) (1): 1977 v Se.
GLASS S. (Aberdeen) (1): 1999 v Fi.
GLEN, A. (Aberdeen) (2): 1956 v E, Ni.
GLEN, R. (Renton, Hibernian) (3): 1895 v W; 1896 v W; 1900 v Ni.
GORAM, A. L. (Oldham, Hibs, Rangers) (42): 1986 v EG, R, Holl; 1987 v Br; 1989 v Y, I; 1990 v EG, Pol, Ma; 1991 v R (2), Sw, Bul (2), USSR, Sm (2); 1992 v Sw, Fin, N, Holl, G, CIS; 1993 v Sw, Por (2), I, Ma; 1994 v Holl; 1995 v Fin, Fi, Ru, Gr; 1996 v Se, D, Holl, Sw, E; 1997 A, La, Est; 1998 v D
GORDON, J. E. (Rangers) (10): 1912 v E, Ni; 1913 v E, Ni, W; 1914 v E, Ni; 1920 v W, E, Ni, U.
GOSSLAND, J. (Rangers) (1): 1884 v Ni.
GOUDLE, J. (Abercorn) (1): 1884 v Ni.
GOUGH, C. R. (Dundee Utd, Tottenham H., Rangers) (61): 1983 v Sw, Ni, W, E, Ca (3); 1984 v U, Bel, EG, Ni, W, E, Fr; 1985 v Sp, E, Ice; 1986 v W, EG, Aus, Is, R, E, D, WG, U; 1987 v Bul, L, Ei (2), Bel, E, Br; 1988 v H, S.Ar, Sp, Co, E; 1989 v Y, I, Cy (2), Fr; 1990 v Fr, Arg, EG, Pol, Ma, Cr; 1991 v USSR, Bul; 1992 v Sm, Ni, Ca, N, Holl, G, CIS; 1993 v Sw, Por.
GOURLAY, J. (Cambuslang) (2): 1886 v Ni; 1888 v W.
GOVAN, J. (Hibernian) (6): 1948 v E, W, Bel, Sw, Fr; 1949 v Ni.
GOW, D. R. (Rangers) (1): 1888 v E.
GOW, J. J. (Queen's Park) (1): 1885 v E.
GOW, J. R. (Rangers) (1): 1888 v Ni.
GRAHAM, A. (Leeds Utd) (10): 1978 v EG; 1979 v A, N, W, Ni, E, Arg, N; 1980 v A; 1981 v W.
GRAHAM, G. (Arsenal, Manchester Utd) (13): 1972 v Por, Sw, Holl, Ni, Y, Cz, Br; 1973 v D (2), E, W, Ni, Br.
GRAHAM, J. (Annbank) (1): 1884 v Ni.
GRAHAM, J. A. (Arsenal) (1): 1921 v Ni.
GRANT, J. (Hibernian) (2): 1959 v W, Ni.
GRANT, P. (Celtic) (2): 1989 v E, Ch.
GRAY, A, (Hibernian) (1): 1903 v Ni.
GRAY, A. M. (Aston Villa, Wolverhampton W., Everton) (20): 1976 v R, Sw; 1977 v Fin, Cz; 1979 v A, N; 1980 v Por, E; 1981 v Se, Por, Is, Ni; 1982 v Se, Ni; 1983 v Ni, W, E, Ca (2); 1985 v Ice.
GRAY, D. (Rangers) (10): 1929 v W, Ni, G, Holl; 1930 v W, E, Ni; 1931 v W; 1933 v W, Ni.
GRAY, E. (Leeds Utd) (12): 1969 v E, Cy; 1970 v WG, A; 1971 v W, Ni; 1972 v Bel, Holl; 1976 v W, E; 1977 v Fin, W.
GRAY, F. T. (Leeds Utd, Nottingham F.) (32): 1976 v Sw; 1979 v N, Por, W, Ni, E, Arg; 1980 v Bel; 1981 v Se, Por, Is (2), Ni, (2), W, E; 1982 v Se, Ni, Por, Sp, Holl, W, Nz, Br, USSR; 1983 v EG, Sw, (2), Bel, W, E, Ca.

GRAY, W. (Pollokshields Ath.) (1): 1886 v E.
GREEN, A. (Blackpool) (6): 1971 v Bel, Por, Ni, E; 1972 v W, E.
GREIG, J. (Rangers) (44): 1964 v E, WG; 1965 v W, Ni, E, Fin (2), Sp, Pol; 1966 v Ni, W, E, Pol, I (2), Por, Holl, Br; 1967 v W, Ni, E; 1968 v Ni, W, E, Holl; 1969 v W, Ni, E, D, A, WG, Cy (2); 1970 v W, E, Ei, WG, A; 1971 v D, Bel, W, Ni, E; 1976 v D.
GROVES, W. (Hibernian, Celtic) (3): 1888 v W; 1889 Ni; 1890 v E.
GUILLILAND, W. (Queen's Park) (4): 1891 v W; 1892 v Ni; 1894 v E; 1895 v E.
GUNN, B. (Norwich City) (6): 1990 v Eg; 1993 v Est (2); 1994 v Sw, I, Holl.
HADDOCK, H. (Clyde) (6): 1955 v E, H (2), Por, Y; 1958 v E.
HADDOW, D. (Rangers) (1): 1894 v E.
HAFFEY, F. (Celtic) (2): 1960 v E; 1961 v E.
HAMILTON, A. (Queen's Park) (4): 1885 v E, W; 1886 v E; 1888 v E.
HAMILTON, A. W. (Dundee) (24): 1962 v Cz, U, W, E; 1963 v W, Ni, E, A, N, Ei; 1964 v Ni, W, E, N, WG; 1965 v Ni, W, E, Fin (2), Pol, Sp; 1966 v Pol, Ni.
HAMILTON, G. (Aberdeen) (5): 1947 v Ni; 1951 v Bel, A; 1954 v N (2).
HAMILTON, G. (Port Glasgow Ath.) (1): 1906 v Ni.
HAMILTON, J. (Queen's Park) (3): 1892 v W; 1893 v E, Ni.
HAMILTON, J. (St Mirren) (1): 1924 v Ni.
HAMILTON, R. C. (Rangers, Dundee) (11): 1899 v E, W, Ni; 1900 v W; 1901 v E, Ni; 1902 v W, Ni; 1903 v E; 1904 v Ni; 1911 v W.
HAMILTON, T. (Hurlford) (1): 1891 v Ni.
HAMILTON, T. (Rangers) (1): 1932 v E.
HAMILTON, W. M. (Hibernian) (1): 1965 v Fin.
HANNAH, A. B., (Renton) (1): 1888 v W.
HANNAH, J. (Third Lanark) (1): 1889 v W.
HANSEN, A. D. (Liverpool) (26): 1979 v W, Arg; 1980 v Bel, Por; 1981 v Se, Por, Is; 1982 v Se, Ni (2), Por, Sp, W, E, Nz, Br, USSR; 1983 v EG, Sw (2), Bel; 1985 v W; 1986 v R; 1987 v Ei (2), L.
HANSEN, J. (Partick Th.) (2): 1972 v Bel, Y.
HARKNESS, J. D. (Queen's Park, Hearts) (12): 1927 v E, Ni; 1928 v E; 1929 v W, E, Ni; 1930 v E, W; 1932 v W, Fr; 1934 v Ni, W.
HARPER, J. M. (Aberdeen, Hibernian) (4): 1973 v D (2); 1976 v D; 1978 v Ir.
HARPER, W. (Hibernian, Arsenal) (11): 1923 v E, Ni, W; 1924 v E, Ni, W; 1925 v E, Ni, W; 1926 v E, Ni.
HARRIS, J. (Partick Th.) (2): 1921 v W, Ni.

HARRIS, N. (Newcastle Utd) (1): 1924 v E.
HARROWER, W. (Queen's Park) (3): 1882 v E; 1884 v Ni; 1886 v W.
HARTFORD, R. A. (WBA, Manchester City, Everton) (50): 1972 v Pe, W, E, Y, Cz, Br; 1976 v D, R, Ni; 1977 v Cz, W, (2), Se, Ni, E, Ch, Arg, Br; 1978 v EG, Cz, W (2), Bul, E, Pe, Ir, Holl; 1979 v A, N, Por, W, Ni, E, Arg, N; 1980 v Pe, Bel; 1981 v Ni (2), Is, W, E; 1982 v Se, Ni (2), Por, Sp, W, E, Br.
HARVEY, D. (Leeds Utd.) (16): 1973 v D; 1974 v Cz, WG, Ni, W, E, Bel, Z, Br, Y; 1975 v EG, Sp (2); 1976 v D (2); 1977 v Fin.
HASTINGS, A. C. (Sunderland) (2): 1936 v Ni; 1938 v Ni.
HAUGHNEY, M. (Celtic) (1): 1954 v E.
HAY, D. (Celtic) (27): 1970 v Ni, W, E; 1971 v D, Bel, W, Por, Ni; 1972 v Por, Bel, Holl; 1973 v W, Ni, E, Sw, Br; 1974 v Cz (2), WG, Ni, W, E, Bel, N, Z, Br.
HAY, J. (Celtic, Newcastle Utd.) (11): 1905 v Ni; 1909 v Ni; 1910 v W, Ni, E; 1911 v Ni, E; 1912 v E, W; 1914 v E, Ni.
HEGARTY, P. (Dundee Utd.) (8): 1979 v W, Ni, E, Arg, N; 1980 v W, E; 1983 v Ni.
HEGGIE, C. (Rangers) (1): 1886 v Ni.
HENDERSON, G. H. (Rangers) (1): 1904 v Ni.
HENDERSON, J. G. (Portsmouth, Arsenal) (7): 1953 v Se; 1954 v Ni, E, N; 1956 v W; 1959 v W, Ni.
HENDERSON, W. (Rangers) (29): 1963 v W, Ni, E, A, N, Ei, Sp; 1964 v W, Ni, E, N, WG; 1965 v Fin, Pol, E, Sp; 1966 v Ni, W, Pol, I, Holl; 1967 v W, Ni; 1968 v Holl; 1969 v Ni, E, Cy; 1970 v Ei; 1971 v Por.
HENDRY C. (Blackburn R.) (39): 1993 v Est (2); 1994 v Ma, Holl (2), A; 1995 v Fin, Fi, Gr, Ru, Sm; 1996 v Fin, Se, Sm, Aus, D, US, U, Holl, E, Sw; 1997 A (2), Se (2), Est (2); 1998 La, D, Fin, Co, US, Br, N, M. 1999 v Lth, Est, Fi, G.
HEPBURN, J. (Alloa Ath.) (1) 1891 v W.
HEPBURN, R. (Ayr Utd) (1): 1932 v Ni.
HERD, A. C. (Hearts): (1): 1935 v Ni.
HERD, D. G. (Arsenal): (5): 1959 v E, W, Ni; 1961 v E, Cz.
HERD, G. (Clyde) (5): 1958 v E; 1960 v H, T; 1961 v W, Ni.
HERRIOT, J. (Birmingham City) (8): 1969 v Ni, E, D, Cy (2), W; 1970 v Ei, WG.
HEWIE, J. D. (Charlton Ath.) (19): 1956 v E, A; 1957 v E, Ni, W, Y, Sp (2), Sw, WG; 1958 v H, Pol, Y, Fr; 1959 v Holl, Por; 1960 v Ni, W, Pol.
HIGGINS, A. (Kilmarnock) (1): 1885 v Ni.
HIGGINS, A. (Newcastle Utd) (4): 1910 v E, Ni; 1911 v E, Ni.
HIGHET, T. C. (Queen's Park) (4): 1875 v E; 1876 v E, W; 1878 v E.
HILL, D. (Rangers) (3): 1881 v E, W; 1882 v W.

HILL, D. A. (Third Lanark) (1): 1906 v Ni.
HILL, F. R. (Aberdeen) (3): 1930 v Fr; 1931 v W, Ni.
HILL, J. (Hearts) (2): 1891 v E; 1892 v W.
HOGG, G. (Hearts) (2): 1896 v E, Ni.
HOGG, J. (Ayr Utd.) (1): 1922 v Ni.
HOGG, R. M. (Celtic) (1): 1937 v Cz.
HOLM, A. H. (Queen's Park) (3): 1882 v W; 1883 v E, W.
HOLT, D. D. (Hearts) (5): 1963 v A, N, Ei, Sp; 1964 v WG.
HOLTON, J. A. (Manchester Utd.) (15): 1973 v W, Ni, E, Sw, Br; 1974 v Cz, WG, Ni, W, E, N, Z, Br, Y; 1975 v EG.
HOPE, R. (WBA) (2): 1968 v Holl; 1969 v D.
HOPKIN, D. (Crystal Palace, Leeds) (5): 1997 v Ma, Blr; 1998 v Blr, La; 1999 v CzR.
HOULISTON, W. (Queen of the South) (3): 1949 v E, Ni; Fr.
HOUSTON, S. M. (Manchester Utd.) (1): 1976 v D.
HOWDEN, W. (Partick Th.) (1): 1905 v Ni.
HOWE, R. (Hamilton Accies) (2): 1929 v N, Holl.
HOWIE, J. (Newcastle Utd.) (3): 1905 v E; 1906 v E; 1908 v E.
HOWIE, H. (Hibernian) (1): 1949 v W.
HOWIESON, J. (St Mirren) (1): 1927 v Ni.
HUGHES, J. (Celtic) (8): 1965 v Pol, Sp; 1966 v Ni, I (2); 1968 v E; 1969 v A; 1970 v Ei.
HUGHES, W. (Sunderland) (1): 1975 v Se.
HUMPHRIES, W. (Motherwell) (1): 1952 v Se.
HUNTER, A. (Kilmarnock, Celtic) (4): 1972 v Pe, Y; 1973 v E; 1974 v Cz.
HUNTER, J. (Dundee) (1): 1909 v W.
HUNTER, J. (Third Lanark, Eastern) (4): 1874 v E, 1875 v E, 1876 v E, 1877 v W.
HUNTER, R. (St Mirren) (1): 1890 v Ni.
HUNTER, W. (Motherwell) (3): 1960 v H, T; 1961 v W.
HUSBAND, J. (Partick Th.) (1): 1947 v W.
HUTCHISON, D. (Everton) (2): 1999 v CzR, G.
HUTCHISON, T. (Coventry City) (17): 1974 v Cz (2), WG (2), Ni, W, Bel, N, Z, Y; 1975 v EG, Sp (2), Por, E, R; 1976 v D.
HUTTON, J. (Aberdeen, Blackburn R.) (10): 1923 v E, W, Ni; 1924 v Ni; 1926 v W, E, Ni; 1927 v Ni; 1928 v W, Ni.
HUTTON, J. (St Bernards) (1): 1887 v Ni.
HYSLOP, T. (Stoke City, Rangers) (2): 1896 v E; 1897 v E.
IMLACH, J. J. S. (Nottingham F.) (4): 1958 v H, Pol, Y. Fr.
IMRIE, W. N. (St Johnstone) (2): 1929 v N, G.
INGLIS, J. (Kilmarnock Ath.) (1): 1884 v Ni.
INGLIS, J. (Rangers) (2): 1883 v E, W.
IRONS, J. H. (Queen's Park) (1): 1900 v W.
IRVINE, B. (Aberdeen) (9): 1991 v R; 1993 v G, Est (2); 1994 v Sw, I, Ma, A, Holl.
JACKSON, A. (Cambuslang) (2): 1886 v W, 1888 v Ni.

JACKSON, A. (Aberdeen, Huddersfield Town) (17): 1925 v E, W, Ni; 1926 v E, W, Ni; 1927 v W, Ni; 1928 v E, W; 1929 v E, W, Ni; 1930 v E, W, Ni, Fr.
JACKSON, C. (Rangers) (8): 1975 v Se, Por, W; 1976 v D, R, Ni, W, E.
JACKSON D. (Hibs, Celtic) (28): 1995 v Ru, Sm, J, Ec, Fi. 1996 v Gr, Fin, Se, Sm, Aus, D, US; 1997 v La, Se (2), Est, A, W, Ma, Blr; 1998 v D, Fin, Co, US, Br, N. 1999 v Lth, Est.
JACKSON, J. (Partick Th., Chelsea) (8): 1931 v A, I, Sw; 1933 v E; 1934 v E; 1935 v E; 1936 v W, Ni.
JACKSON, T. A. (St Mirren) (6): 1904 v W, E, Ni; 1905 v W; 1907 v W, Ni.
JAMES, A. (Preston NE, Arsenal) (8): 1926 v W; 1928 v E; 1929 v E, Ni; 1930 v E, W, Ni; 1933 v W.
JARDINE, A. (Rangers) (38): 1971 v D; 1972 v Por, Bel, Holl; 1973 v E, Sw, Br; 1974 v Cz (2), WG (2), Ni, W, E, Bel, N, Z, Br, Y; 1975 v EG, Sp (2), Se, Por, W, Ni, E; 1977 v Se, Ch, Br; 1978 v Cz, W, Ni, Ir; 1980 v Pe, A. Bel (2).
JARVIE, A. (Airdrie) (3): 1971 v Por, Ni, E.
JESS, E. (Aberdeen) (18): 1993 v I, Ma; 1994 v Sw, I, Holl (2), A; 1995 v Fin; 1996 v Se, Sm, US, U, E; 1998 v D; 1999 v CzR (2), G, Fi.
JENKINSON, T. (Hearts) (1): 1887 v Ni.
JOHNSTON, A. (Sunderland) (6): 1999 v Est, Fi, CzR (2), G, Fi.
JOHNSTON, L. H. (Clyde) (2): 1948 v Bel, Sw.
JOHNSTON, M. (Watford, Celtic, Nantes, Rangers) (38): 1984 v W, E, Fr; 1985 v Y, Ice, Sp (2), W; 1986 v EG; 1987 v Bul, Ei (2), L; 1988 v H, Bel, L. S.Ar, Sp, Co, E; 1989 v N, Y, I, Cy (2), Fr, E, Ch; 1990 v Fr, N, EG, Pol, Ma, Cr, Se, Br; 1992 v Sw, Sm.
JOHNSTON, R. (Sunderland) (1): 1938 v Cz.
JOHNSTON, W. (Rangers, WBA) (22): 1966 v W, E, Pol, Holl; 1968 v W, E; 1969 v Ni; 1970 v Ni; 1971 v D; 1977 v Se, W, Ni, E, Ch, Arg, Br; 1978 v EG, Cz, W (2), E, Pe.
JOHNSTONE, D. (Rangers) (14): 1973 v W, Ni, E, Sw, Br; 1975 v EG, Se; 1976 v Sw, Ni, E; 1978 v Bul, Ni, W; 1980 v Bel.
JOHNSTONE, J. (Abercorn) (1): 1888 v W.
JOHNSTONE, J. (Celtic) (23): 1965 v W, Fin; 1966 v E; 1967 v W, USSR; 1968 v W; 1969 v A, WG; 1970 v E, WG; 1971 v D, E; 1972 v Por, Bel, Holl, Ni, E; 1974 v W, E, Bel, N; 1975 v EG, Sp.
JOHNSTONE, JAS. (Kilmarnock) (1): 1894 v W.
JOHNSTONE, J. A. (Hearts) (3): 1930 v W; 1933 v W, Ni.
JOHNSTONE, R. (Hibernian, Manchester City) (17): 1951 v E, D, Fr; 1952 v Ni, E; 1953 v E, Se; 1954 v W, E, N, Fin; 1955 v Ni, H, E; 1956 v E, Ni, W.
JOHNSTONE, W. (Third Lanark) (3): 1887 v Ni; 1889 v W; 1890 v E.
JORDAN, J. (Leeds Utd, Manchester Utd, AC Milan) (52): 1973 v E, Sw, Br; 1974 v Cz (2), WG, Ni, W, E, Bel, N, Z, Br, Y; 1975 v EG, Sp (2); 1976 v Ni, W, E; 1977 v Cz, W, Ni, E; 1978 v EG, Cz, W, Bul, Ni, E, Pe, Ir, Holl; 1979 v A, Por, W, Ni, E, N; 1980 v Bel, Ni, W, E, Pol; 1981 v Is, W, E; 1982 v Se, Holl, W, E, USSR.

KAY, J. L. (Queen's Park) (6): 1880 v E; 1882 v E, W; 1883 v E, W; 1884 v W.
KEILLOR, A. (Montrose, Dundee) (6): 1891 v W; 1892 v Ni; 1894 v Ni; 1895 v W; 1896 v W; 1897 v W.
KEIR, L. (Dumbarton) (5): 1885 v W: 1886 v Ni; 1887 v E, W; 1888 v E.
KELLY, H. T. (Blackpool) (1): 1952 v USA.
KELLY, J. (Renton, Celtic) (8): 1888 v E; 1889 v E; 1890 v E; 1892 v E; 1893 v E, Ni; 1894 v W; 1896 v Ni.
KELLY, J. C. (Barnsley) (2): 1949 v W, Ni.
KELSO, R. (Renton, Dundee) (8): 1885 v W, Ni; 1886 v W; 1887 v E, W; 1888 v E, Ni; 1898 v Ni.
KELSO, T. (Dundee) (1): 1914 v W.
KENNAWAY, J. (Celtic) (1): 1934 v A.
KENNEDY, A. (Eastern, Third Lanark) (6): 1875 v E; 1876 v E, W; 1878 v E; 1882 v W; 1884 v W.
KENNEDY, J. (Celtic) (6): 1964 v W, Fr, WG; 1965 v W, Ni, Fin.
KENNEDY, J. (Hibernian) (1): 1897 v W.
KENNEDY, S. (Aberdeen) (8): 1978 v Bul, W, E, Pe, Holl; 1979 v A, Por; 1982 v Por.
KENNEDY, S, (Partick Th.) (1): 1905 v W.
KENNEDY, S. (Rangers) (5): 1975 v Se, Por, W, Ni, E.
KER, G. (Queen's Park) (5): 1880 v E; 1881 v E, W; 1882 v W, E.
KER, W. (Granville, Queen's Park) (2): 1872 v E; 1873 v E.
KERR, A. (Partick Th.) (2): 1955 v A, H.
KERR, P. (Hibernian) (1): 1924 v Ni.
KEY, G. (Hearts) (1): 1902 v Ni.
KEY, W. (Queen's Park) (1): 1907 v Ni.
KING, A. (Hearts, Celtic) (6): 1896 v E, W; 1897 v Ni; 1898 v Ni; 1899 v Ni, W.
KING, J. (Hamilton Accies) (2): 1933 v Ni; 1934 v Ni.
KING, W. S. (Queen's Park) (1): 1929 v W.
KINLOCH, J. D. (Partick Th.) (1): 1922 v Ni.
KINNAIRD, A. F. (Wanderers) (1): 1873 v E.
KINNEAR, D. (Rangers) (1): 1938 v Cz.
LAMBERT, P. (Motherwell, Borussia Dortmund, Celtic) (20): 1995 v J, Ec; 1997 v La, Se (2), A, Blr; 1998 v Blr, La, Fin, Co, US, Br, N, M. 1999 v Lth, CzR (2), G, Fi.
LAMBIE, J. A. (Queen's Park) (3): 1886 v Ni; 1887 v Ni; 1888 v E.
LAMBIE, W. A. (Queen's Park) (9): 1892 v Ni; 1893 v W; 1894 v E; 1895 v E, Ni; 1896 v E, Ni; 1897 v E, Ni.
LAMONT, D. (Pilgrims): 1885 v Ni.
LANG, A. (Dumbarton) (1): 1880 v W.
LANG, J. J. (Clydesdale, Third Lanark) (2): 1876 v W; 1878 v W.
LATTA, A. (Dumbarton) (2): 1888 v W; 1889 v E.

LAW, D. (Huddersfield Town, Manchester Utd, Torino, Manchester City) (55): 1959 v W, Ni, Holl, Por; 1960 v Ni, W; 1960 v E, Pol, A; 1961 v E, Ni; 1962 v Cz (2), E; 1963 v W, Ni, E, A, N, Ei, Sp; 1964 v W, E, N, WG;1965 v W, Ni, E, Fin (2), Pol, Sp; 1966 v Ni, E, Pol; 1967 v W, E, USSR; 1968 v Ni; 1969 v Ni, A, WG; 1972 v Pe, Ni, W, E, Y, Cz, Br; 1974 v Cz (2), WG (2), Ni, Z.
LAW, G. (Rangers) (3): 1910 v E, Ni, W.
LAW, T. (Chelsea) (2): 1928 v E, 1930 v E.
LAWRENCE, J. (Newcastle Utd.) (1): 1911 v E.
LAWRENCE, T. (Liverpool) (3): 1963 v Ei; 1969 v W, WG.
LAWSON, D. (St Mirren) (1): 1923 v E.
LECKIE, R. (Queen's Park) (1): 1872 v E.
LEGGAT, G. (Aberdeen, Fulham) (18): 1956 v E; 1957 v W; 1958 v Ni, H, Pol, Y, Par; 1959 v E, W, Ni, WG, Holl; 1960 v E, Ni, W, Pol, A, H.
LEIGHTON, J. (Aberdeen, Manchester Utd, Hibernian, Aberdeen) (91): 1983 v EG, Sw (2), Bel, W, E, Ca (2); 1984 v U, Bel, Ni, W, E, Fr; 1985 v Y, Ice, Sp (2), W, E, Ice; 1986 v W, EG, Aus (2), Is, D, WG, U; 1987 v Bul, Ei (2), L, Bel, E; 1988 v H, Bel, Bul, L, S.Ar, Ma, Sp, Co, E; 1989 v N, Cy (2), Fr, E, Ch; 1990 v Y, Fr, N, Arg, Ma, Cr, Se, Br; 1994 v Ma, A, Holl; 1995 v Gr, Ru, Sm, J, Ec, Fi. 1996 v Gr, Fin, Se, Sm, Aus, D, US;1997 v Se (2), Est, A, W, Ma, Blr.1998 v Blr, La, D, Fin, US, Br, N, M. 1999 v Lth, Est.
LENNIE, W. (Aberdeen) (2): 1908 v W, Ni.
LENNOX, R. (Celtic) (10): 1967 v Ni, E, USSR; 1968 v W, L; 1969 v D, A. WG, Cy; 1970 v W.
LESLIE, L. G. (Airdrie) (5): 1961 v W, Ni, Ei (2), Cz.
LEVEIN, C. (Hearts) (16): 1990 v Arg, EG, Eg, Pol, Ma, Se; 1991 R, Sm; 1993 v Por (2), G; 1994 v Sw, Holl; 1995 v Fin, Fi, Ru.
LIDDELL, W. (Liverpool) (28): 1947 v W, Ni; 1948 v E, W, Ni; 1950 v E, W, Por, Fr; 1951 v W, Ni, E, A; 1952 v W, Ni, E, USA, D, Se; 1953 v W, Ni, E; 1954 v W; 1955 v Por, Y, A, H; 1956 v Ni.
LIDDLE, D. (East Fife) (3): 1931 v A, I, Sw.
LINDSAY, D. (St Mirren) (1): 1903 v Ni.
LINDSAY, J. (Dumbarton) (8): 1880 v W; 1881 v W, E; 1884 v W, E; 1885 v W, E; 1886 v E.
LINDSAY, J. (Renton) (3): 1888 v E; 1893 v E, Ni.
LINWOOD, A. B. (Clyde) (1): 1950 v W.
LITTLE, R. J. (Rangers) (1): 1953 v Se.
LIVINGSTONE, G. T. (Manchester City, Rangers) (2): 1906 v E; 1907 v W.
LOCHHEAD, A. (Third Lanark) (1): 1889 v W.
LOGAN, J. (Ayr Utd) (1): 1891 v W.
LOGAN, T. (Falkirk) (1): 1913 v Ni.
LOGIE, J. T. (Arsenal) (1): 1953 v Ni.
LONEY, W. (Celtic) (2): 1910 v W, Ni.

LONG, H. (Clyde) (1): 1947 v Ni.
LONGAIR, W. (Dundee) (1): 1894 v Ni.
LORIMER, P. (Leeds Utd) (21): 1970 v A; 1971 v W, Ni; 1972 v Ni, W, E; 1973 v D (2), E (2); 1974 v WG, E, Bel, N, Z, Br, Y; 1975 v Sp; 1976 v D (2), R.
LOVE, A. (Aberdeen) (3): 1931 v A, I, Sw.
LOW, A. (Falkirk) (1): 1934 v Ni.
LOW, T. P. (Rangers) (1): 1897 v Ni.
LOW, W. L. (Newcastle Utd) (5): 1911 v E, W; 1912 v Ni; 1920 v E, Ni.
LOWE, J. (Cambuslang) (1): 1891 v Ni.
LOWE, J. (St Bernards) (1): 1887 v Ni.
LUNDIE, J. (Hibernian) (1): 1886 v W.
LYALL, J. (Sheffield W.) (1): 1905 v E.
McADAM, J. (Third Lanark) (1): 1880 v W.
McALLISTER, B. (Wimbledon) (3): 1997 v W, Ma, Blr.
McALLISTER, G. (Leicester City, Leeds Utd, Coventry) (57): 1990 v EG, Pol, Ma; 1991 v R, Sw (2), Bul, USSR, Sm, (2); 1992 v Ni, Fin, US, Ca, N, Holl, G, CIS; 1993 v Sw, Por, I, Ma; 1994 v Sw, I, Ma, Holl (2), A; 1995 v Fin, Ru (2), Gr, Sm. 1996 v Gr, Fin, Se, Sm, Aus, D, US, U, Holl, E, Sw; 1997 v A (2), La, Est (2), Se, W, Ma, Blr; 1998 v Blr, La, Fr; 1999 v CzR.
McARTHUR, D. (Celtic) (3): 1895 v E, Ni; 1899 v W.
McATEE, A. (Celtic) (1): 1913 v W.
McAULAY, J. (Dumbarton, Arthurlie) (2): 1882 v W; 1884 v Ni.
McAULAY, J. (Dumbarton) (8): 1883 v E, W; 1884 v E; 1885 v E, W; 1886 v E; 1887 v E, W.
McAULEY, R. (Rangers) (2): 1932 v Ni, W.
McAVENNIE, F. (West Ham Utd., Celtic) (5): 1986 v Aus (2), D, WG; 1988 v S.Ar.
McBAIN, E. (St Mirren) (1): 1894 v W.
McBAIN, N. (Manchester Utd., Everton) (3): 1922 v E; 1923 v Ni; 1924 v W.
McBRIDE, J. (Celtic) (2): 1967 v W, Ni.
McBRIDE, P. (Preston NE) (6): 1904 v E; 1906 v E; 1907 v E, W; 1908 v E; 1909 v W.
McCALL, J. (Renton) (5): 1886 v W; 1887 v E, W; 1888 v E; 1890 v E.
McCALL, S. M. (Everton, Rangers) (40) 1990 v Arg, EG, Eg, Pol, Ma, Cr, Se, Br; 1991 v Sw, USSR, Sm (2); 1992 v Sw, R, US, Ca, N, Holl, G, CIS; 1993 v Sw, Por (2); 1994 v I, Holl (2), A; 1995 v Fin, Ru, Gr; 1996 v Gr, D, US, U, Holl, E, Sw; 1997 v A, La; 1998 v D.
McCALLIOG, J. (Sheffield W., Wolverhampton W.) (5): 1967 v E, USSR; 1968 v Ni; 1969 v D; 1971 v Por.
McCALLUM, N. (Renton) (1): 1888 v Ni.
McCANN, R. J. (Motherwell) (5): 1959 v WG; 1960 v E, Ni, W; 1961 v E.
McCANN, N. (Hearts, Rangers) (2): 1999 v Lth, CzR.
McCARTNEY, W. (Hibernian) (1): 1902 v Ni.

McCLAIR, B. (Celtic, Manchester Utd) (30): 1987 v L, Ei, E, Br; 1988 v Bul, Ma, Sp; 1989 v N, Y, I, Cy, Fr; 1990 v N, Arg; 1991 v Bul (2), Sm; 1992 v Sw, R, Ni, US, Ca, N, Holl, G, CIS; 1993 v Sw, Por, Est (2).
McCLORY, A. (Motherwell) (3): 1927 v W; 1928 v Ni; 1935 v W.
McCLOY, P. (Ayr Utd) (2): 1924 v E; 1925 v E.
McCLOY, P. (Rangers) (4): 1973 v W, Ni, Sw, Br.
McCOIST, A. (Rangers) (61): 1986 v Holl; 1987 v L, Ei, Bel, E, Br; 1988 v H, Bel, Ma, Sp, Co, E; 1989 v Y, Fr, Cy, E; 1990 v Y, Fr, N, EG, Eg, Pol, Ma, Cr, Se, Br; 1991 v R, Sw, Bul (2), USSR; 1992 v Sw, Sm, Ni, Fin, US, Ca, N, Holl, G, CIS; 1993 v Sw, Por (2), I, Ma. 1996 v Gr, Fin, Sm, Aus, D, U, E, Sw; 1997 v A (2), Se, Est; 1998 v Blr. 1999 v Lth, Est.
McCOLL, A. (Renton) (1): 1888 v Ni.
McCOLL, I. M. (Rangers) (14): 1950 v E, Fr; 1951 v W, Ni, Bel; 1957 v E, Ni, W, Y, Sp, Sw, WG; 1958 v Ni, E.
McCOLL, R. S. (Queen's Park, Newcastle Utd.) (13): 1896 v W, Ni; 1897 v Ni; 1898 v Ni; 1899 v Ni; E, W; 1900 v E, W; 1901 v E, W; 1902 v E; 1908 v Ni.
McCOLL, W. (Renton) (1): 1895 v W.
McCOMBIE, A. (Sunderland, Newcastle Utd.) (4): 1903 v E, W; 1905 v E, W.
McCORKINDALE, J. (Partick Th.) (1): 1891 v W.
McCORMICK, R. (Abercorn) (1): 1886 v W.
McCRAE, D. (St Mirren) (2): 1929 v N, G.
McCREADIE, A. (Rangers) (2): 1893 v W; 1894 v E.
McCREADIE, E. G. (Chelsea) (23): 1965 v E, Sp, Fin, Pol; 1966 v Por, Ni, W, Pol, I; 1967 v E, USSR; 1968 v Ni, W, E, Holl; 1969 v W, Ni, E, D, A. WG, Cy (2).
McCULLOCH, D. (Hearts, Brentford, Derby Co.) (7): 1935 v W; 1936 v E; 1937 v W, Ni; 1938 v Cz; 1939 v H, W.
MacDONALD, A. (Rangers) (1): 1976 v Sw.
McDONALD, J. (Edinburgh University) (1): 1886 v E.
McDONALD, J. (Sunderland) (2): 1956 v W, Ni.
MacDOUGALL, E. J. (Norwich City) (7): 1975 v Se, Por, W, Ni, E; 1976 v D, R.
McDOUGALL, J. (Liverpool) (2): 1931 v I, A.
McDOUGALL, J. (Airdrie) (1): 1926 v Ni.
McDOUGALL, J. (Vale of Leven) (5): 1877 v E, W; 1878 v E; 1879 v E, W.
McFADYEN, W. (Motherwell) (2): 1934 v A, W.
MACFARLANE, A. (Dundee) (5): 1904 v W; 1906 v W; 1908 v W; 1909 v Ni; 1911 v W.
McFARLANE, R. (Morton) (1): 1896 v W.
MACFARLANE, W. (Hearts) (1): 1947 v L.
McGARR, E. (Aberdeen) (2): 1970 v Ei, A.

McGARVEY, F. (Liverpool, Celtic) (7): 1979 v Ni, Arg; 1984 v U, Bel, EG, Ni, W.
McGEOCH, A. (Dumbreck) (4): 1876 v E, W; 1877 v E, W.
McGHEE, J. (Hibernian) (1): 1886 v W.
McGHEE, M. (Aberdeen) (4): 1983 v Ca (2); 1984 v Ni, E.
McGINLAY, J. (Bolton W.) (13): 1994 v A, Holl; 1995 v Fi (2), Ru (2), Gr, Sm; 1996 v Se; 1997 v Se, Est (2), A.
McGONAGLE, W. (Celtic) (6): 1933 v E; 1934 v A, E, Ni; 1935 v Ni, W.
McGRAIN, D. (Celtic) (62): 1973 v W, Ni, E, Sw, Br; 1974 v Cz (2), WG, W, E, Bel, N, Z, Br, Y; 1975 v Sp, Se, Por, W, Ni, E, R; 1976 v D (2), Sw, Ni, W, E; 1977 v Fin, Cz, W (2), Se, Ni, E, Ch, Arg, Br; 1978 v EG, Cz; 1980 v Bel, Por, Ni, W, E, Pol, H; 1981 v Se, Por, Is, (2), Ni (2), W, E; 1982 v Se, Sp, Holl, Ni, E, Nz, USSR.
McGREGOR, J. C. (Vale of Leven) (4): 1877 v E, W; 1878 v E; 1880 v E.
McGRORY, J. E. (Kilmarnock) (3): 1965 v Ni, Fin; 1966 v Por.
McGRORY, J. (Celtic) (7): 1928 v Ni; 1931 v E; 1932 v Ni, W; 1933 v E, Ni; 1934 v Ni.
McGUIRE, W. (Beith) (2): 1881 v E, W.
McGURK, F. (Birmingham City) (1): 1934 v W.
McHARDY, H. (Rangers) (1): 1885 v Ni.
McINALLY, A. (Aston Villa, Bayern Munich) (8): 1989 v Cy, Ch; 1990 v Y, Fr, Arg, Pol, Ma, Cr.
McINALLY, J. (Dundee Utd) (10): 1987 v Bel, Br; 1988 v Ma; 1991 v Bul (2); 1992 v US, N, CIS; 1993 v G, Por.
McINALLY, T. B. (Celtic) (2): 1926 v Ni; 1927 v W.
McINNES, T. (Cowlairs) (1): 1889 v Ni.
McINTOSH, W. (Third Lanark) (1): 1905 v Ni.
McINTYRE, A. (Vale of Leven) (2): 1878 v E; 1882 v E.
McINTYRE, H. (Rangers) (1): 1880 v W.
McINTYRE, J. (Rangers) (1): 1884 v W.
McKAY, D. (Celtic) (14): 1959 v E, WG, Holl, Por; 1960 v E, Pol, A, H, T; 1961 v W, Ni; 1962 v Ni, Cz, U.
MACKAY, D. C. (Hearts, Tottenham H.) (22): 1957 v Sp; 1958 v Fr; 1959 v W, Ni, WG, E; 1960 v W, Ni, A, Pol, H, T; 1961 v W, Ni, E; 1963 v E, A, N; 1964 v Ni, W, N; 1966 v Ni.
MACKAY, G. (Hearts) (4): 1988 v Bul, L, S.Ar, Ma.
McKAY, J. (Blackburn R.) (1): 1924 v W.
McKAY, R. (Newcastle Utd.) (1): 1928 v W.
McKEAN, R. (Rangers) (1): 1976 v Sw.
McKENZIE, D. (Brentford) (1): 1938 v Ni.
MACKENZIE, J. A. (Partick Th.) (9): 1954 v W, E, N, Fin, A, U; 1955 v E, H; 1956 v A.

McKEOWN, M. (Celtic) (2): 1889 v Ni; 1890 v E.
McKIE, J. (East Stirling) (1): 1898 v W.
McKILLOP, T. R. (Rangers) (1): 1938 v Holl.
McKIMMIE, S. (Aberdeen) (40): 1989 v E, Ch; 1990 v Arg, Eg, Cr, Br; 1991 v R (2), Sw, Bul, Sm; 1992 v Sw, Ni, Fin, US, Ca, N, Holl, G, CIS. 1993 v Por, Est; 1994 v Sw, I, Holl (2), A; 1995 v Fin, Fi (2), Ru (2), Gr. 1996 v Gr, Fin, Se, D, U, Holl, E.
McKINLAY, D. (Liverpool) (2): 1922 v W, Ni.
McKINLAY, T. (Celtic) (22): 1996 v Gr, Fin, D, U, E, Sw; 1997 v A (2), La, Se (2), Est (2), W, Ma, Blr; 1998 v Blr, La, Fr, US, Br, M.
McKINLAY, W. (Dundee Utd, Blackburn R.) (29): 1994 v Ma, Holl (2), A; 1995 v Fi (2), Ru (2), Gr, Sm, J, Ec; 1996 v Fin, Se, Sm, Aus, D, Holl; 1997 v Se, Est; 1998 v La, Fr, D, Fin, Co, US, Br. 1999 v Est, Fi.
McKINNON, A. (Queen's Park) (1): 1874 v E.
McKINNON, R. (Rangers) (28): 1966 v W, E, I (2), Holl, Br; 1967 v W, Ni, E; 1968 v Ni, W, E, Holl; 1969 v D, A, WG, Cy; 1970 v Ni, W, E, Ei, WG, A; 1971 v D, Bel, Por, USSR, D.
McKINNON, R. (Motherwell) (3): 1994 v Ma; 1995 v J, Fi.
MACKINNON, W. (Dumbarton) (4): 1883 v E, W; 1884 v E, W.
McKINNON, W. W. (Queen's Park) (9): 1872 v E; 1873 v E; 1874 v E; 1875 v E; 1876 v E, W; 1877 v E; 1878 v E; 1879 v E.
McLAREN, A. (St Johnstone) (5): 1929 v N, G, Holl; 1933 v W, Ni.
McLAREN, A. (Preston NE) (4): 1947 v E, Bel, L; 1948 v W.
McLAREN, A. (Hearts, Rangers) (24): 1992 v US, Ca, N; 1993 v I, Ma, G, Est (2); 1994 v I, Ma, Holl, A; 1995 v Fin, Fi (2), Ru (2), Gr, Sm, J, Ec; 1996 v Fin, Se, Sm.
McLAREN, J. (Hibernian, Celtic) (3): 1888 v W; 1889 v E; 1890 v E.
McLEAN, A. (Celtic) (4): 1926 v W, Ni; 1927 v W, E.
McLEAN, D. (St Bernards) (2): 1896 v W; 1897 v Ni.
McLEAN, D. (Sheffield W.) (1): 1912 v E.
McLEAN, G. (Dundee) (1): 1968 v Holl.
McLEAN, T. (Kilmarnock) (6): 1969 v D. Cy, W; 1970 v Ni, W; 1971 v D.
McLEISH, A. (Aberdeen) (77): 1980 v Por, Ni, W, E, Pol, H; 1981 v Se, Is (2), Ni (2), E; 1982 v Se, Sp, Ni, Br; 1983 v Bel, Sw, W, E, Ca (3); 1984 v U, Bel, EG, Ni, W, E, Fr; 1985 v Y, Ice, (2), Sp (2), W, E; 1986 v W, EG, Aus (2), E, Holl, D; 1987 v Bel, E, Br; 1988 v Bel, Bul, L, S.Ar, Ma, Sp, Co, E; 1989 v N, Y, I, Cy (2), Fr, E, Ch; 1990 v Y, Fr, N, Arg, EG, Eg, Cr, Se, Br; 1991 v R, Sw, USSR, Bul; 1993 v Ma.
McLEOD, D. (Celtic) (4): 1905 v Ni; 1906 v E, W, Ni.
McLEOD, J. (Dumbarton) (5): 1888 v Ni; 1889 v W; 1890 v Ni; 1892 v E; 1893 v W.
MacLEOD, J. M. (Hibernian) (4): 1961 v E, Ei (2), Cz.
MACLEOD, M. (Celtic, Borussia Dort., Hibernian) (20): 1985 v E; 1987 v Ei, L, E, Br; 1988 v Co, E; 1989 v I, Ch; 1990 v Y, Fr, N, Arg, EG, Pol, Se, Br; 1991 v R, Sw, USSR.
McLEOD, W. (Cowlairs) (1): 1886 v Ni.
McLINTOCK, A. (Vale of Leven) (3): 1875 v E; 1876 v E; 1880 v E.
McLINTOCK, F. (Leicester City, Arsenal) (9): 1963 v N, Ei, Sp; 1965 v Ni; 1967 v USSR; 1970 v Ni; 1971 v W, Ni, E.

McMAHON, A. (Celtic) (6): 1892 v E; 1893 v E, Ni; 1894 v E; 1901 v Ni. 1902 v W.
McMENEMY, J. (Celtic) (12): 1905 v Ni; 1909 v Ni; 1910 v E, W; 1911 v Ni, W, E; 1912 v W; 1914 v W, Ni, E; 1920 v Ni.
McMENEMY, J. (Motherwell) (1): 1934 v W.
McMILLAN, J. (St Bernards) (1): 1897 v W.
McMILLAN, I. L. (Airdrie, Rangers) (6): 1952 v E, USA, D; 1955 v E; 1956 v E; 1961 v Cz.
McMILLAN, T. (Dumbarton) (1): 1887 v Ni.
McMULLAN, J. (Partick Th., Manchester City) (16): 1920 v W; 1921 v W, Ni, E; 1924 v E, Ni; 1925 v E; 1926 v W, E; 1927 v E, W; 1928 v E, W; 1929 v W, E, Ni.
McNAB, A. (Morton) (2): 1921 v E, Ni.
McNAB, A. (Sunderland, WBA) (2): 1937 v A; 1939 v E.
McNAB, C. D. (Dundee) (6): 1931 v E, W, A, I, Sw; 1932 v E.
McNAB, J. S. (Liverpool) (1): 1923 v W.
McNAIR, A. (Celtic) (15): 1906 v W; 1907 v Ni; 1908 v E, W; 1909 v E; 1910 v W; 1912 v E, W, Ni; 1913 v E; 1914 v E, Ni; 1920 v E, W, Ni.
McNAMARA J. (Celtic) (9): 1997 v La, Se, Est, W; 1998 v D, Co, US, N, M.
J. McNAUGHT, W. (Raith R.) (5): 1951 v A, W, Ni; 1952 v E; 1955 v Ni.
McNEIL, H. (Queen's Park) (10): 1874 v E; 1875 v E; 1876 v E, W; 1877 v W; 1878 v E; 1879 v E, W; 1881 v E, W.
McNEIL, M. (Rangers) (2): 1876 v W; 1880 v E.
McNEILL, W. (Celtic) (29): 1961 v E, Ei (2), Cz; 1962 v Ni, E, Cz, U; 1963 v Ei, Sp; 1964 v W, E, WG; 1965 v E, Fin, Pol, Sp; 1966 v Ni, Pol; 1967 v USSR; 1968 v E; 1969 v Cy (2), W, E; 1970 v WG; 1972 v Ni, W, E.

McPHAIL, J. (Celtic) (5): 1950 v W; 1951 v W, Ni, A; 1954 v Ni.
McPHAIL, R. (Airdrie, Rangers) (17): 1927 v E; 1929 v W; 1931 v E, Ni; 1932 v W, Ni, Fr; 1933 v E, Ni; 1934 v A, Ni; 1935 v E; 1937 v G, E, Cz; 1938 v W, Ni.
McPHERSON, D. (Kilmarnock) (1): 1892 v Ni.
McPHERSON, D. (Hearts, Rangers) (27): 1989 v Cy, E; 1990 v N, Ma, Cr, Se, Br; 1991 v Sw, Bul (2), USSR, Sm (2); 1992 v Sw, R, Ni, Fin, US, Ca, N, Holl, G, CIS; 1993 v Sw, I, Ma, Por.
McPHERSON, J. (Clydesdale) (1): 1875 v E.
McPHERSON, J. (Vale of Leven) (8): 1879 v E, W; 1880 v E; 1881 v W; 1883 v E, W; 1884 v E; 1885 v Ni.
McPHERSON, J. (Kilmarnock, Cowlairs, Rangers) (9): 1888 v W; 1889 v E; 1890 v Ni, E; 1892 v W; 1894 v E; 1895 v E, Ni; 1897 Ni.
McPHERSON, J. (Hearts) (1): 1891 v E.

McPHERSON, R. (Arthurlie) (1): 1882 v E.
McQUEEN, G. (Leeds Utd., Manchester Utd.) (30): 1974 v Bel; 1975 v Sp (2), Por, W, Ni, E, R; 1976 v D; 1977 v Cz, W (2), Ni, E; 1978 v EG, Cz, W, Bul, Ni, W; 1979 v A, N, Por, Ni, E, N; 1980 v Pe, A, Bel; 1981 v W.
McQUEEN, M. (Leith Ath.) (2): 1890 v W; 1891 v W.
McRORIE, D. M. (Morton) (1): 1931 v W.
McSPADYEN, A. (Partick Th.) (2): 1939 v E, H.
McSTAY, P. (Celtic) (76): 1984 v U, Bel, EG, Ni, W, E; 1985 v Ice, Sp (2), W; 1986 v EG, Aus, Is, U, Y; 1987 v Bul, Ei (2), L, Bel, E, Br; 1988 v H, Bel, Bul, L, S.Ar, Sp, Co, E; 1989 v N, Y, I, Cy (2), Fr, E, Ch; 1990 v Y, Fr, N, Arg, EG, Eg, Pol, Ma, Cr, Se, Br; 1991 v R, USSR, Bul; 1992 v Sm, Fin, US, Ca, N, Holl, G, CIS; 1993 v Sw, Por (2), I, Ma, Est (2); 1994 v I, Holl; 1995 v Fin, Fi, Ru; 1996 v Aus, 1997 v Est (2), A.
McSTAY, W. (Celtic) (13): 1921 v W, Ni; 1925 v E, Ni, W; 1926 v E, Ni, W; 1927 v E, Ni, W; 1928 v W, Ni.
McTAVISH, J. (Falkirk) (1): 1910 v Ni.
McWHATTIE, G. C. (Queen's Park) (2): 1901 v W, Ni.
McWILLIAM, P. (Newcastle Utd.) (8): 1905 v E; 1906 v E; 1907 v E, W; 1909 v E, W; 1910 v E; 1911 v W.
MACARI, L. (Celtic, Manchester Utd.) (24): 1972 v W, E, Y, Cz, Br; 1973 v D, E (2), W, Ni; 1975 v Se, Por, W, E, R; 1977 v Ni, E, Ch, Arg; 1978 v EG, W, Bul, Pe, Ir.
MACAULEY, A. R. (Brentford, Arsenal) (7): 1947 v E; 1948 v E, W, Ni, Bel, Sw, Fr.
MADDEN, J. (Celtic) (2): 1893 v W; 1895 v W.
MAIN, F. R. (Rangers) (1): 1938 v W.
MAIN, J. (Hibernian) (1): 1909 v Ni.
MALEY, W. (Celtic) (2): 1893 v E, Ni.
MALPAS, M. (Dundee Utd.) (55): 1984 v Fr; 1985 v E, Ice; 1986 v W, Aus (2), Is, R, E, Holl, D, WG; 1987 v Bul, Ei, Bel; 1988 v Bel, Bul, L, S.Ar, Ma; 1989 v N, Y, I, Cy (2), Fr, E, Ch; 1990 v Y, Fr, N, Eg, Pol, Ma, Cr, Se, Br; 1991 v R (2), Bul (2), USSR, Sm (2); 1992 v Sw, Ni, Fin, US, Ca, N, Holl, G; 1993 v Sw, Por, I.
MARSHALL, H. (Celtic) (2): 1899 v W; 1900 v Ni.
MARSHALL, G. (Celtic) (1): 1992 v US.
MARSHALL, J. (Middlesbrough, Llanelly) (7): 1921 v E, W, Ni; 1922 v E, W, Ni; 1924 v W.
MARSHALL, J. (Third Lanark) (4): 1885 v Ni; 1886 v W; 1887 v E, W.
MARSHALL, J. (Rangers) (3): 1932 v E; 1933 v E; 1934 v E.
MARSHALL, R. W. (Rangers) (2): 1892 v Ni; 1894 v Ni.
MARTIN, B. (Motherwell) (2): 1995 v. J, Ec.
MARTIN, F. (Aberdeen) (6): 1954 v N (2), A, U; 1955 v E, H.
MARTIN, N. (Hibernian, Sunderland) (3): 1965 v Fin, Pol; 1966 v I.
MARTIS, J. (Motherwell) (1): 1961 v W.

MASON, J. (Third Lanark) (7): 1949 v E, W, Ni; 1950 v Ni; 1951 v Ni, Bel, A.
MASSIE, A. (Hearts, Aston Villa) (18): 1932 v Ni, W, Fr; 1933 v Ni; 1934 v E, Ni; 1935 v E, Ni, W; 1936 v W, Ni, E; 1937 v G, E, W, Ni, A; 1938 v W.
MASSON, D. S. (QPR, Derby Co.) (17): 1976 v Ni, W, E; 1977 v Fin, Cz, W, Ni, E, Ch, Arg, Br; 1978 v EG, Cz, W, Ni, E, Pe.
MATHERS, D. (Partick Th.) (1): 1954 v Fin.
MAXWELL, W. S. (Stoke City) (1): 1898 v E.
MAY, J. (Rangers) (5): 1906 v W, Ni; 1908 v E, Ni; 1909 v W.
MEECHAN, P. (Celtic) (1): 1896 v Ni.
MEIKLEJOHN, D. D. (Rangers) (15): 1922 v W; 1924 v W; 1925 v W, Ni, E; 1928 v W, Ni; 1929 v E, Ni; 1930 v E, Ni; 1931 v E; 1932 v W, Ni; 1934 v A.
MENZIES, A. (Hearts) (1): 1906 v E.
MERCER, R. (Hearts) (2): 1912 v W; 1913 v Ni.
MIDDLETON, R. (Cowdenbeath) (1): 1930 v Ni.
MILLAR, A. (Hearts) (1): 1939 v W.
MILLAR, J. (Rangers) (3): 1897 v E; 1898 v E, W.
MILLAR, J. (Rangers) (2): 1963 v A, Ei.
MILLER, J. (St Mirren) (5): 1931 v E, I, Sw; 1932 v Fr; 1934 v E.
MILLER, P. (Dumbarton) (3): 1882 v E; 1883 v E, W.
MILLER, T. (Liverpool, Manchester Utd.) (3): 1920 v E; 1921 v E, Ni.
MILLER, W. (Third Lanark) (1): 1876 v E.
MILLER, W. (Celtic) (6): 1947 v E, W, Bel, L; 1948 v W, Ni.
MILLER, W. (Aberdeen) (65): 1975 v R; 1978 v Bul; 1980 v Bel, W, E, Pol, H; 1981 v Se, Por, Is, Ni (2), W, E; 1982 v Ni, Por, Holl, Br, USSR; 1983 v EG, Sw (2), W, E, Ca (3); 1984 v U, Bel, EG, W, E, Fr; 1985 v Y, Ice, Sp (2), W, E, Ice; 1986 v W, EG, Aus (2), Is, R, E, Holl, D, WG, U; 1987 v Bul, E, Br; 1988 v H, L, S.Ar, Ma, Sp, Co, E; 1989 v N, Y; 1990 Y, N.
MILLS, W. (Aberdeen) (3): 1936 v W, Ni; 1937 v W.
MILNE, J. V. (Middlesbrough) (2): 1938 v E; 1939 v E.
MITCHELL, D. (Rangers) (5): 1890 v Ni; 1892 v E; 1893 v E, Ni; 1894 v E.
MITCHELL, J. (Kilmarnock) (3): 1908 v Ni; 1910 v Ni, W.
MITCHELL, R. C. (Newcastle Utd.) (2): 1951 v D, Fr.
MOCHAN, N. (Celtic) (3): 1954 v N, A, U.
MOIR, W. (Bolton) (1): 1950 v E.
MONCUR, R. (Newcastle Utd.) (16): 1968 v Holl; 1970 v Ni, W, E, Ei; 1971 v D, Bel, W, Por, Ni, E, D; 1972 v Pe, Ni, W, E.

MORGAN, H. (St Mirren, Liverpool) (2): 1898 v W; 1899 v E.
MORGAN, W. (Burnley, Manchester Utd.) (21): 1968 v Ni; 1972 v Pe, Y, Cz, Br; 1973 v D (2), E (2), W, Ni, Sw, Br; 1974 v Cz (2), WG (2), Ni, Bel, Br, Y.
MORRIS, D. (Raith R.) (6): 1923 v Ni; 1924 v E, Ni; 1925 v E, W, Ni.
MORRIS, H. (East Fife) (1): 1950 v Ni.
MORRISON, T. (St Mirren) (1): 1927 v E.
MORTON, A. L. (Queen's Park, Rangers) (31): 1920 v W, Ni; 1921 v E; 1922 v E, W; 1923 v E, W, Ni; 1924 v E, W, Ni; 1925 v E, W, Ni; 1927 v E, Ni; 1928 v E, W, Ni; 1929 v E, W, Ni; 1930 v E, W, Ni; 1931 v E, W, Ni; 1932 v E, W, Fr.
MORTON, H. A. (Kilmarnock) (2): 1929 v G, Holl.
MUDIE, J. K. (Blackpool) (17): 1957 v W, Ni, E, Y, Sw, Sp (2), WG; 1958 v Ni, E, W, Sw, H, Pol, Y, Par, Fr.
MUIR, W. (Dundee) (1): 1907 v Ni.
MUIRHEAD, T. A. (Rangers) (8): 1922 v Ni; 1923 v E; 1924 v W; 1927 v Ni; 1928 v Ni; 1929 v W, Ni; 1930 v W.
MULHALL, G. (Aberdeen, Sunderland) (3): 1960 v Ni; 1963 v Ni; 1964 v Ni.
MUNRO, A. D. (Hearts, Blackpool) (3): 1937 v W, Ni; 1938 v Holl.
MUNRO, F. M. (Wolverhampton W.) (9): 1971 v Ni, E, D, USSR; 1975 v Se, W, Ni, E, R.
MUNRO, I. (St Mirren) (7): 1979 v Arg, N; 1980 v Pe, A, Bel, W, E.
MUNRO, N. (Abercorn) (2): 1888 v W; 1889 v E.
MURDOCH, J. (Motherwell) (1): 1931 v Ni.
MURDOCH, R. (Celtic) (12): 1966 v W, E, I (2); 1967 v Ni; 1968 v Ni; 1969 v W, Ni, E, WG, Cy; 1970 v A.
MURPHY, F. (Celtic) (1): 1938 v Holl.
MURRAY, J. (Renton) (1): 1895 v W.
MURRAY, J. (Hearts) (5): 1958 v E, H, Pol, Y, Fr.
MURRAY, J. W. (Vale of Leven) (1): 1890 v W.
MURRAY, P. (Hibernian) (2): 1896 v Ni; 1897 v W.
MURRAY, S. (Aberdeen) (1): 1972 v Bel.
MUTCH, G. (Preston NE) (1): 1938 v E.
NAPIER, C. E. (Celtic, Derby County) (5): 1932 v E; 1935 v E, W; 1937 v Ni, A.
NAREY, D. (Dundee Utd.) (35): 1977 v Se; 1979 v Psor, Ni, Arg; 1980 v Por, Ni, Pol, H; 1981 v W, E; 1982 v Holl, W, E, Nz, Br, USSR; 1983 v EG, Sw, Bel, Ni, W, E, Ca (3); 1986 v Is, R, Holl, WG, U; 1987 v Bul, E, Bel; 1989 v I, Cy.
NEIL, R. G. (Hibernian, Rangers) (2): 1896 v W; 1900 v W.

NEILL, R. W. (Queen's Park) (5): 1876 v W; 1877 v E, W; 1878 v W; 1880 v E.
NELLIES, P. (Hearts) (2): 1914 v W, Ni.
NELSON, J. (Cardiff C.) (4): 1925 v W, Ni; 1928 v E; 1930 v Fr.
NEVIN, P. (Chelsea, Everton, Tranmere) (28): 1986 v R, E; 1987 v L, Ei, Bel; 1988 v L; 1989 v Cy, E; 1991 v R, Bul, Sm; 1992 v US, G, CIS; 1993 v Ma, Por, Est; 1994 v Sw, Ma, Holl (2), A. 1995 v Fi, Ru, Sm; 1996 v Se, Sm, Aus.
NIBLO, T. (Aston Villa) (1): 1904 v E.
NIBLOE, J. (Kilmarnock) (11): 1929 v E, N, Holl; 1930 v W; 1931 v E, Ni, A, I, Sw; 1932 v E, Fr.
NICHOLAS, C. (Celtic, Arsenal, Aberdeen) (20): 1983 v Sw, Ni, E, Ca (3); 1984 v Bel, Fr; 1985 v Y, Ice, Sp, W; 1986 v Is, R, E, D, U; 1987 v Bul, E; 1989 v Cy.
NICOL, S. (Liverpool) (27): 1985 v Y, Ice, Sp, W; 1986 v W, EG, Aus, E, D, WG, U; 1988 v H, Bul, S.Ar, Sp, Co, E; 1989 v N, Y, Cy, Fr; 1990 v Y, Fr; 1991 v Sw, USSR, Sm; 1992 Sw.
NISBET, J. (Ayr Utd.) (3): 1929 v N, G, Holl.
NIVEN, J. B. (Moffat) (1): 1885 v Ni.
O'DONNELL, F. (Preston NE, Blackpool) (6): 1937 v E, A, Cz; 1938 v E, W, Holl.
O'DONNELL, P. (Motherwell) (1): 1994 v Sw.
OGILVIE, D. H. (Motherwell) (1): 1934 v A.
O'HARE, J. (Derby County) (13): 1970 v W, Ni, E; 1971 v D, Bel, W, Ni; 1972 v Por, Bel, Holl, Pe, Ni, W.
O'NEILL, B. (Celtic, Wolfsburg) (2): 1996 v Aus; 1999 v G.
ORMOND, W. E. (Hibernian) (6): 1954 v E, N, Fin, A, U; 1959 v E.
O'ROURKE, F. (Airdrie) (1): 1907 v Ni.
ORR, J. (Kilmarnock) (1): 1892 v W.
ORR, R. (Newcastle Utd.) (2): 1902 v E; 1904 v E.
ORR, T. (Morton) (2): 1952 v Ni, W.
ORR, W. (Celtic) (3): 1900 v Ni; 1903 v Ni; 1904 v W.
ORROCK, R. (Falkirk) (1): 1913 v W.
OSWALD, J. (Third Lanark, St Bernards, Rangers) (3): 1889 v E; 1895 v E; 1897 v W.
PARKER, A. H. (Falkirk, Everton) (15): 1955 v Por, Y, A; 1956 v E, Ni, W, A; 1957 v Ni, W, Y; 1958 v Ni, W, E, Sw, Par.
PARLANE, D. (Rangers) (12): 1973 v W, Sw, Br; 1975 v Sp, Se, Por, W, Ni, E, R; 1976 v D; 1977 v W.
PARLANE, R. (Vale of Leven) (3): 1878 v W; 1879 v E, W.
PATERSON, G. D. (Celtic) (1): 1939 v Ni.
PATERSON, J. (Leicester City) (1): 1920 v E.
PATERSON, J. (Cowdenbeath) (3): 1931 v A, I, Sw.
PATON, A. (Motherwell) (2): 1952 v D, Se.
PATON, D. (St Bernards) (1): 1896 v W.
PATON, M. (Dumbarton) (5): 1883 E; 1884 v W; 1885 v W, E; 1886 v E.

PATON, R. (Vale of Leven) (2): 1879 v E, W.
PATRICK, J. (St Mirren) (2): 1897 E, W.
PAUL, J. McD. (Queen's Park) (3): 1909 v E, W, Ni.
PAUL, W. (Partick Th.) (3): 1888 v W; 1889 v W; 1890 v W.
PAUL, W. (Dykebar) (1891 v Ni.
PEARSON, T. (Newcastle Utd.) (2): 1947 v E, Bel.
PENMAN, A. (Dundee) (1): 1966 v Holl.
PETTIGREW, W. (Motherwell) (5): 1976 v Sw, Ni, W; 1977 v W, Se.
PHILLIPS, J. (Queen's Park) (3): 1877 v E, W; 1878 v W.
PLENDERLEITH, J. B. (Manchester City) (1): 1961 v Ni.
PORTEOUS, W. (Hearts) (1): 1903 v Ni.
PRINGLE, C. (St Mirren) (1): 1921 v W.
PROVAN, D. (Rangers) (5): 1964 v Ni, N; 1966 v I (2), Holl.
PROVAN, D. (Celtic) (10): 1980 v Bel (2), Por, Ni; 1981 v Is, W, E; 1982 v Se, Por, Ni.
PURSELL, P. (Queen's Park) (1): 1914 v W.
QUINN, J. (Celtic) (11): 1905 v Ni; 1906 v Ni, W; 1908 v Ni, E; 1909 v E; 1910 v E, Ni, W; 1912 v E, W.
QUINN, P. (Motherwell) (4): 1961 v E, Ei (2); 1962 v U.
RAE, J. (Third Lanark) (2): 1889 v W; 1890 v Ni.
RAESIDE, J. S. (Third Lanark) (1): 1906 v W.
RAISBECK, A. G. (Liverpool) (8): 1900 v E; 1901 v E; 1902 v E; 1903 v E, W; 1904 v E; 1906 v E; 1907 v E.
RANKIN, G. (Vale of Leven) (2): 1890 v Ni; 1891 v E.
RANKIN, R. (St Mirren) (3): 1929 v N, G, Holl.
REDPATH, W. (Motherwell) (9): 1949 v W, Ni; 1951 v E, D, Fr, Bel, A; 1952 v Ni, E.
REID, J, G. (Airdrie) (3): 1914 v W; 1920 v W; 1924 v Ni.
REID, R. (Brentford) (2): 1938 v E, Ni.
REID, W. (Rangers) (9): 1911 v E, W, Ni; 1912 v Ni; 1913 v E, W, Ni; 1914 v E, Ni.
REILLY, L. (Hibernian) (38): 1949 v E, W, Fr; 1950 v W, Ni, Sw, Fr; 1951 v W, E, D, Fr, Bel, A; 1952 v Ni, W, E, USA, D, Se; 1953 v Ni, W, E, Se; 1954 v W; 1955 v H (2), Por, Y, A, E; 1956 v E, W, Ni, A; 1957 v E, Ni, W, Y.
RENNIE, H. G. (Hearts, Hibernian) (13): 1900 v E, Ni; 1901 v E; 1902 v E, Ni, W; 1903 v Ni, W; 1904 v Ni; 1905 v W; 1906 v Ni; 1908 v Ni, W.
RENNY-TAILYOUR, H. W. (Royal Engineers) (1): 1873 v E.
RHIND, A. (Queen's Park) (1): 1872 v E.
RICHMOND, A. (Queen's Park) (1): 1906 v W.

RICHMOND, J. T. (Clydesdale, Queen's Park) (3): 1877 v E; 1878 v E; 1882 v W.
RING, T. (Clyde) (12): 1953 v Se; 1955 v W, Ni, E, H; 1957 v E, Sp (2), Sw, WG; 1958 v Ni, Sw.
RIOCH, B. D. (Derby County, Everton) (24): 1975 v Por, W, Ni, E, R; 1976 v D (2), R, Ni, W, E; 1977 v Fin, Cz, W (2), Ni, E, Ch, Br; 1978 v Cz, Ni, E, Pe, Holl.
RITCHIE, A. (East Stirling) (1): 1891 v W.
RITCHIE, H. (Hibernian) (2): 1923 v W; 1928 v Ni.
RITCHIE, J. (Queen's Park) (1): 1897 v W.
RITCHIE, P. (Hearts) (2): 1999 v G, Czr.
RITCHIE, W. (Rangers) (1): 1962 v U.
ROBB, D. T. (Aberdeen) (5): 1971 v W, E, Por, D, USSR.
ROBB, W. (Rangers, Hibernian) (2): 1926 v W; 1928 v W.
ROBERTSON, A. (Clyde) (5): 1955 v Por, A, H; 1958 v Sw, Par.
ROBERTSON, D. (Rangers) (3): 1991 v Ni; 1994 v Sw, Holl.
ROBERTSON, G. (Motherwell, Sheffield W.) (4): 1910 v W; 1912 v W; 1913 v E, Ni.
ROBERTSON, G. (Kilmarnock) (1): 1938 v Cz.
ROBERTSON, H. (Dundee) (1): 1962 v Cz.
ROBERTSON, J. (Dundee) (2): 1931 v A, I.
ROBERTSON, J. (Hearts) (16): 1991 v R, Sw, Bul, Sm (2); 1992 v Ni, Fin; 1993 v I, Ma, G, Est; 1995 v J, Ec, Fi. 1996 v Gr, Se.
ROBERTSON, J. N. (Nottingham F., Derby County) (28): 1978 v Ni, W, Ir; 1979 v Por, N; 1980 v Pe, A, Bel (2), Por; 1981 v Se, Por, Is, Ni (2), E; 1982 v Se, Ni (2), E, Nz, Br, USSR; 1983 v EG, Sw; 1984 v U, Bel.
ROBERTSON, J. G. (Tottenham H.) (1): 1965 v W.
ROBERTSON, J. T. (Everton, Southampton, Rangers) (16): 1898 v E; 1899 v E; 1900 v E, W; 1901 v W, Ni, E; 1902 v W, Ni, E; 1903 v E, W; 1904 v E, W, Ni; 1905 v W.
ROBERTSON, P. (Dundee) (1): 1903 v Ni.
ROBERTSON, T. (Queen's Park) (4): 1889 v Ni; 1890 v E; 1891 v W; 1892 v Ni.
ROBERTSON, T. (Hearts) (1): 1898 v Ni.
ROBERTSON, W. (Dumbarton) (2): 1887 v E, W.
ROBINSON, R. (Dundee) (4): 1974 v WG; 1975 v Se, Ni, R.
ROUGH, A. (Partick Th, Hibernian) (53): 1976 v Sw, Ni, W, E; 1977 v Fin, Cz, W (2), Se, Ni, E, Ch, Arg, Br; 1978 v Cz, W, Ni, E, Pe, Ir, Holl; 1979 v A, Por, W, Arg, N; 1980 v Pe, A, Bel (2), Por, W, E, Pol, H; 1981 v Se, Por, Is (2), Ni, W, E; 1982 v Se, Ni, Sp, Holl, W, E, Nz, Br, USSR; 1986 v W, E.
ROUGVIE, D. (Aberdeen) (1): 1984 v Ni.
ROWAN, A. (Caledonian, Queen's Park) (2): 1880 v E; 1882 v W.

RUSSELL, D. (Hearts, Celtic) (6): 1895 v E, Ni; 1897 v W; 1898 v Ni; 1901 v W, Ni.
RUSSELL, J. (Cambuslang) (1): 1890 v Ni.
RUSSELL W. F. (Airdrie) (2): 1924 v W; 1925 v E.
RUTHERFORD, E. (Rangers) (1): 1948 v F.
ST JOHN, I. (Motherwell, Liverpool) (21): 1959 v WG; 1960 v E, Ni, W, Pol, A; 1961 v E; 1962 v Ni, W, E, Cz (2), U; 1963 v W, Ni, E, N, Ei, Sp; 1964 v Ni; 1965 v E.
SAWERS, W. (Dundee) (1): 1895 v W.
SCARFF, P. (Celtic) (1): 1931 v Ni.
SCHAEDLER, E. (Hibernian) (1): 1974 v WG.
SCOTT, A. S. (Rangers, Everton) (16): 1957 v Ni, Y, WG; 1958 v W, Sw; 1959 v Por; 1962 v Ni, W, E, Cz, U; 1964 v W, N; 1965 v Fin; 1966 v Por, Br.
SCOTT, J. (Hibernian) (1): 1966 v Holl.
SCOTT, J. (Dundee) (2): 1971 v D, USSR.
SCOTT, M. (Airdrie) (1): 1898 v W.
SCOTT, R. (Airdrie) (1): 1894 v Ni.
SCOULAR, J. (Portsmouth) (9): 1951 v D, Fr, A; 1952 v E, USA, D, Se; 1953 v W, Ni.
SELLAR, W. (Battlefield, Queen's Park) (9): 1885 v E; 1886 v E; 1887 v E, W; 1888 v E; 1891 v E; 1892 v E; 1893 v E, Ni.
SEMPLE, J. (Cambuslang) (1): 1886 v W.
SHANKLY, W. (Preston NE) (5): 1938 v E; 1939 v E, W, Ni, H.
SHARP, G. M. (Everton) (12): 1985 v Ice; 1986 v W, Aus (2), Is, R, U; 1987 v Ei; 1988 v Bel, Bul, L, Ma.
SHARP, J. (Dundee, Woolwich Arsenal, Fulham) (5): 1904 v W; 1907 v W, E; 1908 v E; 1909 v W.
SHAW, D. (Hibernian) (8): 1947 v W, Ni; 1948 v E, Bel, Sw, Fr; 1949 v W, Ni.
SHAW, F. W. (Pollokshields Ath.) (2): 1884 v E, W.
SHAW, J. (Rangers) (4): 1947 v E, Bel, L; 1948 v Ni.
SHEARER, D. (Aberdeen) (7) 1994 v A, Holl; 1995 v Fin, Ru, Sm, Fi. 1996 v Gr.
SHEARER, R. (Rangers) (4): 1961 v E, Ei (2), Cz.
SILLARS, D. C. (Queen's Park) (5): 1891 v Ni; 1892 v E; 1893 v W; 1894 v E; 1895 v W.
SIMPSON, J. (Third Lanark) (3): 1895 v E, W, Ni.
SIMPSON, J. (Rangers) (14): 1935 v E, W, Ni; 1936 v E, W, Ni; 1937 v G, E, W, Ni, A, Cz; 1938 v W, Ni.
SIMPSON, N. (Aberdeen) (4): 1983 v Ni; 1984 v Fr; 1987 v E; 1988 v E.
SIMPSON, R. C. (Celtic) (5): 1967 v E, USSR; 1968 v Ni, E; 1969 v A.
SINCLAIR, G. L. (Hearts) (3): 1910 v Ni; 1912 v W, Ni.

SINCLAIR, J. W. E. (Leicester City) (1): 1966 v Por.
SKENE, L. H. (Queen's Park) (1): 1904 v W.
SLOAN, T. (Third Lanark) (1): 1904 v W.
SMELLIE, R. (Queen's Park) (6): 1887 v Ni; 1888 v W; 1889 v E; 1891 v E; 1893 v E, Ni.
SMITH, A. (Rangers) (20): 1898 v E; 1900 v E, Ni, W; 1901 v E, Ni, W; 1902 v E, Ni, W; 1903 v E, Ni, W; 1904 v Ni; 1905 v W; 1906 v E, Ni; 1907 v W; 1911 v E, Ni.
SMITH, D. (Aberdeen, Rangers) (2): 1966 v Holl; 1968 v Holl.
SMITH, G. (Hibernian) (18): 1947 v E, Ni; 1948 v W, Bel, Sw, Fr; 1952 v E, USA; 1955 v Por, Y, A, H; 1956 v E, Ni, W; 1957 v Sp (2), Sw.
SMITH, H. G. (Hearts) (3): 1988 v S.Ar; 1991 Ni; 1992 v Ca.
SMITH, J. (Rangers) (2): 1935 v Ni; 1938 v Ni.
SMITH, J. (Ayr United) (1): 1924 v E.
SMITH, J. (Aberdeen, Newcastle Utd.) (4): 1968 v Holl; 1974 v WG, Ni, W.
SMITH, J. E. (Celtic) (2); 1959 v H, Por.
SMITH, Jas (Queen's Park) (1): 1872 v E.
SMITH, J. (Mauchline, Edinburgh University, Queen's Park) (10): 1877 v E, W; 1879 v E, W; 1880 v E; 1881 v W, E; 1883 v E, W; 1884 v E.
SMITH, N. (Rangers) (12): 1897 v E; 1898 v W; 1899 v E, W, Ni; 1900 v E, W, Ni; 1901 v Ni, W; 1902 v E, Ni.
SMITH, R, (Queen's Park) (2): 1872 v E; 1873 v E.
SMITH, T. M. (Kilmarnock, Preston NE) (2): 1934 v E; 1938 v E.
SOMERS, P. (Celtic) (4): 1905 v E, Ni; 1907 v Ni; 1909 v W.
SOMERS, W. S. (Third Lanark, Queen's Park) (3): 1879 v E, W; 1880 v W.
SOMERVILLE, G. (Queen's Park) (1): 1886 v E.
SOUNESS, G. J. (Middlesbrough, Liverpool, Sampdoria) (54): 1975 v EG, Sp, Se; 1978 v Bul, W, E, Holl; 1979 v A. N, W, Ni, E; 1980 v Pe, A, Bel, Por, Ni; 1981 v Por, Is (2); 1982 v Ni, Por, Sp, W, E, Nz, Br, USSR; 1983 v EG, Sw (2), Bel, W, E, Ca (3); 1984 v U, Ni, W; 1985 v Y, Ice (2), Sp (2), W, E; 1986 v EG, Aus (2), R, E, D, WG.
SPEEDIE, D. R. (Chelsea, Coventry City) (10): 1985 v E; 1986 v W, EG, Aus, E; 1989 v Y, I, Cy (2), Ch.
SPEEDIE, F. (Rangers) (3): 1903 v E, W, Ni.
SPENCER, J. (Chelsea) (14): 1995 v Ru, Gr, Sm, J; 1996 v Fin, Aus, D, US, U, Holl, E, Sw; 1997 v La, W.
SPIERS, J. H. (Rangers) (1): 1908 v W.
STANTON, P. (Hibernian) (16): 1966 v Holl; 1969 v Ni; 1970 v Ei, A; 1971 v D, Bel, Por, USSR, D; 1972 v Por, Bel, Holl, W; 1973 v W, Ni; 1974 v WG.

STARK. J. (Rangers) (2): 1909 v E, Ni.
STEEL, W. (Morton, Derby County, Dundee) (30): 1947 v E, Bel, L; 1948 v Fr, E, W, Ni; 1949 v E, W, Ni, Fr; 1950 v E, W, Ni, Sw, Por, Fr; 1951 v W, Ni, E, A (2), D, Fr, Bel; 1952 v W; 1953 v W, E, Ni, Se.
STEELE, D. M. (Huddersfield) (3): 1923 v E, W, Ni.
STEIN, C. (Rangers, Coventry City) (21): 1969 v W, Ni, D, E, Cy (2); 1970 v A, Ni, W, E, Ei, WG; 1971 v D. USSR, Bel, D; 1972 v Cz; 1973 v E (2), W, Ni.
STEPHEN, J. F. (Bradford) (2): 1947 v W; 1948 v W.
STEVENSON, G. (Motherwell) (12): 1928 v W, Ni; 1930 v Ni, E, Fr; 1931 v E, W; 1932 v W, Ni; 1933 v Ni; 1934 v E; 1935 v Ni.
STEWART, A. (Queen's Park) (2): 1888 v Ni; 1889 v W.
STEWART, A. (Third Lanark) (1): 1894 v W.
STEWART, D. (Dumbarton) (1): 1888 v Ni.
STEWART, D. (Queen's Park) (3): 1893 v W; 1894 v Ni; 1897 v Ni.
STEWART, D. S. (Leeds Utd.) (1): 1978 v EG.
STEWART, G. (Hibernian, Manchester City) (4): 1906 v W, E; 1907 v E, W.
STEWART, J. (Kilmarnock, Middlesbrough) (2): 1977 v Ch; 1979 v N.
STEWART, R. (West Ham Utd.) (10): 1981 v W, Ni, E; 1982 v Ni, Por, W; 1984 v Fr; 1987 v Ei (2), L.
STEWART, W. E. (Queen's Park) (2): 1898 v Ni; 1900 v Ni.
STORRIER, D. (Celtic) (3): 1899 v E, W, Ni.
STRACHAN, G. (Aberdeen, Manchester Utd., Leeds Utd.) (50): 1980 v Ni, W, E, Pol, H; 1981 v Se, Por; 1982 v Ni, Por, Sp, Holl, Nz, Br, USSR; 1983 v EG, Sw (2), Bel, Ni, W, E, Ca (3); 1984 v EG, Ni, E, Fr; 1985 v Sp, E, Ice; 1986 v W, Aus, R, D, WG, U; 1987 v Bul, Ei (2); 1988 v H; 1989 v Fr; 1990 v Fr; 1991 v USSR, Bul, Sm; 1992 v Sw, R, Ni, Fin.
STURROCK, P. (Dundee Utd.) (20): 1981 v W, Ni, E; 1982 v Por, Ni, W, E; 1983 v EG, Sw, Bel, Ca (3); 1984 v W; 1985 v Y; 1986 v Is, Holl, D, U; 1987 v Bel.
SULLIVAN, N. (Wimbledon) (8): 1997 v W; 1998 Fr, Co. 1999 v Fi, CzR (2), G, Fi.
SUMMERS, W. (St Mirren) (1): 1926 v E.
SYMON, J. S. (Rangers) (1): 1939 v H.
TAIT, T. S. (Sunderland) (1): 1911 v W.
TAYLOR, J. (Queen's Park) (6): 1872 v E; 1873 v E; 1874 v E; 1875 v E; 1876 v E, W.
TAYLOR, J. D. (Dumbarton, St Mirren) (4): 1892 v W; 1893 v W; 1894 v Ni; 1895 v Ni.
TAYLOR, W. (Hearts) (1): 1892 v E.
TELFER, W. (Motherwell) (2): 1933 v Ni; 1934 v Ni.
TELFER, W. D. (St Mirren) (1): 1954 v W.

TEMPLETON, R. (Aston Villa, Newcastle Utd., Woolwich Arsenal, Kilmarnock) (11): 1902 v E; 1903 v E, W; 1904 v E; 1905 v W; 1908 v Ni; 1910 v E, Ni; 1912 v E, Ni; 1913 v W.
THOMSON, A. (Arthurlie) (1): 1886 v Ni.
THOMSON, A. (Third Lanark) (1): 1889 v W.
THOMSON, A. (Airdrie) (1): 1909 v Ni.
THOMSON, A. (Celtic) (3): 1926 v E; 1932 v Fr; 1933 v W.
THOMSON, C. (Hearts, Sunderland) (21): 1904 v Ni; 1905 v E, Ni, W; 1906 v W, Ni; 1907 v E, W, Ni; 1908 v E, W, Ni; 1909 v W; 1910 v E; 1911 v Ni; 1912 v E, W; 1913 v E, W; 1914 v E, Ni.
THOMSON, C. (Sunderland) (1): 1937 v Cz.
THOMSON, D. (Dundee) (1): 1920 v W.
THOMSON, J. (Celtic) (4): 1930 v Fr; 1931 v E, W, Ni.
THOMSON, J. J. (Queen's Park) (3): 1872 v E; 1873 v E; 1874 v E.
THOMSON, J. R. (Everton) (1): 1933 v W.
THOMSON, R. (Celtic) (1): 1932 v W.
THOMSON, R. W. (Falkirk) (1): 1927 v E.
THOMSON, S. (Rangers) (2): 1884 v W, Ni.
THOMSON, W. (Dumbarton) (4): 1892 v W; 1893 v W; 1898 v Ni, W.
THOMSON, W. (Dundee) (1): 1896 v W.
THOMSON, W. (St Mirren) (7): 1980 v Ni; 1981 v Ni (2); 1982 v Por; 1983 v Ni, Ca; 1984 v EG.
THORNTON, W. (Rangers) (7): 1947 v W, Ni; 1948 v E, Ni; 1949 v Fr; 1952 v D, Se.
TONER, W. (Kilmarnock) (2): 1959 v W, Ni.
TOWNSLEY, T. (Falkirk) (1926 v W.
TROUP, A. (Dundee, Everton) (5): 1920 v E; 1921 v W, Ni; 1922 v Ni; 1926 v E.
TURNBULL, E. F. (Hibernian) (8): 1948 v Bel, Sw; 1951 v A; 1958 v H, Pol, Y, Par, Fr.
TURNER, T. (Arthurlie) (1): 1884 v W.
TURNER, W. (Pollokshields Ath.) (2): 1885 v Ni; 1886 v Ni.
URE, J. F. (Dundee, Arsenal) (11): 1962 v W, Cz; 1963 v W, Ni, E, A, N, Sp; 1964 v Ni, N; 1968 v Ni.
URQUHART, D. (Hibernian) (1): 1934 v W.
VALLANCE, T. (Rangers) (7): 1877 v E, W; 1878 v E; 1879 v E, W; 1881 v E, W.
VENTERS, A. (Cowdenbeath, Rangers) (3): 1934 v Ni; 1936 v E; 1939 v E.
WADDELL, T. S. (Queen's Park) (6): 1891 v Ni; 1892 v E; 1893 v E, Ni; 1895 v E, Ni.

WADDELL, W. (Rangers) (17): 1947 v W; 1949 v E, W, Ni, Fr; 1950 v E, Ni; 1951 v E, D, Fr, Bel, A; 1952 v Ni, W; 1954 v Ni; 1955 v W, Ni.
WALES, H. M. (Motherwell) (1): 1933 v W.
WALKER, A. (Celtic) (3): 1988 v Co; 1995 v Fin, Fi.
WALKER, F. (Third Lanark) (1): 1922 v W.
WALKER, G. (St Mirren) (4): 1930 v Fr; 1931 v Ni, A, Sw.
WALKER, J. (Hearts, Rangers) (5): 1895 v Ni; 1897 v W; 1898 v Ni; 1904 v W, Ni.
WALKER, J. (Swindon T.) (9): 1911 v E, W, Ni; 1912 v E, W, Ni; 1913 v E, W, Ni.
WALKER, N. (Hearts) (2): 1993 v G, 1996 US.
WALKER, R. (Hearts) (29): 1900 v E, Ni; 1901 v E, W; 1902 v E, W, Ni; 1903 v E, W, Ni; 1904 v E, W, Ni; 1905 v E, W, Ni; 1906 v Ni; 1907 v E, Ni; 1908 v E, W, Ni; 1909 v E, W; 1912 v E, W, Ni; 1913 v E, W.
WALKER, T. (Hearts) (20): 1935 v E, W; 1936 v E, W, Ni; 1937 v G, E, W, Ni, A, Cz; 1938 v E, W, Ni, Cz, Holl; 1939 v E, W, Ni, H.
WALKER, W. (Clyde) (2): 1909 v Ni; 1910 v Ni.
WALLACE, I. A. (Coventry City) (3): 1978 v Bul; 1979 v Por, W.
WALLACE, W. S. B. (Hearts, Celtic) (7): 1965 v Ni; 1966 v E, Holl; 1967 v E, USSR; 1968 v Ni; 1969 v E.
WARDHAUGH, J. (Hearts) (2): 1955 v H; 1957 v Ni.
WARK, J. (Ipswich Town, Liverpool) (29): 1979 v W, Ni, E, Arg, N; 1980 v Pe, A, Bel (2); 1981 v Is, Ni; 1982 v Se, Sp, Holl, Ni, Nz, Br, USSR; 1983 v EG, Sw (2), Ni, E; 1984 v U, Bel, EG, E, Fr; 1985 v Y.
WATSON, A. (Queen's Park) (3): 1881 v E, W; 1882 v E.
WATSON, J. (Sunderland, Middlesbrough) (6): 1903 v E, W; 1904 v E; 1905 v E; 1909 v E, Ni.
WATSON, J. (Motherwell, Huddersfield Town) (2): 1948 v Ni; 1954 v Ni.
WATSON, J. A. K. (Rangers) (1878 v W.
WATSON, P. R. (Blackpool) (1): 1934 v A.
WATSON, R. (Motherwell) (1): 1971 v USSR.
WATSON, W. (Falkirk) (1): 1898 v W.
WATT, F. (Kilbirnie) (4): 1889 v W, Ni; 1890 v W; 1891 v E.
WATT, W. W. (Queen's Park) (1): 1887 v Ni.
WAUGH, W. (Hearts) (1): 1938 v Cz.
WEIR, A. (Motherwell) (6): 1959 v WG; 1960 v E, Por, A, H, T.
WEIR, D. (Hearts, Everton) (12): 1997 v W; 1998 Fr, D, Fin, N, M. 1999 v Est. Fi, CzR (2), G, Fi.
WEIR, J. (Third Lanark) (1): 1887 v Ni.
WEIR, J. B. (Queen's Park) (4): 1872 v E; 1874 v E; 1875 v E; 1878 v W.

WEIR, P. (St Mirren, Aberdeen) (6): 1980 v N, W, Pol, H; 1983 v Sw; 1984 v Ni.
WHITE, J. (Albion Rovers, Hearts) (2): 1922 v W; 1923 v Ni.
WHITE, J. A. (Falkirk, Tottenham H.) (22): 1959 v WG, Holl, Por; 1960 v Ni, W, Pol, A, T; 1961 v W; 1962 v Ni, W, E, Cz (2); 1963 v W, Ni, E; 1964 v Ni, W, E, N, WG.
WHITE, W. (Bolton W.) (2): 1907 v E; 1908 v E.
WHITELAW, A. (Vale of Leven) (2): 1887 v Ni; 1890 v W.
WHYTE, D. (Celtic, Middlesbrough, Aberdeen) (12): 1988 v Bel, L; 1989 v Ch; 1992 v US; 1993 v Por, I; 1995 v J, Ec, US; 1997 v La; 1998 v Fin: 1999 v G.
WILSON, A. (Sheffield W.) (6): 1907 v E; 1908 v E; 1912 v I; 1913 v E, W; 1914 v Ni.
WILSON, A. (Portsmouth) (1): 1954 v Fin.
WILSON, A. N. (Dunfermline, Middlesbrough) (12): 1920 v E, W, Ni; 1921 v E, W, Ni; 1922 v E, W, Ni; 1923 v E, W, Ni.
WILSON, D. (Queen's Park) (1): 1900 v W.
WILSON, D. (Oldham) (1): 1913 v E.
WILSON, D. (Rangers) (22): 1961 v E, W, Ni, Ei (2), Cz; 1962 v Ni, W, E, Cz, U; 1963 v W, E, A, N, Ei, Sp; 1964 v E, WG; 1965 v Ni, E, Fin.
WILSON, G. W. (Hearts, Everton, Newcastle Utd.) (6): 1904 v W; 1905 v E, Ni; 1906 v W; 1907 v E; 1909 v E.
WILSON, H. (Newmilns, Sunderland, Third Lanark) (4): 1890 v W; 1897 v E; 1902 v W; 1904 v Ni.
WILSON, I. A. (Leicester City, Everton) (5): 1987 v E, Br; 1988 v Bel, Bul, L.
WILSON, J. (Vale of Leven) (4): 1888 v W; 1889 v E; 1890 v E; 1891 v E.
WILSON, P. (Celtic) (4): 1926 v Ni; 1930 v Fr; 1931 v Ni; 1933 v E.
WILSON, P. (Celtic) (1): 1975 v Sp.
WILSON, R. P. (Arsenal) (2): 1972 v Por, Holl.
WINTERS, R. (Aberdeen) (1): 1999 v G.
WISEMAN, W. (Queen's Park) (2): 1927 v W; 1930 v Ni.
WOOD, G. (Everton, Arsenal) (4): 1979 v Ni, E, Arg; 1982 v Ni.
WOODBURN, W. A. (Rangers) (24): 1947 v E, Bel, L; 1948 v W, Ni; 1949 v E, Fr; 1950 v E, W, Ni, Por, Fr; 1951 v E, W, Ni, A (2), D, Fr, Bel; 1952 v E, W, Ni, USA.
WOTHERSPOON, D. N. (Queen's Park) (2): 1872 v E; 1873 v E.
WRIGHT, K. (Hibs) (1): 1992 v Ni.
WRIGHT, S. (Aberdeen) (2): 1993 v G, Est.
WRIGHT, T. (Sunderland) (3): 1953 v W, Ni, E.
WYLIE, T. G. (Rangers) (1): 1890 v Ni.
YEATS, R. (Liverpool) (2): 1965 v W; 1966 v I.
YORSTON, B. C. (Aberdeen) (1): 1931 v Ni.
YORSTON, H. (Aberdeen) (1): 1955 v W.

YOUNG, A. (Hearts, Everton) (8): 1960 v E, A, H, T; 1961 v W, Ni, Ei; 1966 v Por.

YOUNG, A. (Everton) (2): 1905 v E; 1907 v W.

YOUNG, G. A. (Rangers) (53): 1947 v E, Ni, Bel, L; 1948 v E, Ni, Bel, Sw, Fr; 1949 v E, W, Ni, Fr; 1950 v E, W, Ni, Sw, Por, Fr; 1951 v E, W, Ni, A (2), D, Fr, Bel; 1952 v E, W, Ni, USA, D, Se; 1953 v W, E, Ni, Se; 1954 v Ni, W; 1955 v W, Ni, Por, Y; 1956 v Ni, W, E, A; 1957 v E, Ni, W, Y, Sp, Sw.

YOUNG, J. (Celtic) (1): 1906 v Ni.

YOUNGER, T. (Hibernian, Liverpool) (24): 1955 v Por, Y, A, H; 1956 v E, Ni, W, A: 1957 v E, Ni, W, Y, Sp (2), Sw, WG; 1958 v Ni, W, E, Sw, H, Pol, Y, Par.

TOMMY YOUNGER . . . won 24 caps for Scotland

THE Bearsden Academy Under-18s show off the Scottish Secondary Shield

WORLD CUP FINALS

Year	Winners		Runners-up		Venue
1930	URUGUAY	4	Argentina	2	Uruguay
1934	ITALY	2	Czechosl'kia	1	Italy, aet
1938	ITALY	4	Hungary	2	France
1950	URUGUAY	2	Brazil	1	Brazil
1954	W GERMANY	3	Hungary	2	Switzerland
1958	BRAZIL	5	Sweden	2	Sweden
1962	BRAZIL	3	Czechosl'kia	1	Chile
1966	ENGLAND	4	W Germany	2	Wembley, aet
1970	BRAZIL	4	Italy	1	Mexico
1974	W GERMANY	2	Holland	1	W Germany
1978	ARGENTINA	3	Holland	1	Argentina, aet
1982	ITALY	3	W Germany	1	Spain
1986	ARGENTINA	3	W Germany	2	Mexico
1990	W GERMANY	1	Argentina	0	Italy
1994	BRAZIL	0	Italy	0	America
	(After extra time) Brazil won 3-2 on penalties				
1998	FRANCE	3	Brazil	0	France

EUROPEAN CHAMPIONSHIPS

Year	Winners		Runners-up		
1960	RUSSIA	2	Yugoslavia	1	France
1964	SPAIN	2	Russia	1	Spain
1968	ITALY	2	Yugoslavia	0	Italy
	(aet in replay after 1-1 draw)				
1972	W GERMANY	3	Russia	0	Belgium
1976	CZECH	2	W Germany	2	Yugoslavia
	(Czechs won 5-3 on penalties)				
1980	W GERMANY	2	Belgium	1	Italt
1984	FRANCE	2	Spain	0	France
1988	HOLLAND	2	Russia	0	West Germany
1992	DENMARK	2	Germany	0	Sweden
1996	GERMANY	2	Czech Rep	1	Wembley
	(1-1 full time. Germany scored Golden Goal in extra time)				

EUROPEAN SUPER CUP

Played annually between the winners of the European Champions Cup and the European Cup-winners' Cup

1972	AJAX	3	Rangers	1
	Rangers	2	AJAX	3
1973	AC Milan	0	AJAX	1
	AJAX	6	AC Milan	0
	1974 – Not contested			
1975	Bayern Munich	0	DYNAMO KIEV	1
	DYNAMO KIEV	2	Bayern Munich	0
1976	Bayern Munich	2	ANDERLECHT	1
	ANDERLECHT	4	Bayern Munich	1
1977	Hamburg	1	LIVERPOOL	1
	LIVERPOOL	6	Hamburg	0
1978	ANDERLECHT	3	Liverpool	1
	Liverpool	2	ANDERLECHT	1
1979	NOTTS FOREST	1	Barcelona	0
	Barcelona	1	NOTTS FOREST	1
1980	Nottingham Forest	2	VALENCIA	1
	VALENCIA	1	Nottingham Forest	0
	1981 – Not contested			
1982	Barcelona	1	ASTON VILLA	0
	ASTON VILLA	3	Barcelona	0
1983	Hamburg	0	ABERDEEN	0
	ABERDEEN	2	Hamburg	0
1984	JUVENTUS	2	Liverpool	0
	1985 Juventus v Everton not played due to UEFA ban on English clubs			
1986	ST BUCHAREST	1	Dynamo Kiev	0
1987	Ajax	0	FC PORTO	1
	FC PORTO	1	Ajax	0
1988	MECHELEN	3	PSV Eindhoven	0
	PSV Eindhoven	1	MECHELEN	0
1989	Barcelona	1	AC MILAN	1
	AC MILAN	1	Barcelona	0
1990	Sampdoria	1	AC MILAN	1
	AC MILAN	2	Sampdoria	0
1991	MANCHESTER UTD	1	Red Star Belgrade	0
1992	Werder Bremen	1	BARCELONA	1
	BARCELONA	2	Werder Bremen	1
1993	PARMA	0	AC Milan	1
	AC Milan	0	PARMA	2
	(aet, 90 min. 0-1, agg.1-2 for Parma)			
1994	Arsenal	0	AC MILAN	0
	AC MILAN	2	Arsenal	0
1995	Real Zaragoza	1	AJAX	1
	AJAX	4	Real Zaragoza	0
1996	Paris St Germain	0	JUVENTUS	1
	JUVENTUS	6	Paris St Germain	1
1997	BARCELONA	0	Borussia Dortmund	0
	Borussia Dortmund	1	BARCELONA	1
1998	Real Madrid	0	CHELSEA	1

EUROPEAN CUP FINALS

Year	Winners		Runners-up	
1956	REAL MADRID	4	Rheims	3
	(Paris, 38,000)			
1957	REAL MADRID	2	Fiorentina	0
	(Madrid, 124,000)			
1958	REAL MADRID	3	AC Milan	2
	After extra time (Brussels, 67,000)			
1959	REAL MADRID	2	Rheims	0
	(Stuttgart, 80,000)			
1960	REAL MADRID	7	Eintracht	3
	(Glasgow, 127,261)			
1961	BENFICA	3	Barcelona	2
	(Berne, 28,000)			
1962	BENFICA	5	Real Madrid	3
	(Amsterdam, 65,000)			
1963	AC MILAN	2	Benfica	1
	(Wembley, 45,000)			
1964	INTER MILAN	3	Real Madrid	1
	(Vienna, 74,000)			
1965	INTER MILAN	1	Benfica	0
	(Milan, 80,000)			
1966	REAL MADRID	2	Partisan Belgrade	1
	(Brussels, 55,000)			
1967	CELTIC	2	Inter Milan	1
	(Lisbon, 56,000)			
1968	MAN UNITED	4	Benfica	1
	(Wembley, 100,000)			
1969	AC MILAN	4	Ajax	1
	(Madrid, 50,000)			
1970	FEYENOORD	2	Celtic	1
	(Milan, 50,000)			
1971	AJAX	2	Panathinaikos	0
	(Wembey, 90,000)			
1972	AJAX	2	Inter Milan	0
	(Rotterdam, 67,000)			
1973	AJAX	1	Juventus	0
	(Belgrade, 93,500)			
1974	BAYERN MUNICH	4	Atletico Madrid	0
	(Brussels, 65,000) (after 1-1 draw			
1975	BAYERN MUNICH	2	Leeds	0
	(Paris, 50,000)			
1976	BAYERN MUNICH	1	St Etienne	0
	(Glasgow, 54,864)			
1977	LIVERPOOL	3	Borussia MG	1
	(Rome, 57,000)			
1978	LIVERPOOL	1	Bruges	0
	(Wembley, 92,000)			

1979	NOTTS FOREST 1	Malmo 0	
	(Munich, 57,500)		
1980	NOTTS FOREST 1	Hamburg 0	
	(Madrid, 50,000)		
1981	LIVERPOOL...............1	Real Madrid 0	
	(Paris, 48,360)		
1982	ASTON VILLA............1	Bayern Munich................0	
	(Rotterdam, 46,000)		
1983	HAMBURG.................1	Juventus 0	
	(Athens, 75,000)		
1984	LIVERPOOL...............1	Roma 1	
	(Rome, 69,693) Liverpool won 4-2 on penalties		
1985	JUVENTUS.................1	Liverpool 0	
	(Brussels, 58,000)		
1986	STEAU BUCHAREST .0	Barcelona........................0	
	Steau Bucharest won 2-0 on penalties (Seveille, 70,000)		
1987	PORTO........................2	Bayern Munich................1	
	(Vienna, 59,000)		
1988	PSV 0	Benfica 0	
	(Stuttgart, 70,000) PSV Eindhoven won 6-5 on penalties		
1989	AC MILAN 4	Steau Bucharest 0	
	(Barcelona, 97,000)		
1990	AC MILAN 1	Benfica 0	
	(Vienna, 57,500)		
1991	R.S. BELGRADE 0	Marseille.........................0	
	(Bari, 56,000) Red Star won 5-3 on penalties		
1992	BARCELONA 1	Sampdoria 0	
	After extra time (Wembley, 70,000)		
1993	MARSEILLE...............1	AC Milan 0	
	(Munich, 65,000)		
1994	AC MILAN 4	Barcelona........................0	
	(Athens, 75,000)		
1995	AJAX 1	AC Milan 0	
	(Vienna, 49,000)		
1996	JUVENTUS.................1	Ajax 1	
	(Rome, 67,000) Juventus won 4-2 on penalties		
1997	B DORTMUND 3	Juventus 1	
	(Munich, 55,500)		
1998	REAL MADRID 1	Juventus 0	
	(Amsterdam, 45,000)		
1999	MANCHESTER UTD ..2	Bayern Munich...............1	
	(Barcelona, 90,000)		

EUROPEAN CUP-WINNERS CUP FINALS

1961	Rangers 0	FIORENTINA	2
	(Ibrox, 80,000)		
	FIORENTINA. 2	Rangers	1
	(Florence, 50,000)		
	Aggregate 4-1		
1962	ATLETICO MADRID . 1	Fiorentina	1
	(Glasgow, 27,389)		
	ATLETICO MADRID . 3	Fiorentina	0
	(Stuttgart, 45,000)		
1963	SPURS 5	Atletico Madrid	1
	(Rotterdam, 25,000)		
1964	SPORTING LISBON . 1	MTK Budapest	0
	(Antwerp, 18,000)		
	After 3-3 draw in Brussels		
1965	WEST HAM 2	Munich 1860	0
	(Wembley, 100,000)		
1966	BOR. DORTMUND. 2	Liverpool	1
	(Hampden, 41,657)		
1967	BAYERN MUNICH . . 1	Rangers	0
	(Nuremberg, 69,480 aet)		
1968	AC MILAN 2	S.V. Hamburg	0
	(Rotterdam, 60,000)		
1969	S BRATISLAVIA. . . . 3	Barcelona	2
	(Basle, 40,000)		
1970	MANCHESTER CITY 2	Gornik	1
	(Vienna, 10,000)		
1971	CHELSEA. 2	Real Madrid	1
	(Athens, 24,000, after 1-1 draw)		
1972	RANGERS. 3	Moscow Dynamo	2
	(Barcelona, 35,000)		
1973	AC MILAN. 1	Leeds United	0
	(Salonika, 45,000)		
1974	AC MAGDEBURG. . . 2	AC Milan	0
	(Rotterdam, 5,000)		
1975	DYNAMO KIEV 3	Ferencvaros	0
	(Basle, 13,000)		
1976	ANDERLECHT 4	West Ham	2
	(Brussels, 58,000)		
1977	SV HAMBURG 2	Anderlecht	0
	(Amsterdam, 65,000)		
1978	ANDERLECHT 4	Austria Wein	0
	(Amsterdam, 48,679)		
1979	BARCELONA 4	Fortuna Dusseldorf	3
	(Basle, 58,000)		
1980	VALENCIA. 0	Arsenal	0
	(Brussels, 40,000, Valencia won 5-4 on penalties)		

1981 DYNAMO TBILISI . . . 2 Carl Zeiss Jena 1
(Dusseldorf, 9,000)
1982 BARCELONA . . . . . . 2 Standard Liege..................1
(Barcelona, 100,000)
1983 ABERDEEN. . . . . 2 Real Madrid.......................1
(Gothenburg, 17,804)
1984 JUVENTUS . . . . 2 FC Porto............................1
(Basle, 60,000)
1985 EVERTON . . . . 3 Vienna Rapide...................1
(Rotterdam, 30,000)
1986 DYNAMO KIEV . . . . . 3 Atletico Madrid.................0.
(Lyon, 39,300)
1987 AJAX. . . . . 1 Lokomotiv Leipzig.............0
(Athens, 35,000)
1988 MICHELEN . . . . 1 Ajax..................................0
(Strasbourg, 39,446)
1989 BARCELONA . . . . . . 2 Sampdoria 0
(Berne, 45,000)
1990 SAMPDORIA. . . . . . . 2 Anderlecht.........................0
(Gothenburg, 20,103)
1991 MANCHESTER UTD . 2 Barcelona..........................1
(Rotterdam, 50,000)
1992 WERDER BREMEN. . 2 Monaco 0
(Lisbon, 50,000)
1993 Antwerp . . . . 1 PARMA..............................3
(Wembley, 50,000)
1994 Parma . . . . 0 ARSENAL..........................1
(Copenhagen, 33,765)
1995 Arsenal . . . . 1 REAL SARAGOZA.............2
(aet, 90 minutes 1-1)(Paris, 42,000)
1996 PARIS ST GERMAIN . 1 Rapid Vienna.....................0
(Brussels, 50,000)
1997 BARCELONA . . . . . . 1 Paris St Germain...............0
(Rotterdam, 40,000)
1998 CHELSEA . . . . 1 VfB Stuttgart 0
(Stockholm)
1999 LAZIO . . . . 2 Real Mallorca 1
Villa Park, 30,000

UEFA CUP FINALS

(FORMERLY FAIR CITIES CUP)

1958	London	2	BARCELONA	2
	BARCELONA	6	London	0
	(agg: 8-2)			
1960	Birmingham	0	BARCELONA	0
	BARCELONA	4	Birmingham	1
	(agg: 4-1)			
1961	Birmingham	2	ROMA	2
	ROMA	2	Birmingham	0
	(agg: 4-2)			
1962	VALENCIA	6	Barcelona	2
	Barcelona	1	VALENCIA	1
	(agg 7-3)			
1963	Dynamo Zagreb	1	VALENCIA	2
	VALENCIA	2	Dynamo Zagreb	0
	(agg: 4-1)			
1964	REAL ZARAGOSSA	2	Valencia	1
	(Barcelona)			
1965	FERENCVAROS	1	Juventus	0
	(Turin)			
1966	BARCELONA	0	Real Zaragossa	1
	Real Zaragossa	2	BARCELONA	4
	(agg: 4-3)			
1967	DINAMO ZAGREB	2	Leeds United	0
	Leeds United	0	DINAMO ZAGREB	0
	(agg: 2-0)			
1968	LEEDS UNITED	1	Ferencvaros	0
	Ferencvaros	0	LEEDS UNITED	0
	(agg: 1-0)			
1969	NEWCASTLE UTD	3	Ujpest Dozsa	0
	Ujpest Dozsa	2	NEWCASTLE UTD	3
	(agg: 6-2)			
1970	Anderlecht	3	ARSENAL	1
	ARSENAL	3	Anderlecht	0
	(agg: 4-3)			
1971	Juventus	2	LEEDS UNITED	2
	LEEDS UNITED	1	Juventus	1
	(agg: 3-3)			
	Leeds won on away goals			
1972	Wolves	1	TOTTENHAM	2
	TOTTENHAM	1	Wolves	1
	(agg: 3-2)			
1973	LIVERPOOL	3	Borussia M	0
	Borussia M	2	LIVERPOOL	0
	(agg: 3-2)			

1974	Tottenham Hostpur	2	FEYENOORD	2
	FEYENOORD	2	Tottenham Hotspur	0
		(agg: 4-2)		
1975	BORUSSIA M	0	Twente	0
	Twente	1	BORUSSIA M	5
		(agg: 5-1)		
1976	LIVERPOOL	3	FC Bruges	2
	Bruges	1	LIVERPOOL	1
		(agg 4-3)		
1977	JUVENTUS	1	Athletic Bilbao	0
	Athletic Bilbao	2	JUVENTUS	1
		(agg: 2-2)		
		Juventus won on away goals		
1978	Bastia	0	PSV EINDHOVEN	0
	PSV EINDHOVEN	3	Bastia	0
		(agg: 3-0)		
1979	Red Star Belgrade	1	BORUSSIA M	1
	BORUSSIA M	1	Red Star Belgrade	0
		(agg: 2-1)		
1980	Borussia M	3	EINTRACHT	2
	EINTRACHT	1	Borussia M	0
		(agg: 3-3)		
		Eintracht won on away goals		
1981	IPSWICH	3	AZ 67	0
	AZ 67	4	IPSWICH	2
		(agg: 5-4)		
1982	GOTHENBURG	1	Hamburg	0
	Hamburg	0	GOTHENBURG	3
		(agg: 4-0)		
1983	ANDERLECHT	1	Benfica	0
	Benfica	1	ANDERLECHT	1
		(agg: 2-1)		
1984	Anderlecht	1	TOTTENHAM	1
	TOTTENHAM	1	Anderlecht	1
		(agg: 2-2)		
		Tottenham won 4-3 on penalties		
1985	Videoton	0	REAL MADRID	3
	REAL MADRID	0	Videoton	1
		(agg: 3-1)		
1986	REAL MADRID	5	Cologne	1
	Cologne	2	REAL MADRID	0
		(agg: 5-3)		
1987	GOTHENBURG	1	Dundee United	0
	Dundee United	1	GOTHENBURG	1
		(agg: 2-1)		

1988	Espanol	3	BAYER LEVERKUSEN	0
	BAYER LEVERKUSEN	3	Espanol	0
	(agg: 3-3)			
	Leverkusen won 3-2 on penalties)			
1989	NAPOLI	2	Stuttgart	1
	Stuttgart	3	NAPOLI	3
	(agg: 5-4)			
1990	JUVENTUS	3	Fiorentina	1
	Fiorentina	0	JUVENTUS	0
	(agg: 3-1)			
1991	INTER MILAN	2	Roma	0
	Roma	1	INTER MILAN	0
	(agg: 2-1)			
1992	Torino	2	AJAX	2
	AJAX	0	Torino	0
	(Ajax win on away goals rule)			
1993	Borussia Dortmund	1	JUVENTUS	3
	JUVENTUS	3	Borussia Dortmund	0
	(agg: 6-1)			
1994	Salsburg	0	INTER MILAN	1
	INTER MILAN	1	Salsburg	0
	(agg 2-0)			
1995	PARMA	1	Juventus	0
	Juventus	1	PARMA	1
	(agg 2-1)			
1996	BAYERN M.	2	Bordeaux	0
	Bordeaux	1	BAYERN M	3
	(agg 5-1)			
1997	Schalke	1	INTER MILAN	0
	INTER MILAN	1	Schalke	0
	(Schalke win 4-1 on penalties)			
1998	INTER MILAN	3	Lazio	0
	(Paris)			
1999	Parma	3	Marseille	0
	(Moscow)			

JUAN VERON . . . the Argentinian played a major role for Parma

SCOTTISH JUNIOR CUP

1886-87	Fairfield (Govan) . . 3	Edin Woodburn 1
	(After protest)	
1887-88	Wishaw Thistle . . . 3	Maryhill 1
1888-89	Burnbank Swifts . . 4	W Benhar Violet 1
1889-90	Burnbank Swifts . . 3	Benburb 1 . . . .
	(After protest)	
1890-91	Vale of Clyde 2	Chryston Ath. 0
	(After a draw)	
1891-92	Minerva 5	W Benhar Violet 2
1892-93	Vale of Clyde 3	Dumbarton Fern 2
	(After a draw)	
1893-94	Ashfield 3	Renfrew V 0
1894-95	Ashfield 2	West Calder Wan. 1
	(After a draw)	
1895-96	Cambuslang Hibs . 3	Parkhead 1
1896-97	Strathclyde 2	Dunfermline Jun. 0
	(After protest)	
1897-98	Dalziel Rovers 2	Parkhead 1
1898-99	Parkhead 4	Westmarch XI 1
1899-00	Maryhill 3	Rugby XI 2
1900-01	Burnbank Ath. 2	Maryhill 0
1901-02	Glencairn 1	Maryhill 0
	(After a draw)	
1902-03	Parkhead 3	Larkhall Th. 0
1903-04	Vale of Clyde 3	Parkhead 0
1904-05	Ashfield 2	Renfrew Vic. 1
1905-06	Dunipace Jun. 1	Rob Roy 0
	(After a draw)	
1906-07	Strathclyde 1	Maryhill XI 0
	(After two draws)	
1907-08	Larkhall Th. 1	Q.P. Hampden XI 0
1908-09	Kilwinning R. 1	Strathclyde 0
	(After a draw)	
1909-10	Ashfield 3	Kilwinning R. 0
	(After protest)	
1910-11	Burnbank Ath. 1	Petershill 0
	(After a draw)	
1911-12	Petershill 5	Denny Hibs 0

1912-13 Inverkeithing Un. . . 1 . . . Dunipace Jun 0
1913-14 Larkhall Th. . . . . . . 1 . . . Ashfield 0
(After two draws)
1914-15 Parkhead . . . . 2 . . . Port Glasgow Ath. . . . 0
1915-16 Petershill. . . . . 2 . . . Parkhead 0
1916-17 St Mirren Jun. . . . . 1 . . . Renfrew Jun. 0
(After a draw)
1917-18 Petershill awarded cup, no final tie.. . . . .
1918-19 Glencairn . . . . 1 . . . St Anthony's 0
(After a draw)
1919-20 Parkhead . . . . 2 . . . Cambuslang R.. 0
1920-21 Rob Roy . . . . 1 . . . Ashfield 0
1921-22 St Roch's . . . . 2 . . . Kilwinning R.. 1
(After protest)
1922-23 Musselb'gh Bruntonian 2 . . . Arniston R. 0
1923-24 Parkhead . . . . 3 . . . Baillieston Jun. 1
(After a draw)
1924-25 Saltcoats Vics . . . 2 . . . St Anthony's 1
(After two draws)
1925-26 Strathclyde . . . . . . 2 . . . Bridgeton Wav. 0
(After a draw)
1926-27 Glencairn . . . . 2 . . . Cambuslang R. 1
1927-28 Maryhill Hibs . . . . . 6 . . . Burnbank Ath. 2
1928-29 Dundee Violet . . . . 4 . . . Denny Hibs. 0
1929-30 Newtongrange Star 3 . . . Hall Russell's 0
1930-31 Denny Hibs . . . . . . 1 . . . Burnbank Ath. 0
(Replay ordered, Denny failed to appear)
1931-32 Perthshire . . . . 2 . . . Rob Roy 1
1932-33 Yoker Ath . . . . 4 . . . Tranent Jun. 2
(After a draw)
1933-34 Benburb . . . . 3 . . . Bridgeton Wav. 1
1934-35 Tranent . . . . 6 . . . Petershill. 1
1935-36 Benburb . . . . 1 . . . Yoker Ath. 0
(After a draw)
1936-37 Arthurlie . . . . 5 . . . Rob Roy 1
1937-38 Cambuslang R. . . . 3 . . . Benburb 2
1938-39 Glencairn . . . . 2 . . . Shawfield 1
1939-40 Maryhill . . . . 1 . . . Morton Jun. 0
1940-41 Perthshire . . . . 3 . . . Armadale Th. 1
(After two draws)
1941-42 Clydebank . . . . 4 . . . Vale of Clyde 2
1942-43 Rob Roy . . . . 3 . . . Benburb 1
(After two draws)
1943-44 Perthshire . . . . 1 . . . Blantyre Vics. 0

1944-45	Burnbank Ath. 3	Cambuslang R.. 1
	(After protest)	
1945-46	Fauldhouse Un. . .2	Arthurlie 0
1946-47	Shawfield 2	Bo'ness Un. 1
	(After a draw)	
1947-48	Bo'ness Un. 2	Irvine Meadow 1
1948-49	Auchinleck Talbot .3	Petershill. 2
1949-50	Blantyre Vics 3	Cumnock 0
1950-51	Petershill 1	Irvine Meadow 0
1951-52	Kilbirnie Ladeside .1	Camelon. 0
1952-53	Vale of Leven 1	Annbank Un 0
1953-54	Sunnybank 2	Lochee Harp. 1
1954-55	Kilsyth R. 4	Duntocher Hibs 1
	(After a draw)	
1955-56	Petershill 4	Lugar Boswell Th.. . . .1
1956-57	A'deen Bnks o' Dee 1	Kilsyth R. 0
1957-58	Shotts Bon Accord 2	Pumpherston 0
1958-59	Irvine Meadow . . .2	Shettleston 1
1959-60	St Andrew's 3	Greenock 1
1960-61	Dunbar United . . .2	Cambuslang R.. 0
	(After a draw)	
1961-62	Rob Roy 1	Renfrew 0
	(After a draw)	
1962-63	Irvine Meadow . . .2	Glenafton Ath. 1
1963-64	Johnstone Burgh .3	Cambuslang R.. 0
	(After a draw)	
1964-65	Linlithgow Rose . .4	Baillieston. 1
1965-66	Bonnyrigg Rose . .6	Whitburn. 1
	(After a draw)	
1966-67	Kilsyth R. 3	Glencairn 1
	(After a draw)	
1967-68	Johnstone Burgh .4	Glenrothes 3
	(After a draw)	
1968-69	Cambuslang R. . . .1	Rob Roy 0
1969-70	Blantyre Vics 1	Penicuick Ath. 0
	(After a draw)	
1970-71	Cambuslang R. . . .2	Newtongrange Star . . 1
1971-72	Cambuslang R. . . .3	Bonnyrigg Rose 2
	(After 1-1 draw)	
1972-73	Irvine Meadow . . .1	Cambuslang R.. 0
	(After two draws)	
1973-74	Cambuslang R. . . .3	Linlithgow Rose 1
1974-75	Glenrothes 1	Glencairn 0
1975-76	Bo'ness Un. 3	Darvel. 0
1976-77	Kilbirnie Ladeside .3	Rob Roy 1

1977-78	Bonnyrigg Rose 1	Stonehouse Violet...........0
1978-79	Cumnock 1	Bo'ness Un. 0
1979-80	Baillieston 2	Benburb 0
	(After a draw)	
1980-81	Pollok 1	Arthurlie 0
1981-82	Baillieston 0	Blantyre Vics 1
1982-83	East Kilbride Th. . . .2	Bo'ness Un. 0
1983-84	Baillieston 0	Bo'ness United 2
1984-85	Pollok 3	Petershill 1
	(After 1-1 draw)	
1985-86	Auchinleck Talbot . .3	Pollok..............................2
1986-87	Auchinleck Talbot . .1	Kilbirnie Ladeside 0
	(After 1-1 draw)	
1987-88	Auchinleck Talbot . .1	Petershill 0
1988-89	Cumnock 1	Ormiston Primrose..........0
1989-90	Hill o' Beath 1	Lesmahagow 0
1990-91	Auchinleck Talbot . .1	Newtongrange Star.........0
1991-92	Auchinleck Talbot . .4	Glenafton 0
1992-93	Glenafton 1	Tayport............................0
1993-94	Largs Thistle 1	Glenafton 0
1994-95	Camelon 2	Whitburn 0
1995-96	Camelon 0	Tayport............................2
	(After 0-0 draw)	
1996-97	Pollok 3	Tayport............................1
1997-98	Arthurlie 4	Pollok..............................0
1998-99	Kilwinning Rangers .1	Kelty Hearts 0

BOBBY DICKSON . . . led Kilwinning to an OVD Scottish Junior Cup triumph

EVENING TIMES CUP-WINNERS' CUP

(Formerly Central League Championship)

1931-32	SHAWFIELD 5	YOKER ATH 2
1932-33	PETERSHILL 3	STRATHCLYDE 1
1933-34	GLENCAIRN 2	YOKER ATH 1
1934-35	CLYDEBANK (74 points for 50 games)	
1935-36	BLANTYRE VICS (70 points for 50 games)	
1936-37	ARTHURLIE 1	SHAWFIELD................ 0
1937-38	MORTON JUN. . . . 4	CAMBUSLANG R. 2
1938-39	PETERSHILL 3	CAMBUSLANG R. 1
1939-40	PETERSHILL 3	STRATHCLYDE 1
1940-41	CLYDEBANK 3	BLANTYRE VICS 1
1941-42	CLYDEBANK 3	MARYHILL HARP 0
1942-43	GLENCAIRN 2	BENBURB.................... 0
1943-44	ST ROCH'S 2	CLYDEBANK................ 1
1944-45	CLYDEBANK 4	PETERSHILL................ 3
1945-46	ARTHURLIE 2	BLANTYRE CELTIC 1
1946-47	VALE OF LEVEN . . 2	PETERSHILL................ 0
1947-48	KILSYTH R. 2	POLLOK....................... 1
1948-49	BLANTYRE C. . . . 3	CLYDEBANK................ 1
1949-50	CLYDEBANK 3	PETERSHILL................ 0
1950-51	DUNTOCHER HIBS1	BENBURB.................... 0
1951-52	PETERSHILL 3	BELLSHILL ATH........... 0
1952-53	ASHFIELD 3	CLYDEBANK................ 1
1953-54	KILSYTH R. 6	BENBURB.................... 0
1954-55	ASHFIELD 4	PETERSHILL................ 3
1955-56	PETERSHILL 4	PARKHEAD 0
1956-57	KILSYTH R. 3	ST ROCH'S.................. 0
1957-58	DUNTOCHER HIBS 5	PARKHEAD 3
1958-59	JOHNSTONE B . . . 4	ASHFIELD.................... 1
1959-60	BAILLIESTON . . . 2	SHETTLESTON............ 0
1960-61	GREENOCK 4	MARYHILL HARP 2
1961-62	ROB ROY 4	SHETTLESTON............ 0
1962-63	ROB ROY 3	SHETTLESTON............ 0
1963-64	PETERSHILL 4	ROB ROY..................... 1
1964-65	JOHNSTONE B . . . 2	SHETTLESTON............ 1
1965-66	GREENOCK 3	CAMBUSLANG R. 2
1966-67	GLENCAIRN 2	CAMBUSLANG R. 1
1967-68	JOHNSTONE B . . . 3	PETERSHILL................ 1
1968-69	PETERSHILL 3	POLLOK....................... 1
	(After draws of 1-1 and 2-2)	
1969-70	RENFREW 1	VALE OF LEVEN 4
	(After 3-3 draw)	

1970-71	CAMBUSLANG R . .2	CUMBERNAULD UN. ..0
1971-72	CAMBUSLANG R . .6	ST ROCH'S..................0
1972-73	CAMBUSLANG R . .4	ST ROCH'S..................1
1973-74	CAMBUSLANG R . .1	MARYHILL..................1
	(Cambuslang won on penalties)	
1974-75	EAST KILBRIDE . . .4	LARKHALL TH 3
	(After extra time)	
1975-76	EAST KILBRIDE . . .3	PORT GLASGOW 1
1976-77	GLAS PERTHSHIRE . . .2	SHETTLESTON............1
1977-78	LESMAHAGOW . . .0	CUMBERNAULD UN ...1
1978-79	PORT GLASGOW . .0	POLLOK.......................2
1979-80	BLANTYRE VICS . .1	EAST KILBRIDE 0
1980-81	POLLOK 1	BLANTYRE VICS 1
	(Pollok won 12-11 on penalties)	
1981-82	EAST KILBRIDE . . .2	LESMAHAGOW 3
1982-83	EAST KILBRIDE . . .3	STONEHOUSE V..........3
	(East Kilbride won 4-3 on penalties)	

1983-84	POLLOK 3	LARKHALL TH. 0
1984-85	POLLOK 3	SHOTTS BON ACC. 2
1985-86	POLLOK 1	SHETTLESTON............0
1986-87	ARTHURLIE 3	POLLOK.......................1
1987-88	MARYHILL 0	POLLOK.......................1
1988-89	ARTHURLIE 2	LESMAHAGOW 1
1989-90	VALE OF CLYDE . .1	DUNIPACE...................0
1990-91	CAMBUSLANG R . .2	POLLOK.......................0
	(After extra time)	
1991-92	PETERSHILL 3	JOHNSTONE BURGH .1
	(After extra time)	
1992-93	LESMAHAGOW . . .4	POLLOK.......................1
1993-94	ARTHURLIE 3	SHOTTS BON ACC. 1
1994-95	ARTHURLIE 3	PETERSHILL...............1
1995-96	MARYHILL 3	BLANTYRE VICS 0
1996-97	MARYHILL 2	POLLOK.......................1
1997-98	MARYHILL 5	GREENOCK.................0
1998-99	DUNIPACE 3	GLENCAIRN 0

JUNIOR SECRETARIES

CENTRAL REGIONAL LEAGUE

ARTHURLIE....J Rooney, 0141 571 4349
ASHFIELD....T Robertson, 0141 944 0571
BAILLIESTON....G Kelly, 0141 643 0104
BELLSHILL....J Love, 01698 341172
BENBURB....T Douglas, 0141 445 3938
BLANTYRE VICS....A McDade, 01698 323790
CAMBUSLANG RANGERS....J Fyfe, 0141 876 1050
CARLUKE ROVERS....Miss C. Kay, 01555 772154
COLTNESS UTD....T Sloan, 01698 383971
CUMBERNAULD UTD....B Duncan, 01236 735582
DUNIPACE....I Duncan, 01324 813463
EAST KILBRIDE TH.....A Barclay, 01355 223770
FORTH WANDERERS....J Kelly, 01555 840861
GLASGOW PERTHSHIRE....G Coyle 0141 336 5772
GREENOCK....W Barbour, 01475 726520
JOHNSTONE BURGH....G Walker, 01505 337252
KILSYTH RANGERS....J Ferguson, 01236 824306
KIRKINTILLOCH ROB ROY....N. McNab, 0141 776 1901
LANARK UNITED....T. Anderson, 01555 663796
LARKHALL THISTLE....D Coffey, 01698 884998
LESMAHAGOW....G Brownlie, 01555 892771
MARYHILL....G Anderson, 0141 563 0969
NEILSTON....H Blair, 0141 881 8282
PETERSHILL....A Sideserf, 0141 552 9554
POLLOK....F McNeill, 0141 881 0026
PORT GLASGOW....R Cabrey, 0141 882 4468
RENFREW....R Cantwell, 0141 561 6010
ROYAL ALBERT....WMilson, 01698 884767
RUTHERGLEN GLENCAIRN....A Forbes, 0141 643 1406
SHETTLESTON....J Gallagher, 0141 774 6722
SHOTTS BON ACCORD....W Quilter, 01505 771165
STONEHOUSE VIOLET....A Brown, 01698 792629
ST ANTHONY'S....F McKenna, 0141 641 9659
ST ROCH'S....C McLean, 0141 558 8976
THORNIEWOOD UTD....W Knox, 01698 817930
VALE OF CLYDE....J Wilson 0141 778 3340
VALE OF LEVEN....H Hamill, 01389 841050
WISHAW....W Paterson, 01698 350498
YOKER ATH.....D Andrew, 01389 872406

AYRSHIRE LEAGUE

ANNBANK..........F Hainey, 01292 520457
ARDEER TH...........B Millar, 01294 601839
ARDROSSAN W. ROVERS..........R Cooper, 01294 468851
AUCHINLECK TALBOT..........H Dumigan, 01290 421785
BEITH..........R McCarter, 01505 503800
CRAIGMARK..........T Farrell, 01292 550093
CUMNOCK..........G Morton, 01290 423992
DALRY..........H Aitken, 01505 683558
DARVEL..........J MacLachlan, 01560 321487
GLENAFTON ATH...........I Bell, 01290 422518
HURLFORD..........W McMahon, 01563 821047
IRVINE MEADOW..........I McQueen, 01560 329393
IRVINE VICTORIA..........H Loach, 01294 274340
KELLO ROVERS..........J Campbell, 01659 67472
KILBIRNIE LADESIDE..........D Gardner, 01505 683548
KILWINNING..........T Moore, 01294 557585
LARGS..........K Smailes, 01475 675511
LUGAR BOSWELL TH...........K Young, 01555 851889
MAYBOLE..........A Meek, 01655 883419
MUIRKIRK..........A McKay, 01290 423022
SALTCOATS VIC...........Mrs Thomson, 01294 468480
TROON..........R Murray, 01292 476530
WHITLETTS..........R Lawrie, 01294 551883

WHERE THEY PLAY

CENTRAL LEAGUE: Arthurlie (Dunterlie Pk), **Ashfield** (Saracen Pk), **Baillieston** (Station Pk), **Bellshill** (Brandon Pk), **Benburb** (Tinto Pk), **Blantyre V** (Castle Pk), **Cambuslang Rangers** (Somervell Pk), **Carluke Rov** (Loch Park Stadium), **Coltness Utd** (Victoria Pk), **Cumbernauld Utd** (Guys Meadow), **Dunipace** (Westefield Pk), **East Kilbride Th** (Showpark), **Forth Wand.** (Kingshill), **Glasgow Perthshire** (Keppoch Pk), **Greenock** (Ravenscraig Stadium), **Johnstone Burgh** (Keanie Pk), **Kilsyth Rangers** (Duncansfield), **Kirkintilloch Rob Rob** (Adamlie Pk), **Lanark Utd** (Moor Pk), **Larkhall Th** (Gasworks Pk), **Lesmahagow** (Craighead Pk), **Maryhill** (Lochburn Pk), **Neilston** (Brig-O-Lea Stadium), **Petershill** (Petershill Pk), **Pollok** (Newlandsfield Pk), **Port Glasgow** (Woodhall Pk), **Renfrew** (Western Pk), **Royal Albert Athletic** (Robert Smillie Memorial), **Rutherglen Glencairn** (Southcroft), **St Anthony's** (Moore Pk), **St Roch's** (Provanmill Pk), **Shettleston** (Greenfield Pk), **Shotts Bon Accord** (Hannah Pk), **Stonehouse Violet** (Tilework Pk), **Thorniewood Utd** (Robertson Pk), **Vale of Clyde** (Fullarton Pk), **Vale of Leven** (Millburn Pk), **Wishaw** (Victoria Pk), **Yoker Athletic** (Holm Pk).
AYRSHIRE LEAGUE: Annbank Utd (Pebble Pk), **Ardeer Th** (Ardeer Stadium), **Ardrossan Winton Rovers** (Winton Pk), **Auchinleck Talbot** (Beechwood Pk), **Beith** (Bellsdale Pk), **Craigmark Burtonians** (Station Pk), **Cumnock** (Townhead Pk), **Dalry Th** (Merskworth Pk), **Darvel** (Recreation Pk), **Glenafton Athletic** (Loch Pk), **Hurlford Utd** (Blair Pk) **Irvine Meadow** (Meadow Pk), **Irvine Vics** (Victoria Pk), **Kello Rovers** (Nithside Pk), **Kilbirnie Ladeside** (Valleyfield), **Kilwinning Rangers** (Abbey Pk), **Largs Th** (Barrfields Pk), **Lugar Boswell Th** (Rosebank Pk), **Maybole** (Ladywell Stadium), **Muirkirk** (Burnside Pk), **Saltcoats Vics** (Campbell Pk), **Troon** (Porstland Pk), **Whitletts Vics** (Voluntary Pk).

LEADING EXECUTIVES

SCOTTISH FOOTBALL ASSOCIATION – D. Taylor, 6 Park Gardens, Glasgow, G3 7YE. Tel: 0141 332 6372/3.

SCOTTISH PREMIER LEAGUE – R Mitchell, The National Stadium, Hampden Park, Glasgow, G42 9BA. 0141 649 6962

SCOTTISH FOOTBALL LEAGUE – P. Donald, 188 West Regent Street, Glasgow, G2 4RY. Tel: 0141 248 3844/5.

ENGLISH FOOTBALL ASSOCIATION – 16 Lancaster Gate, London, W2 3LW. Tel: 0171 262 4542.

ENGLISH PREMIER LEAGUE – P. Leaver, 11 Connaught Place, London, W2 2ET. Tel: 0171 298 1600.

ENGLISH FOOTBALL LEAGUE – J. D. Dent, F.C.I.S., Football League Ltd., Lytham St Annes, Lancs, FY8 1JG. Tel: 01253 729421.

FOOTBALL ASSOCIATION OF WALES – D. Collins, Plymouth Chambers, 3 Westgate Street, Cardiff, CF1 1JF. Tel: 01222 372325.

FOOTBALL ASSOCIATION OF IRELAND – B. O'Byrne ,80 Merrion Square South, Dublin 2. Tel: 003531 6766864.

FOOTBALL LEAGUE OF IRELAND – E. Morris, 80 Merrion Square South, Dublin 2. Tel: 003531 765120.

NORTHERN IRELAND FOOTBALL ASSOCIATION – D. I. Bowen, 20 Windsor Avenue, Belfast, BT9 6EG. Tel: 01232 669458.

IRISH LEAGUE – H. Wallace, 87 University Street, Belfast, BT7 1HP. Tel: 01232 242888.

FIFA – S. Blatter, PO Box 85 8030, Zurich, Switzerland. 0041 1384 9595.

UEFA: G. Aigner, Chemin de la Redoute 54, Case Postale 303 CH-1260 Nyon, Switzerland. Tel: 01041 22994 4444.

SCOTTISH PROFESSIONAL FOOTBALLERS' ASSOCIATION – A. Higgins, Fountain House, 1/3 Woodside Crescent, Glasgow, G3 74J. 0141 332 8641 (ext 213).

SCOTTISH JUNIOR FA – T Johnston, 0141 248 1095

REEBOK CENTRAL REGIONAL LEAGUE – J. Scott Robertson, Tel: 01698 266725.

WEST OF SCOTLAND JUNIOR FA – M. Spiers, Tel: 01563 527408.

SCOTTISH WOMEN'S FA – Ms M McGonigle, 0141 353 1162.

SCOTTISH CLUBS IN EUROPE - A COMPLETE HISTORY

Abbreviations EC (European Champions Cup), ECWC (European Cup Winners Cup), FC (Fair Cities Cup) UEFA (UEFA Cup) w (won) l (lost)

ABERDEEN

Opponents	Venue	Res	Scorers	Rnd
		1967-68 ECWC		
KR Reykjavic	H	W10-1	Munro 3, Storrie 2	1
Iceland			Smith 2, McMillan, Petersen,Taylor	
	A	W4-1	Storrie 2 Buchan, Munro	
Standard Liege	A	L0-3		2
Belgium	H	W2-0	Munro, Melrose	
		1968-69 FC		
Slavia Sofia	A	D0-0		1
Bulgaria	H	W2-0	Robb, Taylor	
Real Zaragossa	H	W2-1	Forrest, Smith	2
Spain	A	L0-3		
		1970-71 ECWC		
Honved	H	W3-1	Graham, Harper, S Murray	1
Hungary	A	L1-3	S Murray	
		1971-72 UEFA		
Celta Vigo	A	W2-0	Harper, o.g.	1
Spain	H	W1-0	Harper	
Juventus	A	L0-2		2
Italy	H	D1-1	Harper	
		1972-73 UEFA		
Borussia Munch.	H	L2-3	Harper, Jarvie	1
W Germany	A	L3-6	Harper (2), Jarvie	
		1973-74 UEFA		
Finns Harp	H	W4-1	R Miller, Jarvie (2), Graham	1
Eire				
	A	W3-1	Robb, Graham, R Miller	
Tottenham H	H	D1-1	Hermiston (pen)	2
England	A	L1-4	Jarvie	
		1977-78 UEFA		
RWD Molenbeek	A	D0-0		1
Belgium	H	L1-2	(Jarvie)	
		1978-79 ECWC		
Marek Stanke	A	L2-3	Jarvie, Harper	1
Bulgaria	H	W3-0	Strachan, Jarvie, Harper	
Fortuna Dusseldorf	A	L0-3		2
West Germany	H	W2-0	McLelland, Jarvie	

Opponents	Venue	Res	Scorers	Rnd
		1979-80 UEFA		
Eintracht Frankfurt	H	D1-1	Harper	1
W Germany	A	L0-1		
		1980-81 EC		
Austria Vienna	H	W1-0	McGhee	1
Austria	A	D0-0		
Liverpool	H	L0-1		2
England	A	L0-4		
		1981-82 UEFA		
Ipswich Town	A	D1-1	Hewitt	1
England	H	W3-1	Strachan, pen, Weir 2	
Arges Pitesti	H	W3-0	Strachan, Weir, Hewit t	2
Romania	A	D2-2	Strachan, pen,Hewitt	
SV Hamburg	H	W3-2	Black, Watson, Hewitt	3
Germany	A	L1-3	McGhee	
		1982-83 ECWC		
Sion Switzerland	H	W7-0	Black 2, Strachan, Hewitt, Simpson, McGhee, Kennedy	Pr
	A	W4-1	Hewitt, Miller, McGhee 2	
Dinamo Tirana	H	W1-0	Hewitt	1
Albania	A	D0-0		
Lech Poznan	H	W2-0	McGhee, Weir	2
Poland	A	W1-0	Bell	
Bayern Munich	A	D0-0		QF
Germany	H	W3-2	Simpson, McLeish, Hewitt	
Waterschei Belgium	H	W5-1	Black, Simpson McGhee 2, Weir	SF
	A	L0-1		
Real Madrid	N	W2-1	Black, Hewitt	F
		1983-94 (European Super Cup)		
Hamburg	A	D0-0		
Germany	H	W2-0	Simpson, McGhee	
		1983-84 ECWC		
Akranes	A	W2-1	McGhee 2	1
Iceland	H	D1-1	Strachan, pen	
Beveren	A	D0-0		2
Belgium		W4-1	Strachan 2, 1 pen, Simpson, Weir	
Ujpest Dozsa	A	L0-2		QF
Hungary	H	W3-0	McGhee 3	
Porto	A	L0-1		SF
Portugal	H	L0-1		
		1984-85 EC		
Dynamo Berlin	H	W2-1	Black 2	1
E. Germany	A	L1-2	Angus	

Opponents	Venue	Res	Scorers	Rnd
		1985-86 (EC)		
Akranes	A	W3-1	Black, Hewitt, Stark	1
Iceland	H	W4-1	Simpson, Hewitt Gray, Falconer	
Servette	A	D0-0		2
Switz.	H	W1-0	McDougall	
IFK Gothenburg	H	D2-2	J Miller, Hewitt	QF
Sweden	A	D0-0		
		1986-87 (ECWC)		
Sion	H	W2-1	Bett (pen), Wright	1
Switzerland	A	L0-3		
		1987-88 (UEFA)		
Bohemians	A	D0-0		1
Eire	H	W1-0	Bett (pen)	
Feyenoord	H	W2-1	Falconer, J Miller	2
Holland	A	L0-1		
		1988-89 (UEFA)		
Dynamo Dresden	H	D0-0		1
East Germany	A	L0-2		
		1989-90 (UEFA)		
Rapid Vienna	H	W2-1	C Robertson, Grant	1
Austria	A	L0-1		
		1990-91 (UCWC)		
Salamis	A	W2-0	Mason, Gillhaus	1
	H	W3-0	C Robertson, Gillhaus, Jess	
Legia Warsaw	H	D0-0		2
Poland	A	L0-1		
		1991-92 (UEFA)		
BK Copenhagen	H	L0-1		1
Denmark	A	L0-2		
		1993-94 (ECWC)		
Valur	A	W3-0	Shearer, Jess 2	1
Iceland	H	W4-0	Jess 2, Miller, Irvine	
Torino	A	L2-3	Paatelainen, Jess	
Italy	H	L1-3	Richardson	
		1994-95 (UEFA)		
Skonto Riga	A	D0-0		P
Latvia	H	D1-1	Kane	
		1996-97 (UEFA)		
Vilnius	A	W4-1	Dodds 2, Glass, Shearer	Q
Latvia	H	L1-3	Irvine	
Barry Town	H	W3-1	Windass, Glass, Young	1
Wales	A	D3-3	Dodds 2, Rowson	
Brondby	H	L0-2		2
Denmark	A	D0-0		

AIRDRIE

1992-93 UCWC

Opponents	Venue	Res	Scorers	Rnd
Sparta Prague	H	L0-1		1
Czechoslovakia	A	L1-2	Black	

CELTIC

Opponents	Venue	Res	Scorers	Rnd
		1962-63 FC		
Valencia	A	L2-4	Carrol 2	1
Spain	H	D2-2	Crerand, o.g.	
		1963-64 UCWC		
Basle	A	W5-1	Divers, Hughes 3, Lennox	1
Switzerland	H	W5-0	Johnstone, Divers 2 Murdoch, Chalmers	
Dynamo Zagreb	H	W3-0	Chalmers 2, Hughes	2
Yugoslavia	A	L1-2	Murdoch	
Slovan Bratislava	H	W1-0	Murdoch pen	QF
Czechoslovakia	A	W1-0	Hughes	
MTK Budapest	H	W3-0	Johnstone, Chalmers 2	SF
Hungary	A	L0-4		
		1964-65 FC		
Leixoes	A	D1-1	Murdoch	1
Portugal	H	W3-0	Murdoch, pen, Chalmers	
Barcelona	A	L1-3	Hughes	2
Spain	H	D0-0		
		1965-66 UCWC		
Go Ahead	A	W6-0	Gallacher 2, Hughes	1
Holland			Johnstone 2 Lennox	
	H	W1-0	McBride	
Aarhus	A	W1-0	McBride	2
Denmark	H	W2-0	McNeill, Johnstone	
Dynamo Kiev	H	W3-0	Gemmell, Murdoch 2	QF
USSR	A	D1-1	Gemmell	
Liverpool	H	W1-0	Lennox	SF
England	A	L0-2		
		1966-67 EC		
Zurich	H	W2-0	Gemmell, McBride	1
Switzerland	A	W3-0	Gemmell 2, 1 pen, McBride	
Nantes	A	W3-1	McBride, Lennox,	2
France			Chalmers	
	H	W3-1	Johnstone, Lennox, Chalmers	
Vojvodina	A	L0-1		QF
Yugoslavia	H	W2-0	Chalmers, McNeill	
Dukla Prague	H	W3-1	Johnstone, Wallace, 2	SF
Czechoslovakia	A	D0-0		
Inter Milan	N	W2-1	Gemmell, Chalmers	F

Opponents	Venue	Res	Scorers	Rnd
		1967-68 EC		
Dymano Kiev	H	L1-2	Lennox	1
USSR	A	D1-1	Lennox	
		1968-69 EC		
St Etienne	A	L0-2		1
France	H	W4-0	Gemmell (pen), Craig Chalmers, McBride	
Red Star Belgrade	H	W5-1	Murdoch, Johnstone 2,	2
Yugoslavia			Lennox, Wallace	
	A	D1-1	Wallace	
AC Milan	A	D0-0		QF
Italy	H	L0-1		
		1969-70 EC		
Basle	A	D0-0		1
Switzerland	H	W2-0	Hood, Gemmell	
Benfica	H	W3-0	Gemmell, Wallace, Hood	2
Portugal	A	L0-3		
Fiorentina	H	W3-0	Auld, Wallace, o.g.	QF
Italy	A	L0-1		
Leeds United	A	W1-0	Connelly	SF
England	H	W2-1	Hughes, Murdoch	
Feyenoord	N	L1-2	Gemmell	F
		1970-71 EC		
KPV Kokkola	H	W9-0	Hood 3, Wilson 2, Hughes	1
Finland			McNeill, Johnstone, Davidson	
	A	W5-0	Wallace 2, Callaghan Davidson, Lennox	
Waterford	A	W7-0	Wallace 3, Murdoch 2	2
Eire			Macari 2	
	H	W3-2	Hughes, Johnstone 2	
Ajax	A	L0-3		QF
Holland	H	W1-0	Johnstone	
		1971-72 EC		
BK 1903	A	L1-2	Macari	1
Copenhagen	H	W3-0	Wallace 2,	
Denmark			Callaghan	
Sliema W	H	W5-0	Gemmell, Macari 2	2
Malta			Hood, Brogan	
	A	W2-1	Hood, Lennox	
Ujpest Dozsa	A	W2-1	Macari, o.g.	QF
Hungary	H	D1-1	Macari	
Inter Milan	A	D0-0		SF
Italy	H	D0-0	lost on penalties	

Opponents	Venue	Res	Scorers	Rnd
		1972-73 EC		
Rosenborg	H	W2-1	Macari, Deans	1
Norway	A	W3-1	Macari, Hood, Dalglish	
Ujpest Dozsa	H	W2-1	Dalglish 2	2
Hungary	A	L0-3		
		1973-74 EC		
Turun	A	W6-1	Callaghan 2, Hood,	1
Finland			Johnstone, Deans,	
			Connelly, pen	
	H	W3-0	Deans, Johnstone 2	
Vejle	H	D0-0		2
Denmark	A	W1-0	Lennox	
Basle	A	L2-3	Wilson, Dalglish	QF
Switzerland	H	W4-2	Dalglish, Deans,	
			Callaghan, Murray	
Atletico Madrid	H	D0-0		SF
Spain	A	L0-2		
		1974-75 EC		
Olympiakos	H	D1-1	Wilson	1
Greece	A	L0-2		
		1975-76 ECWC		
Valur	A	W2-0	Wilson McDonald	1
Iceland	H	W7-0	Edvaldsson, Dalglish	
			McCluskey, pen, Deans	
			Hood 2, Callaghan	
Boavista	A	D0-0		2
Portugal	H	W3-1	Dalglish, Edvaldsson, Deans	
Zwickau	H	D1-1	Dalglish	QF
East Germany	A	L0-1		
		1976-77 UEFA		
Wisla Krakow	H	D2-2	McDonald, Dalglish	1
Poland	A	L0-2		
		1977-78 EC		
Jeunesse D'Esch	H	W5-0	McDonald, Wilson,	1
Luxembourg			Craig 2, McLaughlin	
	A	W6-1	Lennox 2, Glavin	
			Edvaldsson 2, Craig	
SW Innsbruck	H	W2-1	Craig, Burns	2
Austria	A	L0-3		
		1979-80 EC		
Partizan Tirana	A	L0-1		1
Albania	H	W4-1	McDonald, Aitken 2	
			Davidson	
Dundalk	H	W3-2	McDonald, Burns	2
Eire			McCluskey	
	A	D0-0		

Opponents	Venue	Res	Scorers	Rnd
Real Madrid	H	W2-0	McCluskey, Doyle	QF
Spain	A	L0-3		
		1980-81 ECWC		
Diosgyor	H	W6-0	McGarvey 2, Sullivan	P
Hungary			McCluskey 2, o.g.	
	A	L1-2	Nicholas	
Timisorara	H	W2-1	Nicholas 2	1
Romania	A	L0-1	lost on away goals	
		1981-82 EC		
Juventus	H	W1-0	MacLeod	1
Italy	A	L0-2		
		1982-83 EC		
Ajax	H	D2-2	Nicholas, McGarvey	1
Holland	A	W2-1	Nicholas, McCluskey	
Real Sociedad	A	L0-2		2
Spain	H	W2-1	MacLeod 2	
		1983-84 UEFA		
Aarhus	H	1-0	Aitken	1
Denmark	A	W4-1	MacLeod, McGarvey, Aitken,Provan	
Sporting Lisbon	A	L0-2		2
Portugal	H	W5-0	Burns, McAdam, McClair MacLeod, McGarvey	
Notts Forest	A	D0-0		3
England	H	L1-2	MacLeod	
		1984-85 ECWC		
Gent	A	L0-1		1
Belgium	H	W3-0	McGarvey 2, McStay	
Rapid Vienna	A	L1-3	McClair	2
Austria	H	W3-0	McClair, MacLeod, Burns	
		(UEFA ordered match to be replayed)		
	N	L0-1		
		1985-86 ECWC		
Atletico Madrid	A	D1-1	Johnston	1
Spain	H	L1-2	Aitken	
		1986-87 EC		
Shamrock Rov	A	W1-0	MacLeod	1
Ireland	H	W2-0	Johnston 2	
Dymano Kiev	H	D1-1	Johnston	2
USSR	A	L1-3	McGhee	
		1987-88 UEFA		
Bor Dortmund	H	W2-1	Walker, Whyte	1
W Germany	A	L0-2		

Opponents	Venue	Res	Scorers	Rnd
		1988-89 EC		
Honved	A	L0-1		1
Hungary	H	W4-0	Stark, Walker, McAvennie, McGhee	
Werder Bremen	H	L0-2		2
W Germany	A	D0-0		
		1989-90 ECWC		
*Part Belgrade	A	L1-2	Galloway	1
Yugoslavia	H	W5-4	Dziekanowski 4 Walker	
		1991-92 UEFA		
Ekeren	H	W2-0	Nicholas 2, 1 pen	1
Belgium	A	D1-1	Galloway	
Neuchatel Xamax	A	L1-5	O'Neill	2
Switzerland	H	W1-0	Miller	
		1992-93 UEFA		
Cologne	A	L0-2		1
Germany	H	W3-0	McStay, Creaney, Collins	
Bor Dortmund	A	L0-1		2
Germany	H	L1-2	Creaney	
		1993-94 UEFA		
Young Boys	A	D0-0		1
Switzerland	W	1-0	og	
Sporting Lisbon	H	W1-0	Creaney	2
Portugal	A	L0-2		
		1995-96 ECWC		
Dinamo Batumi	A	W3-2	Thom 2, Donnelly	1
Georgia	H	W4-0	Thom 2, Donnelly, Walker	
Paris St Germain	A	L0-1		2
France	H	L0-3		
		1996-97 UEFA		
Kosice	A	D0-0		Q
Poland	H	W1-0	Cadete	
Hamburg	H	L0-2		1
Germany	A	L0-2		
		1997-98 UEFA		
Inter Cable-Tel Wales	A	W3-0	Thom pen, Johnson pen, Wieghorst	Q
	H	W5-0	Thom pen, Jackson, Johnson, Hannah, Hay	
Tirol Innsbruck	A	L1-2	Stubbs	Q
Austria	H	W6-3	Donnelly 2, 1 pen, Thom Burley 2, Wieghorst	

Opponents	Venue	Res	Scorers	Rnd
Liverpool	H	D2-2	McNamara, Donnelly	1
England	A	D0-0		
		1998-99 EC		
St Patrick's	H	D0-0		P
Eire	A	W2-0	Brattbakk, Larsson	
Croatia Zagreb	H	W1-0	Jackson	P
Croatia	A	L0-3		
		UEFA		
FC Zurich	H	D1-1	Brattbakk	1
Switzerland	A	L4-2	O'Donnell, Larsson	

MARK VIDUKA . . . played againtst Celtic for Croatia Zagreb

DUNDEE

Opponents	Venue	Res	Scorers	Rnd
		1962-63 EC		
FC Cologne	H	W8-1	Gilzean 3, Wishart, Smith	P
W Germany			Robertson, Penman, og	
	A	L0-4		
Sporting Lisbon	A	L0-1		1
Portugal	H	W4-1	Gilzean 3, Cousin	
Anderlecht	A	W4-1	Gilzean 2, Cousin, Smith	QF
Belgium	H	W2-1	Cousin, Smith	
AC Milan	A	L1-5	Cousin	SF
Italy	H	W1-0	Gilzean	
		1964-65 ECWC		
Bye				1
Real Zaragossa	H	D2-2	Murray, Houston	2
Spain	A	L1-2	Robertson	
		1967-68 FC		
DWS Amsterdam	A	L1-2	McLean	1
Holland	H	W3-0	Wilson, McLean 2, 1 pen	
FC Liege	H	W3-1	Stuart 2, Wilson	2
Belgium	A	W4-1	McLean 4	
		Bye in Round 3		
Zurich	H	W1-0	Easton	QF
Switzerland	A	W1-0	Wilson	
Leeds United	H	D1-1	Wilson	SF
England	A	L0-2		
		1971-72 UEFA		
Akademisk	H	W4-2	Bryce 2, Wallace, Lambie	1
Denmark	A	W1-0	Duncan	
Cologne	A	L1-2	Kinninmonth	2
W Germany	H	W4-2	Duncan 3, Wilson	
AC Milan	A	L0-3		3
Italy	H	W2-0	Wallace, Duncan	
		1973-74 UEFA		
Twente Ensch.	H	L1-3	Stewart	1
Holland	A	L2-4	Johnston, Scott	
		1974-75 UEFA		
RWD Molenbeek	A	L0-1		1

DUNDEE UNITED

Opponents	Venue	Res	Scorers	Rnd
		1966-67 FC		
Bye				1
Barcelona	A	W2-1	Hainey, Seeman	2
Spain	H	W2-0	Mitchell, Hainey	
Juventus	A	L0-3		3
Italy	H	W1-0	Dossing	
		1969-70 FC		
Newcastle Utd	H	L1-2	Scott	1
England	A	L0-1		
		1970-71 FC		
Grasshoppers	H	W3-2	Reid I, Markland, Reid A	1
Switzerland	A	D0-0		
Sparta Prague	A	L1-3	Traynor	2
Czechoslovakia	H	W1-0	Gordon	
		1974-75 ECWC		
Jiul Petrosani	H	W3-0	Narey, Copland, Gardner	1
Romania	A	L0-2		
Bursaspor	H	D0-0		2
Turkey	A	L0-1		
		1975-76 UEFA		
Keflavik	A	W2-0	Narey 2	1
Iceland	H	W4-0	Hall 2, Hegarty, pen, Sturrock	
Porto	H	L1-2	Rennie	2
Portugal	A	D1-1	Hegarty	
		1977-78 UEFA		
KB Copenhagen	H	W1-0	Sturrock	1
Denmark	A	L0-3		
		1978-79 UEFA		
Standard Liege	A	L0-1		1
Belgium	H	D0-0		
		1979-80 UEFA		
Anderlecht	H	D0-0		1
Belgium	A	D1-1	Kopel	
Diosgyor	H	L0-1		2
Hungary	A	L1-3	Kopel	
		1980-81 UEFA		
Slask Wroclaw	A	D0-0		1
Poland	H	W7-2	Dodds 2, Pettigrew, Stark, Hegarty, Payne pen	
Lokeren	H	D1-1	Pettigrew 2	
Belgium	A	D0-0		
		1981-82 UEFA		
Monaco (France)	A	W5-2	Bannon 2, 1 pen, Dodds 2, Kirkwood	1
	H	L1-2	Milne	

Opponents	Venue	Res	Scorers	Rnd
Borussia M.	A	L0-2		2
(W. Germany)	H	W5-0	Milne, Kirkwood, Hegarty, Sturrock, Bannon	
Winterslag	A	D0-0		3
(Belgium)	H	W5-0	Bannon, Narey, Hegarty Milne 2	
Rankicki Nis	H	W2-0	Narey, Dodds	QF
(Yugoslavia)	A	L0-3		
		1982-83 UEFA		
PSV Eindhoven	H	D1-1	Dodds	1
(Holland)	A	W2-0	Kirkwood, Hegarty	
Viking Stavanger	A	W3-1	Milne 2, Sturrock	2
(Norway)	H	D0-0		
Werder Bremen	H	W2-1	Milne, Narey	3
(W. Germany)	A	D1-1	Hegarty	
Bohemians	A	L0-1		QF
(Czech)	H	D0-0		
		1983-84 EC		
Hamrun Spartans	A	W3-0	Reilly, Bannon, Stark	1
(Malta)	H	W3-0	Milne, Kirkwood 2	
Standard Liege	A	D0-0		2
(Belgium)	H	W4-0	Milne 2, Hegarty, Dodds	
Rapid Vienna	A	L1-2	Stark	QF
(Austria)	H	W1-0	Dodds	
AS Roma	H	W2-0	Dodds, Stark	SF
(Italy)	A	L0-3		
		1984-85 UEFA		
AIK Stockholm	A	L0-1		1
(Sweden)	H	W3-0	Sturrock, Milne 2	
ASK Linz	A	W2-1	Kirkwood, Bannon pen 2	
(Austria)	H	W5-1	Hegarty, Coyne 2, Gough Beaumont	
Man United	A	D2-2	Hegarty, Sturrock	3
(England)	H	L2-3	Dodds, Hegarty	
		1985-86 UEFA		
Bohemians	A	W5-2	Sturrock 3, Bannon 2	1
Eire	H	D2-2	Milne, Redford	
Vardar Skopje	H	W2-0	Redford, Gough	2
(Yugoslavia)	A	D1-1	Hegarty	
Neuchatel Xamax	H	W2-1	Dodds, Redford	3
Switzerland	A	L1-3	Redford	
		1986-87 UEFA		
Lens	A	L0-1		1
France	H	W2-0	Milne, Coyne	
Uni Craiova	H	W3-0	Redford 2, Clark	2
Romania	A	L0-1		

Opponents	Venue	Res	Scorers	Rnd
Hadjuk Split	H	W2-0	McInally, Clark	3
Yugoslavia	A	D0-0		
Barcelona	H	W1-0	Gallacher	QF
Spain	A	W2-1	Clark, Ferguson	
Borussia Munch.	H	D0-0		SF
W. Germany	A	W2-0	Ferguson, Redford	
IFK Gothenburg	A	L0-1		F
Sweden	H	D1-1		
		1987-88 UEFA		
Coleraine	A	W1-0	Sturrock	1
N. Ireland	H	W3-1	Gallacher, Sturrock, Clark	
Vitkovice	H	L1-2	Ferguson	2
Czechoslovakia	A	D1-1	og	
		1988-89 ECWC		
Floriana	A	D0-0		1
Malta	H	W1-0	Meade	
Din. Bucharest	H	L0-1		2
Romania	A	D1-1	Beaumont	
		1989-90 UEFA		
Glentoran	A	W3-1	Clelland, McInally, Hinds	1
N. Ireland	H	W2-0	Clark, Gallacher	
Antwerp	A	L0-4		2
Belgium	H	W3-2	Paatelainen, O'Neill, Clark	
		1990-91 UEFA		
Harnfjardar	A	W3-1	Jackson, Clelland, og	1
	H	D2-2	Connolly, og	
Arnhem	A	L1-0		2
	H	L0-4		
		1993-94 UEFA		
Brondby	A	L0-2		1
Denmark	H	W3-1	McKinlay, Crabbe, Clark	
		1994s-95 UCWC		
Tatran Presov	H	W3-2	Petric, Nixon, Hannah	1
Slovakia	A	L3-1	Nixon	

DUNFERMLINE

Opponents	Venue	Res	Scorers	Rnd
		1961-62 ECWC		
St Patrick's Ath.	H	W4-1	Melrose, Peebles,	1
Eire			Dickson, Macdonald	
	A	W4-0	Peebles 2, Dickson 2	
Vardar Skopje	H	W5-0	Smith, Dickson 2,	2
Yugoslavia			Melrose, Peebles	
	A	L0-2		
Ujpest Dozsa	A	L3-4	Smith, Macdonald 2	QF
Hungary	H	L0-1		
		1962-63 FC		
Everton	A	L0-1		1
England	H	W2-0	Miller, Melrose	
Valencia	A	L0-4		2
Spain	H	W6-2	Melrose, Sinclair 2	
			McLean, Peebles, Smith	
	N	L0-1		
		1964-65 FC		
Oergryte	H	W4-2	McLaughlin 2, Sinclair 2	1
Sweden	A	D0-0		
Stuttgart	H	W1-0	Callaghan	2
W Germany	A	D0-0		
Athletico Bilbao	A	L0-1		3
Spain	H	W1-0	Smith	
	A	L1-2	Smith	
		1965-66 FC		
Bye				1
KB Copenhagen	H	W5-0	Fleming, Paton 2,	2
Denmark			Robertson, Callaghan	
	A	W4-2	Edwards, Paton, Fleming,	
			Ferguson	
Spartak Brno	H	W2-0	Paton, Ferguson, pen	3
Czechoslovakia	A	D0-0		
Real Zaragossa	H	W1-0	Paton	QF
Spain	A	L2-4	Ferguson 2	
		1966-67 FC		
Frigg Oslo	A	W3-1	Fleming 2, Callaghan	1
Norway	H	W3-1	Delaney 2 Callaghan	
Dynamo Zagreb	H	W4-2	Delaney, Edwards,	2
Yugoslavia			Ferguson 2	
	A	L0-2		
		1968-69 ECWC		
Apoel	H	W10-1	Robertson 2, Renton 2	1
Cyprus			Barry, Callaghan W 2, Gardner	
			Edwards, Callaghan T	
	A	W2-0	Gardner, Callaghan W	

Opponents	Venue	Res	Scorers	Rnd
Olymp. Piraeus	H	W4-0	Edwards 2, Fraser,	2
Greece			Mitchell	
	A	L0-3		
West Bromwich	H	D0-0		QF
England	A	W1-0	Gardner	
Slovan Bratislava	H	D1-1	Fraser	SF
Czechoslovakia	A	L0-1		
		1969-70 FC		
Bordeaux	H	W4-0	Paton 2, Mitchell, Gardner	1
France	A	L0-2		
Gwardia Warsaw	H	W2-1	McLean, Gardner	2
Poland	A	W1-0	Renton	
Anderlecht	A	L0-1		3
Belgium	H	W3-2	McLean 2, Mitchell	

ALEX EDWARDS . . . a star of the Dunfermline team of the 1960s.

HEARTS

Opponents	Venue	Res	Scorers	Rnd
		1958-59 EC		
Standard Liege	A	L1-5	Crawford	P
Belgium	H	W2-1	Bauld	
		1960-61 EC		
Benfica	H	L1-2	Young	P
Portugal	A	L0-3		
		1961-62 FC		
Union St Gilloise	A	W3-1	Blackwood, Davidson 2	1
Belgium	H	W2-0	Wallace, Stenhouse	
Inter Milan	H	L0-1		2
Italy	A	L0-4		
		1963-64 FC		
Lausanne	A	D2-2	Traynor, Ferguson	1
Switzerland	H	D2-2	Cumming, Hamilton J	
	A	L2-3	Wallace, Ferguson	
		1965-66 FC		
Bye				1
Valerengen	H	W1-0	Wallace	2
Norway	A	W3-1	Kerrigan 2, Traynor	
Real Zaragossa Spain	H	D3-3	Anderson, Wallace, Kerrigan	3
	A	D2-2	Anderson, Wallace	
	A	L0-1		
		1976-77 ECWC		
Lokomotiv Leipzig	A	L0-2		1
East Germany	H	W5-1	Kay, Gibson 2, Brown, Busby	
SV Hamburg	A	L2-4	Park, Busby	2
West Germany	H	L1-4	Gibson	
		1984-85 UEFA		
Paris St Germain	A	L0-4		1
France	H	D2-2	Robertson 2	
		1986-87 UEFA		
Dukla Prague	H	W3-2	Foster, Clark, Robertson	1
Czechoslovakia	A	L0-1		
		1988-89 UEFA		
St Patrick's Ath	A	W2-0	Foster pen, Galloway	1
Eire	H	W2-0	Black, Galloway	
FK Austria	H	D0-0		2
Austria	A	W1-0	Galloway	
Velez Mostar Yugoslavia	H	W3-0	Bannon, Galloway, Colquhoun	3
	A	L1-2	Galloway	
Bayern Munich	H	W1-0	Ferguson	QF
West Germany	A	L0-2		

Opponents	Venue	Res	Scorers	Rnd
		1990-91 UEFA		
Dnepr	A	D1-1	Robertson	1
	H	W3-1	McPherson, Robertson 2	
Bologna	H	W3-1	Foster 2, Ferguson	2
Italy	A	L0-3		
		1992-93 UEFA		
Slavia Prague	A	L0-1		1
Czech Rep	H	W4-2	Mackay, Baird, Levein, Snodin	
Standard Liege	H	L0-1		2
Belgium	A	L0-1		
		1993-94 UEFA		
Atletico Madrid	H	W2-1	Robertson, Colquhoun	1
Spain	A	L0-3		
		1996-97 ECWC		
Red Star Belgrade	A	D0-0		1
Yugoslavia	H	D1-1	McPherson	
		1998-99 ECWC		
Lantana	A	W1-0	Makel	Q
Estonia	H	W5-0	Hamilton, Fulton, McCann, Flogel, Holmes	
Real Mallorca	H	L0-1		1
Spain	A	D1-1	Hamilton	

STEVE FULTON . . . scored for Hearts against Estonian side Lantana

HIBERNIAN

Opponents	Venue	Res	Scorers	Rnd
1955-56 EC				
Rot-Weiss Essen	A	W4-0	Turnbull 2, Reilly, Ormond	1
West Germany	H	D1-1	Buchanan J	
Djurgaarden	H	W3-1	Combe, Mulkerrin, og	QF
Sweden	A	W1-0	Turnbull pen	
Reims	A	L0-2		SF
France	H	L0-1		
1960-61 FC				
Barcelona	A	D4-4	McLeod, Preston Baker 2	QF
Spain	H	W3-2	Kinloch 2, 1 pen, Baker	
AS Roma	H	D2-2	Baker, McLeod	SF
Italy	A	D3-3	Baker 2, Kinloch	
	A	L0-6		
1961-62 FC				
Belenenses	H	D3-3	Fraser 2, Baird pen	1
Portugal	A	W3-1	Baxter 2, Stevenson	
Red Star Belgrade	A	L0-4		2
Yugoslavia	H	L0-1		
1962-63 FC				
Stavenet	H	W4-0	Byrne 2, Baker, og	1
Denmark	A	W3-2	Stevenson 2, Byrne	
DOS Utrecht	A	W1-0	Falconer	2
Holland	H	W2-1	Baker, Stevenson	
Valencia	A	L0-5		QF
Spain	H	W2-1	Preston, Baker	
1965-66 FC				
Valencia	H	W2-0	Scott, McNamee	1
Spain	A	L0-2		
	A	L0-3		
1967-68 FC				
Porto	H	W3-0	Cormack 2, Stevenson	1
Portugal	A	L1-3	Stanton pen	
Napoli	A	L1-4	Stein	2
Italy	H	W5-0	Duncan, Quinn, Cormack Stanton, Stein	
Leeds United	A	L0-1		3
England	H	D1-1	Stein	
1968-69 FC				
Ljubljana	A	W3-0	Stevenson, Stein, Marinello	1
Yugoslavia	H	W2-1	Davis 2	
Lokomotiv Leipzig	H	W3-1	McBride 3	2
East Germany	A	W1-0	Grant	
SV Hamburg	A	L0-1		3
West Germany	H	W2-1	McBride 2	

Opponents	Venue	Res	Scorers	Rnd
		1970-71 FC		
Malmo FF	H	W6-0	McBride 3 Duncan 2, Blair	1
Sweden	A	W3-2	Duncan, McEwan, Stanton	
Vitoria Giumaraes	H	W2-0	Duncan, Stanton	2
Portugal	A	L1-2	Graham	
Liverpool	H	L0-1		3
England	A	L0-2		
		1972-73 ECWC		
Sporting Lisbon	A	L1-2	Duncan	1
Portugal	H	W6-1	Gordon 2, O'Rourke 3, og	
Besa	H	W7-1	Cropley, O'Rourke 3,	2
Albania			Duncan 2, Brownlie	
	A	D1-1	Gordon	
Hadjuk Split	H	W4-2	Gordon 3, Duncan	QF
Yugoslavia	A	L0-3		
		1973-74 UEFA		
Keflavik	H	W2-0	Black, Higgins	1
Iceland	A	D1-1	Stanton	
Leeds United	A	D0-0		2
England	H	D0-0		
		1974-75 UEFA		
Rosenborg	A	W3-2	Stanton, Gordon, Cropley	1
Norway	H	W9-1	Harper 2, Munro 2, Stanton 2, Cropley 2 pens, Gordon	
Juventus	H	L2-4	Stanton, Cropley	2
Italy	A	L0-4		
		1975-76 UEFA		
Liverpool	H	W1-0	Harper	1
England	A	L1-3	Edwards	
		1976-77 UEFA		
Sochaux	H	W1-0	Brownlie	1
France	A	D0-0		
Osters Vaxjo	H	W2-0	Blackley, Brownlie pen	2
Sweden	A	L1-4	Smith	
		1978-79 UEFA		
Norrkoping	H	W3-2	Higgins 2, Temperley	1
Sweden	A	D0-0		
Strasbourg	A	L0-2		2
France	H	W1-0	McLeod pen	
		1989-90 UEFA		
Videoton	H	W1-0	Mitchell	1
Hungary	A	W3-0	Houchen, Evans, Collins	
FC Liege	H	D0-0		
Belgium	A	L0-1		

Opponents	Venue	Res	Scorers	Rnd
		1992-93	**UEFA**	
Anderlecht	H	D2-2	Beaumont, McGinlay	1
Belgium	A	D1-1	Jackson	

KILMARNOCK

Opponents	Venue	Res	Scorers	Rnd
		1964-65	**FC**	
Ein. Frankfurt	A	L0-3		1
West Germany	H	W5-1	Hamilton, McIlroy, Sneddon McFadzean, McInally	
Everton	H	L0-2		2
England	A	L1-4	McIlroy	
		1965-66	**EC**	
Nendori Tirana	A	D0-0		P
Albania	H	W1-0	Black	
Real Madrid	H	D2-2	McLean pen, McInally	1
Spain	A	L1-5	McIlroy	
		1966-67	**FC**	
Bye				1
Antwerp	A	W1-0	McInally	2
Belgium	H	W7-2	McInally 2, Queen 2 McLean 2, Watson	
La Gantoise	H	W1-0	Murray	3
Belgium	A	W2-1	McInally, McLean	
Lokomotiv Leipzig	A	L0-1		QF
East Gemany	H	W2-0	McFadzean, McIlroy	
Leeds United	A	L2-4	McIlroy 2	SF
England	H	D0-0		
		1969-70	**FC**	
Zurich	A	L2-3	McLean J, Mathie	1
Switzerland	H	W3-1	McGrory, Morrison, McLean	T
Slavia Sofia	H	W4-1	Mathie 2, Cook, Gilmour	2
Bulgaria	A	L0-2		
Dynamo Bacau	H	D1-1	Mathie	3
Romania	A	L0-2		
		1970-71	**FC**	
Coleraine	A	D1-1	Mathie	1
N. Ireland	H	L2-3	McLean T, Morrison	
		1997-98	**ECWC**	
Shelbourne	H	W2-1	Wright 2	Q
Eire	A	D1-1	McIntyre	
Nice	A	L1-3	Wright	1
France	H	D1-1	Reilly	

Opponents	Venue	Res	Scorers	Rnd
		1998-99 UEFA		
Zeljeznicar	A	D1-1	McGowne	P
Bosnia	H	W1-0	Mahood	
Sigma Olomouc	A	L0-2		P
Czech Rep	H	L0-2		

MORTON

Opponents	Venue	Res	Scorers	Rnd
		1968-69 FC		
Chelsea	A	L0-5		1
England	H	L3-4	Thorop, Mason, Taylor	

MOTHERWELL

Opponents	Venue	Res	Scorers	Rnd
		1991-92 FC		
Katowice	A	L0-2		1
Poland	H	W3-1	Kirk 2, Cusack	
		1994-95 UEFA		
Hanvar	H	W3-0	Coyne, McGrillen, Kirk	P
Faroe Islands	A	W4-1	Kirk 2, Davies, Burns	
Bor Dortmund	A	L0-1		1
Germany	H	L0-2		
		1995-96 UEFA		
My-Pa 47	H	L1-3	McSkimming	P
Finland	A	W2-0	Burns, Arnott	

PARTICK THISTLE

Opponents	Venue	Res	Scorers	Rnd
		1963-64 FC		
Glentoran	A	W4-1	Hainey, Yard 2, Wright	1
N. Ireland	H	W3-0	Smith 2, Harvey, pen,	
Spartak Brno	H	W3-2	Yard, Harvey, pen,	2
Czechoslovakia			Ferguson	
	A	L0-4		
		1972-73 UEFA		
Honved	A	L0-1		1
Hungary	H	L0-3		

RAITH ROVERS

Opponents	Venue	Res	Scorers	Rnd
		1995-96 FC		
Gotu	H	W4-0	Dairs, Rougier, Cameron	P
Faroe Islands			McAnespie	
	A	D2-2	Lennon, Crawford	
Akranes	H	W3-1	Lennon 2, Wilson	1
Iceland	A	L0-1		
Bayern Munich	H	L0-2		2
Germany	A	L1-2	Lennon	

RANGERS

Opponents	Venue	Res	Scorers	Rnd
		1956-57 EC		
Bye				P
Nice	H	W2-1	Murray, Simpson	1
France	A	L1-2	Hubbard pen	
	N	L1-3	og	
		1957-58 EC		
St Etienne	H	W3-1	Kichenbrand, Scott,	P
France			Simpson	
	A	L1-2	Wilson	
AC Milan	H	L1-4	Murray	1
Italy	A	L0-2		
		1959-60 EC		
Anderlecht	H	W5-2	Millar, Scott, Matthew,	P
Belgium			Baird 2	
	A	W2-0	Matthew, McMillan	
Red Star	H	W4-3	McMillan, Scott, Wilson	1
Bratislava			Millar	
Czechoslovakia	A	D1-1	Scott	
Sparta Rotterdam	A	W3-2	Wilson, Baird, Murray	QF
Holland	H	L0-1		
	N	3-2	Baird 2, og	
Eintracht Frank.	A	L1-6	Caldow pen	SF
West Germany	H	L3-6	McMillan 2, Wilson	
		1960-61 ECWC		
Ferencvaros	H	W4-2	Davis, Millar 2, Brand	P
Hungary	A	L1-2	Wilson	
Borussia Munch.	A	W3-0	Millar, Scott, McMillan	QF
West Germany	H	W8-0	Baxter, Brand 3, Millar 2	
			Davis, og	
Wolves	H	W2-0	Scott, Brand	SF
England	A	D1-1	Scott	
Fiorentina	H	L0-2		F
Italy	A	L1-2	Scott	
		1961-62 EC		
Monaco	A	W3-2	Baxter, Scott 2	P
France	H	W3-2	Christie 2, Scott	
Vorwaerts	A	W2-1	Caldow pen, Brand	1
East Germany	H	W4-1	McMillan 2 Henderson, og	
Standard Liege	A	L1-4	Wilson	
Belgium	H	W2-0	Brand, Caldow	
		1962-63 ECWC		
Seville	H	W4-0	Millar 3, Brand	1
Spain	A	L0-2		
Tottenham	A	L2-5	Brand, Millar	2
England	H	L2-3	Brand, Wilson	

Opponents	Venue	Res	Scorers	Rnd
		1963-64 EC		
Real Madrid	H	L0-1		P
Spain	A	L0-6		
		1964-65 EC		
Red Star Belgrade	H	W3-1	Brand 2, Forrest	P
Yugoslavia	A	L2-4	Greig, McKinnon	
	N	W3-1	Forrest 2, Brand	
Rapid Vienna	H	W1-0	Wilson	1
Austria	A	W2-0	Forrest, Wilson	
Inter Milan	A	L1-3	Forrest	QF
Italy	H	W1-0	Forrest	
		1966-67 ECWC		
Glentoran	A	D1-1	McLean	1
Northern Ireland	H	W4-0	Johnston, Smith D, Setterington, McLean	
Bor Dortmund	H	W2-1	Johansen, Smith A	2
West Germany	A	D0-0		
Real Zaragossa	H	W2-0	Smith, Willoughby	QF
Spain	A	L0-2		
Slavia Sofia	A	W1-0	Wilson	SF
Bulgaria	H	W1-0	Henderson	
Bayern Munich	N	L0-1		F
West Germany				
		1967-68 FC		
Dynamo Dresden	A	D1-1	Ferguson	1
East Germany	H	W2-1	Penman, Greig	
FC Cologne	H	W3-0	Ferguson 2, Henderson	2
West Germany	A	L1-3	Henderson	
		Bye		3
Leeds United	H	D0-0		QF
England	A	L0-2		
		1968-69 FC		
Vojvodina	H	W2-0	Greig pen, Jardine	1
Yugoslavia	A	L0-1		
Dundalk	H	W6-1	Henderson 2, Greig	2
Eire			Ferguson 2, og	
	A	W3-0	Mathieson, Stein 2	
DWS Amsterdam	A	W2-0	Johnstone, Henderson	3
Holland	H	W2-1	Smith, Stein	
Athletic Bilbao	H	W4-1	Ferguson, Penman,	QF
Spain			Persson, Stein	
	A	L0-2		
Newcastle Utd	H	D0-0		SF
England	A	L0-2		

GAMES TO REMEMBER

1967 CELTIC .... 2 Inter Milan 1

(Lisbon, May 25, 1967. Attendance 56,000)

CELTIC: Simpson, Craig, Gemmell, Murdoch, McNeill, Clark, Johnstone, Wallace, Chalmers, Auld, Lennox.
Scorers: Gemmell (63), Chalmers (85).
INTER MILAN: Sarti, Burgnich, Facchetti, Bedin, Guarneri, Picchi, Domenghini, Cappellini, Mazzola, Bicicli, Corso.
Scorer: Mazzola (7 pen).

1967 England.......... 2 SCOTLAND........................3

(Wembley, 1967. Att: 100,000)

SCOTLAND: Simpson, Gemmell, McCreadie, Greig, McKinnon, Baxter, Wallace, Bremner, McCalliog, Law, Lennox.
Scorers: Law, Lennox, McCalliog.
ENGLAND: Banks, Cohen, Wilson, Stiles, J Charlton, Moore, Ball, Greaves, R Charlton, Hurst, Peters.
Scorers: J. Charlton, Hurst.

1972 RANGERS........ 3 Moscow Dynamo..............2

(Barcelona, May 24, 1972. Att: 35,000)

RANGERS: McCloy, Jardine, Mathieson, Greig, D Johnstone, Smith, McLean, Conn, Stein, MacDonald, W Johnston.
Scorers: Stein (24), Johnston (40, 49).
MOSCOW DYNAMO: Pilgui, Basalev, Dolmatov, Zykov, Dobbonosov, (Gerschkovitch), Zhukov, Baidatchini, Jakubik (Eschtrekov), Sabo, Makovikov, Evryuzhikbin.
Scorers: Eschtrekov (55) Makovikov (87).

1983 ABERDEEN....... 2 Real Madrid......................1

(Gothenburg, May 11, 1983. Att: 17,804)

ABERDEEN: Leighton, Rougvie, McMaster, Cooper, McLeish, Miller, Strachan, Simpson, McGhie, Black (Hewitt), Weir. Subs: Kennedy, Gunn, Watson, Hewitt, Angus.
Scorers: Black (7), Hewitt (112).
REAL MADRID: Agustin, Jan jose, Camacho, Metgod, Bonet, Gallego, Jaunito, Angel, Santillana, Stielike, Isidro.
Scorer: Juanito (14 pen).

1983 SV HAMBURG .... 0 ABERDEEN........................0

(Hamburg, November 22. Att: 15,000)

HAMBURG: Stein, Schroder, Wehmeyer, Jacobs, Hieronymus, Hartwig, (Wuttke), Roff, Groh, Schatzschneider, Magath, Von Heeson.
ABERDEEN: Leighton, Cooper, Rougvie, Simpson, McLeish, Miller, Strachan, Hewitt, McGhee, Bell, Weir.

1983 ABERDEEN....... 2 HAMBURG........................0

(Aberdeen, December 20. Att: 22,500)

ABERDEEN: Leighton, McKimmie, McMaster, Simpson, McLeish, Miller, Strachan, Hewitt (Black), McGhee, Bell, Weir.
Scorers: Simpson (47) McGhee (64).
HAMBURG: Stein, Kaltz (Hanson) Wehmeyer, Jacobs, Hieronymus, Hartwig, Schroder, Groh, Schatzschneider (Wuttke), Magath, Roff.

Opponents	Venue	Res	Scorers	Rnd
		1969-70 ECWC		
Steaua Bucharest	H	W2-0	Johnston 2	1
Romania	A	D0-0		
Gornik Zabrze	A	L1-3	Persson	2
Poland	H	L1-3	Baxter	
		1970-71 FC		
Bayern Munich	A	L0-1		1
West Germany	H	D1-1	Stein	
		1971-72 ECWC		
Rennes	A	D1-1	Johnston	1
France	H	W1-0	MacDonald	
Sporting Lisbon	H	W3-2	Stein 2, Henderson	2
Portugal	A	L3-4	Stein 2, Henderson	
Torino	A	D1-1	Johnston	QF
Italy	H	W1-0	MacDonald	
Bayern Munich	A	D1-1	og	SF
West Germany	H	W2-0	Jardine, Parlane	
Dynamo Moscow	N	W3-2	Johnston 2, Stein	F
USSR				
		1972-73 (European Super Cup)		
Ajax	H	L1-3	MacDonald	
Holland	A	L2-3	MacDonald, Young	
		1973-74 ECWC		
Ankaragucu	A	W2-0	Conn, McLean	1
Turkey	H	W4-0	Greig 2, O'Hara, Johnstone	
Borussia Munch.	A	L0-3		2
West Germany	H	W3-2	Conn, Jackson, MacDonald	
		1975-76 EC		
Bohemians	H	W4-1	Fyfe, Johnstone, O'Hara	1
Eire			og	
	A	D1-1	Johnstone	
St Etienne	A	L0-2		2
France	H	L1-2	MacDonald	
		1976-77 EC		
Zurich	H	D1-1	Parlane	1
Switzerland	A	L0-1		
		1977-78 ECWC		
Young Boys	H	W1-0	Greig	P
Switzerland	A	D2-2	Johnstone, Smith	
Twente Enschede	H	D0-0		1
Holland	A	L0-3		
		1978-79 EC		
Juventus	A	L0-1		1
Italy	H	W2-0	MacDonald, Smith	

Opponents	Venue	Res	Scorers	Rnd
PSV Eindhoven	H	D0-0		2
Holland	A	W3-2	MacDonald, Johnstone Russell	
FC Cologne	A	L0-1		QF
West Germany	H	D1-1	McLean	
		1979-80 ECWC		
Lillestrom	H	W1-0	Smith	P
Norway	A	W2-0	MacDonald A, Johnstone	
Fortuna Dussel.	H	W2-1	MacDonald A, McLean	1
West Germany	A	D0-0		
Valencia	A	D1-1	McLean	2
Spain	H	L1-3	Johnstone	
		1981-82 ECWC		
Dukla Prague	A	L0-3		1
Czechoslovakia	H	W2-1	Bett, MacDonald J	
		1982-83 UEFA		
Borussia Dort.	A	D0-0		1
West Germany	H	W2-0	Cooper, Johnstone	
FC Cologne	H	W2-1	Johnstone, McClelland	2
West Germany	A	L0-5		
		1983-84 ECWC		
Valetta	A	W8-0	Paterson, McPherson 4	1
Malta			MacDonald, Prytz 2	
	H	W10-0	Mitchell 2, MacDonald 3 Dawson, MacKay, Davis 2, Redford	
Porto	H	W2-1	Clark, Mitchell	2
Portugal	A	L0-1		
		1984-85 UEFA		
Bohemians	A	L2-3	McCoist, McPherson	1
Eire	H	W2-0	Paterson, Redford	
Inter Milan	A	L0-3		2
Italy	H	W3-1	Mitchell, Ferguson 2	
		1985-86 UEFA		
Osasuna	H	W1-0	Paterson	1
Spain	A	L0-2		
		1986-87 UEFA		
Ilves	H	W4-0	Fleck 3, McCoist	1
Finland	A	L0-2		
Boavista	H	W2-1	McPherson, McCoist	2
Portugal	A	W1-0	Ferguson	
Borussia Munch.	H	D1-1	Durrant	3
West Germany	A	D0-0		

Opponents	Venue	Res	Scorers	Rnd
			1987-88 EC	
Dynamo Kiev	A	L0-1		1
USSR	H	W2-0	Falco, McCoist	
Gornik Zabrze	H	W3-1	McCoist, Durrant, Falco	2
Poland	A	D1-1	McCoist pen	
Steaua Buch.	A	L0-2		QF
Romania	H	W2-1	Gough, McCoist pen	
			1988-89 UEFA	
Katowice	H	W1-0	Walters	1
Poland	A	W4-2	Butcher 2, Durrant Ferguson	
FC Cologne	A	L0-2		2
W. Germany	H	D1-1	Drinkell	
			1989-90 EC	
Bayern Munich	H	L1-3	Walters, pen	1
W. Germany	A	D0-0		
			1990-91 EC	
Valetta	A	W4-0	McCoist, Hateley, Johnston 2	1
Malta				
	H	W6-0	Dodds, Spencer, Johnston 3, McCoist	
Red Star Belgrade	A	L0-3		2
Yugoslavia	H	D1-1	McCoist	
			1991-92 EC	
Sparta Prague	A	L0-1		1
Czechoslovakia	H	W2-1	McCall 2	
			1992-93 EC	
Lyngby	H	W2-0	Hateley, Huistra	1
Denmark	A	W1-0	Durrant	
Leeds United	H	W2-1	og, McCoist	
England	A	W2-1	Hateley, McCoist	
			GROUP STAGE	
Marseille	H	D2-2	McSwegan, Hateley	
CSKA Moscow	A	W1-0	Ferguson	
FC Bruges	A	D1-1	Huistra	
FC Bruges	H	W2-1	Durrant, Nisbet	
Marseille	A	D1-1	Durrant	
CSKA Moscow	H	D0-0		
			1993-94 EC	
Levski Sofia	H	W3-2	McPherson, Hateley 2	1
Bulgaria	A	L2-1	Durrant	
			1994-95 EC	
AEK Athens	A	L2-0		1
Greece	H	L0-1		

Opponents	Venue	Res	Scorers	Rnd
			1995-96 EC	
Anorthosis	H	W1-0	Durie	P
Cyprus	A	D0-0		
			GROUP STAGES	
Steau Bucharest	A	L0-1		
Borussia Dort	H	D2-2	Gough, Ferguson	
Juventus	A	L1-4	Gough	
Juventus	H	L0-4		
Steau Bucharest	H	D1-1	Gascoigne	
Borussia Dort	A	D2-2	Laudrup, Durie	
			1996-97 EC	
Vladikavkaz	H	W3-1	McInnes, McCoist, Petric	Q
Russia	A	W7-2	McCoist 3, van Vossen Laudrup 2, Miller	
			GROUP STAGES	
Grasshoppers	A	L0-3		
Auxerre	H	L1-2	Gascoigne	
Ajax	L	4-1	Durrant	
Ajax	H	L0-1		
Grasshoppers	H	W2-1	McCoist 2, 1 pen	
Auxerre	A	L1-2	Gough	
			1997-98 EC	
Gotu	A	W5-0	Negri, Durie 2, McCoist 2	Q
Faroe Islands	H	W6-0	Durie, Negri 2, McCoist Albertz, Ferguson	
Gothenburg	A	L0-3		Q
Sweden	H	D1-1	Miller	
			UEFA	
Strasbourg	A	L1-2	Albertz	1
France	H	L1-2	Gattuso	
			1998-99 UEFA	
Shelbourne	A	W5-3	Albertz 2, 1 pen,	Q
Eire			Amato 2, van Bronckhorst	
	H	W2-0	Johansson 2	
PAOK Salonika	H	W2-0	Kanchelskis, Wallace	Q
Greece	A	D0-0		
Beitar	A	D1-1	Albertz	1
Israel	H	W4-2	Gattuso, Porrini, Johansson, Wallace	
B Leverkusen	A	W2-1	van Bronckhorst,	2
Germany			Johansson	
	H	D1-1	Johansson	
Parma	H	D1-1	Wallace	3
Italy	A	L1-3	Albertz	

ST JOHNSTONE

Opponents	Venue	Res	Scorers	Rnd
		1971-72 UEFA		
SV Hamburg	A	L1-2	Pearson	1
West Germany	H	W3-0	Hall, Pearson, Whitelaw	
Vasas Budapest	H	W2-0	Connolly pen, Pearson	2
Hungary	A	L0-1		
Zeljeznicar	H	W1-0	Connolly	3
Yugoslavia	A	L1-5	Rooney	

ST MIRREN

Opponents	Venue	Res	Scorers	Rnd
		1980-81 UEFA		
Elfsborg	A	W2-1	Somner, Abercromby	1
Sweden	H	D0-0		
St Etienne	H	D0-0		2
France	A	L0-2		
		1983-84 UEFA		
Feyenoord	H	L0-1		1
Holland	A	L0-2		
		1985-86 UEFA		
Slavia Prague	A	L0-1		1
Czechoslovakia	H	W3-0	Gallagher, McGarvey 2	
Hammarby	A	D3-3	Gallagher 3	2
Sweden	H	L1-2	McGarvey	
		1987-88 UCWC		
Tromso	H	W1-0	McDowall	1
Norway	A	D0-0		
Mechelen	A	D0-0		2
Belgium	H	L0-2		

Ties finishing level on goals have been settled by: play-offs, toss of the coin, away goals rule (from 1966-67), or penalty kicks.

KENNY McDOWALL . . . netted for St Mirren in the Cup-Winners' Cup

AUTOGRAPHS